More praise for

Of Tigers and Men

"A highly gripping account of a Melvillean quest."

—*St. Louis Post-Dispatch*

"There are some books, a few, that are so passionate, so mesmerizing, they transport you entirely—letting you share an author's obsession. Richard Ives does that for me and for the last wild tigers. We both stand in his debt."

—Lyall Watson, author of *Supernature*

"For readers reaching for the feeling of staring a tiger in the eye, without a zoo barrier in between, Ives succeeds marvelously."

—*Booklist*

"A sad story and a powerful book, one that avoids platitudes and romantic cant to deliver its bracing insights."

—P.J. O'Rourke, author of *All the Trouble in the World*

"For all the story's subcurrent of despair, Ives has managed to infuse it with a bouncy, adventurous air, full of daring episodes, reckless happenings, even a love story . . . This isn't so much a caution as it is an elegy—beautifully etched, picaresque even, but a sadder song for all that."

—*Kirkus Reviews*

"Exciting . . . eloquent, moving . . . a terrific book . . . replete with exotic locales, mystery, suspense, and downright terror . . . It casts a spell as complete and irresistible as a tiger's steady gaze."

—Valerie Martin, author of *Mary Reilly*

OF TIGERS AND MEN

ENTERING THE AGE OF EXTINCTION

RICHARD IVES

AVON BOOKS NEW YORK

AVON BOOKS
A division of
The Hearst Corporation
1350 Avenue of the Americas
New York, New York 10019

Cover photo by Tony Stone Images/New York Inc.
Inside cover author photo by Jeffrey Blondes
Published by arrangement with Doubleday
Visit our website at **http://AvonBooks.com**
Library of Congress Catalog Card Number: 95-15421
ISBN: 0-380-72936-9

Library of Congress Cataloging in Publication Data:

Ives, Richard, 1946–
Of tigers and men: entering the age of extinction / Richard Ives.
p. cm.
1. Tigers—Asia. 2. Endangered species—Asia. 3. Wildlife conservation—Asia. 4. Ives, Richard, 1946– . I. Title.
QL737.C23I94 1996
599.74′428—dc20 95-15421
CIP

First Avon Books Trade Printing: March 1997

Printed in the U.S.A.

OPM 10 9 8 7 6 5 4 3 2 1

For Christina

And God blessed them, and God said unto them, Be fruitful, and multiply, and replenish the earth, and subdue it: and have dominion over the fish of the sea, and over the fowl of the air, and over every living thing that moveth upon the earth.

Genesis 1:28

Après d'innombrables dynasties de créatures gigantesques, après des races de poissons et des clans de mollusques, arrive enfin le genre humain, produit dégénéré d'un type grandiose, brisé peut-être par Le Créateur.

Honoré de Balzac, *Le Peau de Chagrin*

Prologue

THE WONDERFUL THING about a chance encounter is that you never know where it may lead.

I had arrived at my hotel in Calcutta in the wake of a train journey that was supposed to require twelve hours but that, in circumstances comic enough to make even the most jaded traveler weep bitter tears, ended up lasting thirty-six. Because I was exhausted, almost out of my mind from lack of sleep, what I wanted most was a hot shower, something decent to eat, something to drink, and a nice bed where I could, quite literally, stretch out and rest in peace.

My first glance at the hotel, however, was not encouraging. Though its name, garnered from a usually dependable guidebook, suggested a charming hostel surrounded by an infinite expanse of greenery bordered by beds of dewy roses, the reality that presented itself was considerably less appealing—an infirmary-green building, seemingly as old as British India itself, squeezed into a narrow corner lot on a filthy side street not far from the Maidan. The "garden" turned out to be nothing more exotic than a patio, which is to say a painted concrete slab equipped with several sets of metal tables and chairs, each set clustered protectively under a gaudy umbrella, the entire ensemble ringed with half a dozen enormous trees and about a thousand potted plants, most of which were liberally spattered with chalky white crow droppings.

Crows, the gray-collard variety so common in Indian towns, were everywhere, scolding, squawking, and pecking, chasing each other from branch to table to potted plant, seemingly involved in some kind of corvid gang warfare, their raucousness almost but not quite sufficient to drown out the blare of automobile horns, the clamor of irate motorists, emanating from the street outside. In my exhausted state, somewhat bug-eyed, all I could do was gaze around and sigh.

Noticing that some thoughtful person had recently hosed off the tables and chairs, I walked over to a table that did not seem too strategically placed under an overhanging branch and took a seat. I ordered a drink from a passing waiter, which arrived rather quickly. It was just as it was crossing my mind that perhaps things were not as bad as they seemed that I heard a voice inquire, "Just arrived?"

Uncertain at first to whom the question was directed, I turned around in my chair and saw an Indian gentleman sitting at a table nearby, half concealed by a wilted potted palm. Movie-star handsome, in his late forties or early fifties, he was elegantly dressed in a sports jacket and pullover. I judged him instantly to be an aristo, or perhaps a movie actor: in India, only people with lots of money dress like this.

"Yes," I said.

"You've come from Delhi?"

"From Nepal."

"Ah, Nepal . . ." He sighed as if the word held for him

some special significance. Sizing me up as he raised his glass, he asked, "First time in India?"

"No, I'm a veteran. This is my sixth visit."

"Sixth!" He smiled. "You must enjoy this country, then. You are American, I think?"

"Is it that obvious?"

"Not really. But at the same time I am quite certain that you are not from Texas."

"How can you tell?" I asked. "No cowboy hat?"

He laughed at the gibe. "Would you care to join me?" he asked after a moment. "I'll have to be going in a few minutes, but I thought I'd have another drink before running off."

It was a friendly offer, one that made me realize that I was perhaps more in the mood for company than I had reckoned. Rising from my chair, drink and bottle in hand, I walked over to his table and introduced myself. Standing to greet me, he shook my hand and told me his name; then, indicating the chair across the table from him, said, "Have a seat."

Spotting one of the plume-turbaned waiters who had suddenly appeared at the back of the garden, my new acquaintance barked an order—whether in Hindi or Bengali or some other Indian tongue, I could not tell—then turned back to me and asked, "Would you like your drink freshened up? Some ice perhaps?" I told him no and the waiter was dismissed with a nod. Settling back in his seat, he said, "So what has brought you to this country a sixth time?"

"Curiosity."

"It killed the cat."

"I'm thinking of writing a book."

"A book about India?"

"A book about tiger."

His eyes flashed, as though perhaps he thought I might be joking. He gazed at me flatly. "You are a biologist, then?"

"A naturalist. I lead wildlife tours."

"You bring tourists to this country from the United States?"

"I'll be leading my first tour here in India in about a week. I've been leading tours to Nepal for the last three years."

"And in Nepal, where do you take your tourists?"

"We go trekking, usually in the Annapurnas. Then sometimes we spend three or four days in Chitwan Park."

"Ah yes, Chitwan . . . A sort of living postcard, isn't it? With the snowy Himalaya as a backdrop? I expect that it shall remain so as long as the army is there to protect it. You stay at Tiger Tops, I imagine?"

"Sometimes."

"You have seen tiger there?"

"Several times."

"Always from a hide, with the tiger attracted to a bullock set out as bait?"

"Yes."

"And what did you think of the baiting?"

"Impressive. But not really so very different from seeing a tiger at the zoo, or at the circus."

"But you were impressed with the cats themselves?"

"Of course. How could one not be?"

"And now that you have seen a tiger, you want to write a book about him . . ."

I started to explain. But at that moment the waiter arrived with the ordered drink. Glancing my way, my interlocutor said "Cheers," and the waiter, interpreting this as a dismissal, turned and walked off. For a moment or two we enjoyed our drinks in silence, my new acquaintance studying me over the rim of his glass. Lowering it at last, he said, "And what do you think of Calcutta?"

Calcutta. Now *there* was a subject for a book.

The memory of the taxi ride that had brought me from Howrah station to the hotel suddenly played before my eyes

—the noise, the drifting fog of automobile exhaust, the tidal movement of the crowds, the handless beggar tapping his knobby stumps against my half-opened window, the wretched family at the side of the road picking its way through a small mountain of suppurating refuse. How could I tell him what I really thought—that Calcutta was the end of the line, the last stop in that part of Asia which was fast becoming a vast human dung pile? Couldn't, obviously. So I hedged. "I've always found it a very interesting city."

"Have you?" My companion smiled, his expression seeming to telegraph his conviction that I was being something less than candid. "Personally," he continued, fingering his glass, "I don't think of it as a city at all anymore. When I was a child, I used to come here from time to time. But the city I knew then has vanished. What remains is something of an exoskeleton, isn't it? The cast-off remains of a once great capital, lying in the midst of what is in all likelihood the largest DP camp in the world."

Ah, well . . .

Sensing my unease perhaps, he tactfully changed the subject. "Now about this book you're planning to write—how will you go about it?"

"I don't know," I said. "I haven't gotten that far. Maybe I'll begin by visiting some of the tiger reserves down here I've been reading about—I've only been to Corbett so far. There are a number of people in India who have been studying unbaited tigers closely for a number of years. I think of them as the Tiger Men. I'd like to meet some of them, if I can. I suppose after that it will be mostly a question of putting pen to paper."

"That simple? You're very confident, aren't you? But I like that. You're really starting at zero, square one."

"Yes, I suppose so."

He raised his glass and took a sip, keeping an eye on me as he did. Then, lowering it, he said, "I must tell you, I find all this very interesting. When it comes to tiger, I am—how shall I put it?—something of an aficionado. I shot my first tiger, a fairly sizable male, two weeks after my sixteenth birthday. He measured nine feet, five inches between pegs. My father was with me. That was in northwestern U.P. at the end of the rains in 1955. Over the course of the next eight years I accounted for another four tigers, the last being a young female that I shot from a tree machan near a tribal area in northern Madhya Pradesh. That was on New Year's Day, 1963. I put up my guns after that. I have done no hunting since."

His words left me feeling excited and slightly stunned. Although it had occurred to me that there must be hundreds, if not thousands, of people in India who had hunted tigers in the days when hunting was still allowed, I had formed no clear idea of who these ex-hunters might be or how I might go about meeting them. Certainly it had never crossed my mind that I would casually stumble across such a person while having a drink in Calcutta.

Taking a long, thoughtful sip from his glass, my companion said, "Your project interests me. I, too, am rather taken with these Tiger Men. Somebody *ought* to write about them. It seems to me that if you really want to learn about them, I could perhaps be of some assistance to you. I have a few contacts in that world."

This seemed to me a very generous offer, particularly in view of the fact that he had known me for all of fifteen minutes. But that is India for you: friendships are often made at the drop of a hat. "I'm flattered," I said at last, "and I would be very appreciative of any help you could give me."

"Good. Then it's settled. You said that you will be leading a tour here in a few days?"

"Yes."

"And the tour will originate in Delhi?"

"Yes."

"Good. Then after your trip, if you have time, you will come and stay with us. I have a house there. I have an extra room or two. You would be welcome to come and stay as long as you like."

"It's very kind of you to offer."

Reaching into an inside jacket pocket, he removed an expensive-looking agenda book (which bore the escutcheon of a well-known Parisian purveyor of leather goods) and a fancy fountain pen. Ripping a page out of the agenda and writing his name, address, and telephone number in letters so perfectly formed that they looked engraved, he said, "Ring me up a day or two before your arrival. Somebody will be there to take your call. Even if I am not there, you will be most welcome to stay."

"This is really very kind of you," I said, folding the paper and sticking it in my shirt pocket.

"And what will you be doing between now and Delhi?" he asked.

"Sunderbans. I am planning to go out there in the next couple of days."

"Research for your book?"

"Yes."

"You've heard about the cyclone, of course."

"No."

"It occurred about three weeks ago. Several hundred people were drowned, a large percentage of them on the Bangladesh side. But you'll hear all about that when you make your inquiry."

My new friend drained his glass in a single draft, then pushed his chair back and stood. "Unfortunately," he said, "I have to meet my wife for dinner. She has been visiting her grandfather here in Calcutta. The old man has been dying for months, but I believe he is about to bring the performance to a dramatic finale. In any case, we will be taking the sleeper to Delhi tonight."

I rose, shook hands, and thanked him again.

"I shall wait to hear from you," he said. Removing several banknotes from his pocket, he tossed them onto the table and walked off. At the edge of the patio he paused and, looking back over his shoulder, said, "Be careful in Sunderbans. Lots of maneaters in those swamps."

"I think I'm probably more worried about wandering around the streets here."

"You may have a point," he said.

And was gone.

The next morning the sky was white, the heat blistering. When I walked into the air-conditioned tourist office near the Great Eastern Hotel, the chill moistness of the air struck me in the face like a damp pillow. The sari-clad lady with crimson lipstick who sat so composedly behind the desk had the anarchic mien of a middle-aged terrorist but turned out to be very pleasant indeed. "Of course we can help you arrange a tour to Sunderbans, if you really want to go," she said, smiling. "But I feel obliged to tell you that this is really not a good time. The cyclone three weeks ago was devastating, you see. Some two thousand people and five hundred head of cattle were drowned. The bodies and carcasses have bloated in the heat, apparently, and in some areas are still floating in the waterways. There is no good drinking water, and the jetties . . ."

She went on for another minute or two at least, but my brain did not register whatever it was that she said. Suddenly aware that she was staring at me rather quizzically, I automatically thanked her for her trouble and headed for the door. In the steambath outside I was greeted by a family of beggars—the wife, not more than sixteen, hugely pregnant and with a milky, bulging eye that leered crazily, the husband, a tattered rag of a man, looking ill, standing hunched over, barely supporting himself on a grimy bamboo cane. Their child lay blissfully asleep on the sidewalk, covered with copper-colored flies.

Dropping a rupee in their cup, I hurried away from them as fast as I could. I needed to think. Plan one had failed. Was there a plan two? In this open-air sauna where seemingly nothing ever happened as it should, might I not need a plan three?

A bus, nearly bursting at the seams with people, roared by, spewing clouds of black exhaust which danced in dervish whirls about my head. My thoughts had wandered back to Sunderbans and the once-brown bodies, swollen and bleached pink by sun and tide, bobbing face down in the mangroves.

Spinning on my heel, breasting the oncoming crowd, I headed for the airline office. It would be cool there, and I could think. I did not know what I was going to do, but if I decided it was the best course, I thought I might try to move up my flight to Delhi, where I was to meet my clients.

Part One

Initiation

One

If, WITH A MAP OF ASIA spread out on a table before you, you were to take a flying stab at pinpointing what you supposed to be the dead center of India, the tip of your extended forefinger (provided your aim was not too far off the mark) would indicate a spot not far removed from Kanha, one of the great national parks of the world. Located on a plateau in the Maikal Range, a spur of the Satpura Hills, in east-central Madhya Pradesh, Kanha is an area of extraordinary beauty which boasts a fine variety of wildlife. Over the last twenty years or so, it has become a place of pilgrimage for biologists, naturalists, and international travelers. And for a very particular reason: it happens to be one of the best remaining areas on earth to observe a tiger in the wild.

On a damp uncomfortable morning, the trees and the spaces between the trees steeped in stone-gray light, I am sitting in the front seat of a jeep, bouncing along a dirt track in an obscure corner of the park in the company of four of my clients and our guide, Amar Singh. Amar and his wife met me and the clients at the airport at Khajuraho. After taking a brief tour of what must be the naughtiest collection of erotic statuary in the world, at the renowned tenth-century temples, we had headed south in three automobiles, toward tiger country, arriving here at the park late yesterday evening. Amar Singh, as it turns out, is a former tiger hunter and naturalist of the old school who has obviously forgotten more about India's wildlife than I could ever hope to learn. Acquainted with him for less than twenty-four hours, I have already grown very fond of him.

The clients, pleasant people for the most part, are the usual mix—a retired professor and his wife from Maine, an art teacher from Colorado, an insurance executive and his wife from Des Moines, a lawyer and his teenage daughter from Florida . . . On this, the fourth day of the tour, they seem pleased at what we have seen so far—blackbuck, swamp deer, jackal, a number of dhole, India's increasingly rare wild dog, and a great many beautiful birds. As always on this sort of tour, however, I am aware of a tangible undercurrent of impatience. The animal they want most, the animal they have flown halfway around the world to see, has not yet chosen to make an appearance.

One of the clients, a retired psychiatrist from San Francisco named Bob, has not hesitated to make known his concerns about this. At the supper table last night he spent fifteen minutes grilling Amar about our chances. Amar, the soul of patience and a gentleman to the soles of his feet, explained that our chances were in fact "very good." But Bob did not appear to be reassured. He gave the distinct impression, in fact, that he would have much preferred odds gauged "excellent" or, to use one of his own favorite words, "great."

Amar downshifts and we head uphill. Pulling out of the woods onto the brushy edge of a flat clearing, we come to a place where a rough track leads through ragged forest to the left. Amar's gaze swings off in a leisurely way in that direction as we pass it, then suddenly snaps back. *"Tiger!"* he cries, jamming on the brakes and jutting out an arm, which barely prevents me from crashing into the windshield. *"Tiger in the road!"*

"Where?" I say, looking all around me.

"Up that track we just passed!"

Wheels keening, we lunge backward, twenty, thirty, forty feet . . .

Once even with the track, Amar stomps on the brakes, slamming us back in our seats. "Hold on!" he cries. Yanking the gearshift into a forward gear, he floors it and we fishtail onto the track.

I stare straight ahead. Sixty or seventy yards away, something *is* standing in the middle of the track. I lift up my binoculars to take a look. But with the jeep bouncing like a jackhammer over the ruts and rills, there is no way to tell what it is. It might be a tiger. It might be a Great Dane. It might be a cardboard box.

At twenty yards, the animal, whatever it is, moves off to the left. Anger flashes through me. Approached in this aggressive manner, no wonder it is hightailing it. Coming even with the place where the animal disappeared, Amar stands on the brake, heaving us forward in our seats. The jeep skids to a halt.

Every head swings left.

At first I see nothing. Then, fifteen feet away, something vibrates the branches of a large spreading shrub. A face, framed by leaves, glares out at us—a face covered not with stripes but spots.

"Leopard," Amar says quietly.

The leopard opens its mouth and bares its fangs. Eyes fixed on us, muscles rippling like cables under its skin, its body flattened against the ground, it squirms and begins an ungainly, crablike retreat. Five feet. Ten. Springing up in a cloud of dust, it bolts, darting off through a wall of bushes and trees.

A dry rattling of leaves in the settling dust. Then silence. The entire episode has lasted less than a minute.

Amar turns around in his seat and smiles at Bob, who, as it happens, is sitting right behind him. "Well, Bob, what do you think?"

"That was *great,*" Bob says with a big grin. Then, his brow wrinkling slightly, he adds, "But I thought you said it was a tiger."

"My eyes are not what they used to be."

"Well, I hope we see a tiger that close," Bob says. "Think that's possible?"

"You want to get close enough to pluck one of its whiskers?"

"Something like that."

"Well," Amar says, "anything is possible. We'll see what we can do."

Two

THROUGH THE TREES, the twisted curling branches, beyond the dappled shadows and dead leaves: a swatch of orange, slashed with black. The elephant lurches to a halt; Bob ducks down to get a better look. "Is that *it?*" he whispers. "Is *that* the tiger?"

Three days have passed since we saw the leopard. During that time the group and I have traveled north by car the 150-odd miles that separate Kanha from Bandhavgarh National Park. Here, because there are no roads to speak of, one looks for tiger not from the seat of a jeep but from an elephant's swaying back.

The mahout clicks his tongue, heels the elephant behind the ears. Shifting her weight under us, she lifts a great rounded foot and thrusts it down onto soft earth, heaving us upward through branches and leaves, which the mahout fends off with his hardwood stick. The orange swatch disappears. We move blindly toward it. I feel my chest muscles tighten. Droplets of sweat streak down the undersides of my arms. Sweeping a barrier of branches aside with her trunk, the elephant carries us up into a small clearing ringed with slender trees.

Fifteen feet away, the tiger, staring straight at us, is stretched out on the ground, forepaws clutching the base of some bizarre, strangely twisted forest plant.

"My God," Bob whispers.

The plant is shimmering, vibrating. An odor like old garbage reaches my nostrils. Then I know what it is. No plant, it is the head and tattered shoulder of a sambar elk, velvet antlers branching up out of a teeming mass of maggots the shape of a skull.

"Jesus," Bob says. His forehead glistening with sweat, he stares. Raising his camera slowly, he peers through the viewfinder, revolves the enormous lens first one way, then the other, then back again, and lowers it at last with an exasperated "Too close."

Claire, a client from Des Moines, twists around in her seat behind us, focuses, and begins to shoot. Shutter and motor drive gnaw the silence—*chickit shhh, chickit shhh, chickit shhh* . . .

The tiger turns its head. Stares. Flicks an ear.

Bob detaches his telephoto lens by feel and drops it into his camera bag, fumbling as he does, nearly sending it over the side. *Lose it here,* I think, *and it will stay here.* After twisting a short, fat lens onto the camera body, he raises the camera and squeezes off half a dozen frenzied shots. The tiger locks its gaze on Bob. Rolling back its lips to expose its fangs, it releases a hiss like freezing steam. "Whoa," Bob says, watching it through the viewfinder. And stops.

For perhaps two minutes we sit watching it, it watching us, us watching it watching us. I try to look away, but I can't stop staring. With a short burst of effort, it could kill all of us. It is, after all, a pure killer. Killing is what it does for a living. Even so, its very aliveness is what impresses.

Waves of it roll over us. Here, in this place, it is almost all of what is.

Amar turns and glances back. Ten yards downhill, the elephant carrying the rest of the clients is weaving and bobbing its way up through the vegetation. Turning back around, Amar leans forward to the mahout and whispers something in his ear. The mahout nods, clicks his tongue, gives the elephant a jab with his heels.

The elephant releases a deep intestinal groan and moves reluctantly ahead three or four steps over soft, broken ground. Shifting her weight, she loses her balance momentarily, compensates, veers slightly to the left, in the direction of the tiger, and comes to a rocking halt less than five feet from it. Bob, seated in front of me, at the corner of the howdah, now sits cantilevered out into space, staring straight into the face of the tiger.

The tiger half rises on its haunches. Muscles tensed, it bares it fangs, leans forward, and releases a short but powerful coughing roar. Recoiling as though shot, Bob climbs halfway out of his seat. In an instant daydream, I see what happens next, the tiger leaping up, hooking a paw over the edge of the howdah, slapping Bob full in the face, Bob cartwheeling away . . .

But the tiger has not moved.

Yellow eyes focused, intent, it awaits some final provocation. Bob sits gray-faced, rigid, holding his camera at the ready in front of him as though it were some last-ditch weapon of defense. The mahout clicks his tongue, and I go cold at the thought that he is urging the elephant *toward* the tiger.

But the elephant knows better. Sidling away with a clumsy step, she takes another step, then another, and another. It is only when we have pushed through the barrier of undergrowth, only when we are nearly out of sight, that the tiger's muscles relax, only then that in a single sensuous movement it settles back onto the still-warm impression of its own bodily form, stamped on the damp leaf litter of the forest floor.

Two minutes later, the howdah steeply tilted, the elephant steps down into a dry streambed dappled with irregular pools of filtering light, the sandy bottom everywhere impressed with tiger tracks. As though we were a group of medieval pilgrims stunned by some holy visitation, no one has uttered a word. At last, it is Amar who breaks the silence. Turning to Bob, a broad grin on his face, he asks, "Well, Bob, was that close enough for you?"

I wince. Though Amar has not noticed it, Bob is still trembling, and I have no idea how he will take this kind of teasing.

"Yes, Amar," he says at last, his voice just slightly shaky, "that was *definitely* close enough."

"Close enough to pluck one of the tiger's whiskers?"

"I'd say so."

"And did you pluck one?"

"No, I didn't, Amar." Bob smiles. "Frankly, I was too worried that I was going to pee my pants."

Three

THAT EVENING, long after supper, Amar, Mrs. Singh, and I are sitting in my room at the lodge, chatting, enjoying a nightcap. The dim silvery glare of a vampire moon lost somewhere behind the clouds; the night is mild, almost warm. I am seated on my bed, my back to the wall, feeling very relaxed. Amar, glass in hand, sits nearby, looking as neatly composed as a choirboy. Next to the partly opened door, Mrs. Singh is perched on a wooden chair, smoking what must be her fortieth cigarette of the day. For the past few minutes the three of us have been discussing the day's events, and for about the fifth time in our conversation, Bob's name has come up.

"Well, Richard," Amar asks, taking a sip of his drink, "do you think Bob got his money's worth today?"

"I wouldn't be a bit surprised."

"He got all the pictures of tiger he wanted when we went out this afternoon, didn't he?"

"I think so."

"And without the aid of his telephoto."

"Yes."

"Do you know what he asked me after we got back this evening?"

"God knows."

"He asked me if I had ever fallen off an elephant."

"And what did you tell him?"

"Well, when he asked the question, I laughed, because, you know, I could read his mind. I could tell what he was thinking. So I told him no. But you know, later on I remembered—once I *did* fall off an elephant."

"When was that?"

"Oh, a long time back—twenty-five years ago. It happened during a tiger hunt. I had brought some people down from Delhi to a place not very far from here and we set up camp. The next morning we went out on a beat. As it turned out, there were only two people riding the elephant I was on, the mahout and myself. It was very hot that morning, not a breath of air moving. As we began to head into some rather thick cover, I remember, we heard a troop of beaters coming up from the right. I had my rifle ready, but the beaters still seemed some distance away, so I was perhaps not quite as prepared as I ought to have been when suddenly, directly in front of us, the tiger broke cover. Not hesitating, he came right at us. I believe he was already in the air before I could swing my rifle round. Well, the tiger landed right on top of the elephant's head, directly in front of the mahout! And the mahout was so startled, he tumbled backwards off the side of the elephant, leaving me sitting there, staring directly into the tiger's mouth! Before I could even move, the elephant pitched violently forward, and I went flying, literally head over heels, and landed flat on my back on the ground. I think I may have been out for a few seconds, because I remember opening my eyes and thinking, *I've got to do something*. But I couldn't. At last, coming to my senses, I realized that my rifle was gone, probably off in a bush somewhere, and that a few inches away the tiger was growling and snarling, crying out in pain. The elephant had pinned it to the ground, you see, and was wrestling with it, attempting to crush it with its forehead. At the same time the tiger was scratching and clawing violently, its hindpaws flinging up dust and leaves and soil."

"So what did you do?"

"It dawned on me at last that I had better clear out. So, managing somehow to struggle to my feet, I slipped away."

"And the elephant?"

"It eventually crushed the tiger to death."

"How long did it take?"

"I couldn't say. I didn't stick around to find out."

"And did the elephant survive?"

"It did. But it was gravely wounded. The tiger had ripped one of its eyes out of the socket, and the poor animal lingered in great pain for about a month or so, I think, before it died."

At the doorway, Mrs. Singh drops her cigarette stub onto the floor and stamps it out with the sole of her shoe. Rising from her chair, she walks over to us and, placing her empty glass on the side table, says, "It's time for me to go to bed." Glancing down at her husband, then at me, she adds, "You two had better turn in soon. Tomorrow morning we shall have to be up with the lark."

"In a few minutes," Amar says.

"All right then," she says turning. "Sleep well, Richard."

"The same to you."

She walks to the door, steps outside, and pulls the door closed behind her.

"One more?" I ask, reaching for the bottle.

Amar holds out his glass and I pour until it is a quarter full, then pour half as much into my own. For several seconds, neither of us speaks. Then Amar, whose eyes have taken on a faraway look, turns to me and says, "It's strange, the things you remember."

"What?"

"While I was lying there on the ground next to the tiger and the elephant as they were fighting, in the midst of the uproar, I heard a sound, or rather a series of sounds, I have never forgotten."

"What sort of sound?"

"The sound a stick makes when you break it in two."

"And what was it?"

"The elephant, you know, was pushing its head down on the tiger."

"Yes?"

"It was the sound of the tiger's ribs cracking, one by one."

Four

"IS THAT *IT?*" I ask, whirling to face my driver, Raj, who is so covered with dust he looks as though he has just survived an explosion in a flour mill. "Is that where we're headed?"

A half-hour before sunset, three days after delivering my clients to the airport for their trip home, I am standing next to my hired automobile (a sturdy Indian make called an Ambassador) on the crumbling shoulder of a dirt road at the foot of the Aravalli hills in eastern Rajasthan, Rajasthan being that mostly arid and mostly very colorful Indian state that lies to the south and west of Delhi. My reason for coming here is really quite simple: to visit the Ranthambor Tiger Reserve, which in recent years has become increasingly recognized as one of the pearls of India's national park system. It has also not escaped me that here I may have my first encounter with India's fabled Tiger Men.

But the journey has been far from easy. Having spent hours and hours being bounced over roads humorously referred to as "surfaced" on the map, I am now as bone tired as I have ever been. My nerves are so dazed and jangled that

I am no longer quite sure whether I am coming or going. Unless I am very mistaken, at this particular moment I am hallucinating. What my eyes report is that atop a barren hill perhaps a mile away as the crow flies, a fairy-tale castle is perched—a castle whose fancy turrets and towers, caught in the final golden light of day, are an ostentatious, warmly delicious, one might even go so far as to say impossible, *pink*.

"Now be honest with me, Raj," I say, turning to my dust-coated driver once again. "Am I seeing things? Have I gone crazy? Or is there a pink castle on the top of that hill?"

"Oh yes," Raj says, his voice for some reason brimming over with secret satisfaction. "Joomar Bhowari. Hunting lodge of maharaja. Maharaja very famous man. Shooting the tiger. Playing the polo. Now Joomar Bhowari belonging to the Rajasthan state. Is there we will be staying."

Glancing down at my hands, realizing suddenly that I am as dustcoated as he is, I feel a stupid smile of satisfaction springing to my lips. Hunting lodge of a maharaja? The tour operator with whom I made arrangements in Delhi had referred to the place as a hotel and left it at that.

As I turn to climb back into the car, however, and look around me, the sense of prospective pleasure fizzles. Once upon a time, not so very long ago, this desolate range of hills was a pleasant tract of verdant forest. No more. The collision of history and human need has left it a bone-dry wasteland of rocks, dust, and twisted, barely rooted trees. Everywhere I look, the sterile ground is impressed with hoof marks, littered with wads of desiccated scat. It is a blasted terrain in which every fragment of greenery has been devoured, chewed, digested, and shat out by grazing animals. In this case, goats.

As people struggling to survive in arid areas the world over are coming to learn, not infrequently to their great distress, the age of pastoralism—a way of life that has endured on this planet for perhaps ten thousand years—is coming to an end. At the close of the twentieth century, to attempt to make a living by herding animals can never amount to anything more than spending one's life dancing on a razor's edge. Such a fragile existence can unravel with horrifying speed. Add a measure of civil strife and any period of prolonged drought, and Ethiopia or Somalia is the result. This place will be a Somalia or an Ethiopia someday. I am sure of it.

"So, tell me, Raj," I say, brushing dust off the sleeves of my shirt, trying to think of something pleasant. "Is there a shower up at this Joomar Bhowari?"

"Shower?" Raj says a little dreamily. "Oh yes . . ." Then, his expression darkening a little, he adds, "A kind of shower."

The words "kind of" do not reassure. But I let it go. In my brain-numbed, dusty state, it is difficult for me to imagine any sort of shower that will not do.

"Let's go."

The dirt road leading up the hill to the pink palace is long, twisting, rutted. In a few stretches it is impossibly steep. Now, at the end of our journey, it does not escape me that one too-casual gear change, one ill-timed glance at the passing scenery, could result in our plunging down the hillside in a fiery ball. Not that I am particularly worried. More than once since our departure early this morning our trusty Ambassador has proved its worth. Designed along aerodynamically plump 1930s English sedan lines—a style not changed for decades—it has gradually led me to think of it over the course of the day as some huge, highly evolved, armored desert organism, utterly adapted to a rigorous environment. I have developed equal confidence in Raj. Not much of a conversationalist, to be sure. But with gearshift, clutch, and accelerator, he is an artist nonpareil.

Through the ever-shifting cloud of rolling dust boiling up around us, I keep looking up the hill, catching a glimpse of the pink palace whenever I can as it vanishes and reappears, each enlarged prospect making it seem not more real but somehow more fantastic. At last, as we grind around a final hairpin turn, the castle gate looms directly ahead, the road levels out, and the Ambassador wheezes with relief as we pass through the gateway and glide onto the comparative smoothness of the paved courtyard.

Swinging the car around in a wide, stylish arc, Raj brings it to a halt in front of an impressively pointy-headed Gothic doorway, one which appears to offer access to the castle's interior precincts. Eager to get an unobstructed look, eager too to escape the confines of the back seat, I give the door handle a yank and push the door open, even before Raj can turn off the ignition. I step out and gaze up, then stumble back several steps to gain perspective.

I blink, but it doesn't go away. With its pink circular crenelated towers and gingerbread windows, the castle is a page from a child's pop-up book—a spun-sugar dream, a marzipan masterpiece. Gazing up at it, I am instantly aware of the vertiginous sensation that somehow I have managed to tumble through a dark space-time corridor and have settled to earth at some abandoned Disneyland East of the future. If a troop of turbaned Mousketeers were suddenly to come prancing out of the shadows, I doubt that I would bat an eyelash.

The paved courtyard into which we have driven is bordered by a low wall or parapet, about three feet high. Sauntering over to one section of it, facing west, I look out across a broad, dry, and mostly barren valley, several miles wide, on the opposite rim of which the swollen orange ball of the sun, lazing in an empty sky, is preparing to extinguish itself beyond a hazy contour of distant hills. Disappointingly the peaceful scene is somewhat marred in the middle distance by a pair of factory smokestacks spouting black pollution at the town of Sawai Madhopur.

Turning slightly, I notice that at the back of the castle the hillside rises several hundred feet to a stony summit. A rocky wilderness punctuated here and there by a few ragged trees and the occasional cactus-resembling euphorbia, the stark terrain brings a smile to my face even before I consciously know why. Then it comes to me. With all those goats grazing just down the hill, this is perfect leopard habitat.

"Greetings," a voice says behind me.

I turn and gape. In the overheated remains of a roasting day, the speaker, a moustached young man in his twenties, stands at attention before me. Decked out in a new pair of jeans, a heavy brown leather jacket, and an expensive-looking pair of wraparound sunglasses, he possesses, it seems to me, the rather studied air of a jaded hipster.

"Mr. Ives?" he asks.

"Yes."

"I am manager. Welcome to Joomar Bhowari. You came from Delhi via Jaipur?" he inquires with a grin.

"Yes, my driver thought we'd better come that way because of the strike."

"Oh yes, strike," the manager says. "We are always having strike. Strike very popular in Rajasthan—rail strike, food strike, post strike, transport strike . . . Road bad, isn't it?"

"Road miserable."

"How long did it take for you to come from Delhi?"

"About seven hours, I think, though it may have been more. It feels like seven days. Might my room be ready?"

"*Ready!*" the manager says, almost singing the word.

"Excellent. And where might that room be located?"

"*Top* floor. Nice room. *Very* nice."

"And the room has a shower?"

"*Every* room has shower, sir."

"Wonderful. Then I think I'd like to go right up."

Hoisting his shoulders in a careless shrug, as though thinking *What's the rush? But if that's what you want,* the manager spins on his heel and marches off across the cobbles like a tin soldier toward the entrance to the castle, I directly at his heels.

Inside the castle, everything is dissolved in brothy gloom. After a moment or two, when my eyes have adjusted to the shadowy light, I see that we are standing in a sort of large, high-ceilinged reception hall, which must have been quite a showpiece in its heyday, fitted out as it would have been with fancy carpets and sturdy furniture, with tiger and leopard trophies grinning down from the walls, crowded with visitors and abuzz with troops of fancily uniformed servants dispensing, according to the hour, copious doses of tea and gin. Unfortunately, this attractive vision seems as distant from the present as the grainy images of a disintegrating newsreel. A junkshop sofa has been parked against one wall; two moth-eaten chairs face it from across the room. A scarred, spindly-legged table jammed into a space beneath the stairs appears to function as a front desk. The room otherwise is as hollow and featureless as an abandoned godown.

Raj, completely done in, stands next to the spindly table. Propped up next to him is a scarecrow-thin old codger whom I take to be about seventy (though this being India, he could just as easily be forty). Wrapped in a threadbare shirt and a dhoti stained with ashes and fat, shod in a pair of sandals that look as though they could have used a retread a few thousand miles ago, he smiles as our eyes meet, putting on display an impressively gaping maw where canines, incisors, and bicuspids were once firmly anchored.

My bag lies in a twisted heap at his feet. It is obviously he who has lugged it in from the car.

In the left wall of the room there is a doorway, the door of which is standing ajar. Walking over to it, I peer into a Stygian gloom. Long experience of traveling the back roads of the subcontinent has taught me a thing or two. "Kitchen?" I venture.

"Yes," the manager says, with what seems to me great satisfaction.

"How is the food here?"

"Good. *He* is cook," the manager says, throwing a nod to the old man, who, I notice, adds a little warmth to his toothless smile, a smile that leaves me suddenly and curiously appalled at the selection of culinary delights this unlikely gastronome might conceivably come up with.

"I see," I say. "Well, is there any chance I can go up to my room now? I'm really pretty tired."

"Certainly," the manager says. "No *problem!* But will you first be so kind as to sign the guestbook register?"

"With pleasure."

Five

Ranthambor

The first time I have looked at this notebook for days . . . After a drive of nearly seven hours from Delhi by car, over what was for the last couple of hours an almost nonexistent road, my driver, Raj, and I have landed at Joomar Bhowari, onetime hunting lodge of the maharaja of Jaipur, a gentleman of questionable taste who possessed his own sense of style nevertheless. Unfortunately, his little fairy-tale castle has fallen on evil days. It pretends to be a hotel; it is in fact a sort of rustic madhouse.

Three items of evidence:

1. There is no running water (one has to flush the toilet with a bucket).

2. There is no electricity (I am writing this by the flickering light of a kerosene lamp).

3. The place is run by a pair of Samuel Beckett characters who are living proof not only that the Creator possesses a great sense of humor but that he has compassionately forgiven himself for his own mistakes.

I have managed a bath, of sorts. The old man who haunts the place brought two buckets of very cold water, with which I have, with some difficulty, managed to splash myself clean. I have changed my clothes, poured myself a large scotch, and am sitting up in bed, sleeping bag tucked around my knees, listening to the gale blowing outside my window. The wind came up with almost supernatural suddenness just after sunset and has been howling ever since.

*Ranthambor. I have read somewhere recently that more tigers are seen here than anywhere else in India. Just before picking up this notebook, I was paging through a book I brought with me from the States—*Tiger: Portrait of a Predator, *written by one Valmik Thapar, with photos supplied by Gunther Ziesler and Fateh Singh Rathore. The photos are absolutely stunning, the best I have ever seen. It seems likely that this is the very best photo book on tiger ever published.*

Just a moment ago, the wind really whipped up and I heard the sound of glass breaking somewhere downstairs. The wind continues to blow so hard that only the fact that the place is constructed of solid rock gives me the confidence that it won't come tumbling down on my head.

Pretty done in.

Drinking whisky on an empty stomach never works very well with me—a fact that does not appear to have much effect on my habits. I'd better go downstairs and search out the toothless gourmet if I expect to get anything to eat tonight. I am, as far as I am able to tell, the sole guest. The manager assures me that a local driver will be here tomorrow morning at seven-thirty sharp to drive me into the park to look for tiger. Exhausted. Eat. Then sleep.

Six

IN THE CHILL DARKNESS of the room, I unlatch the cracked and peeling shutters and swing them open to reveal a dripping world, drowned in a fine gray mist. Two minutes later, daypack slung over my shoulder, I am creeping down the stairwell, hand outstretched, fingers splayed, sliding a palm over the clammy wall, trying my damnedest not to go flying head over heels into the darkness. A pale suffusion of yellowy light wells up from below, flairs into intensity, a familiar face looming out of it. That of the old man. "Good morning, sa'b," he gums with a depressing cheerfulness. "Driver is waiting."

"Driver can bloody well go on waiting," I say, with a not-yet-awake irritability. "He's not supposed to be here for another fifteen minutes."

"Driver is waiting, sa'b."

Edging past him, I bounce on down the stairs to the emptiness of the reception hall, where a feathery stratus of pale blue smoke hangs suspended in the cool stillness. A thickset human figure standing hunched over in one corner like an out-of-work marionette unbends, comes alive, steps into the light, revealing itself to be a moustached Indian man half a head shorter than I, so bulkily wrapped in a down jacket and woolen cap he looks as though he might just have wiggled out of an igloo. "Good morning, sir," he says, a toothy, civilized smile flourishing on his face. There is such a pleasant air about him and his greeting that my irritation at his early arrival vanishes.

"Good morning," I say, extending my hand. "What's your name?"

"Shafi, sir. Shafi Mohammed."

"The name of the Prophet."

"The same, sir."

"Shafi, I have just rolled out of bed. Any chance I could get a cup of tea before we head out?"

"Of course," he says. "There is time." Turning to the old man standing nearby, he says, "Ek cup chai sa'b ke liye."

"You don't want one yourself?" I ask.

"Thank you very much, sir. I have had my breakfast."

The tea arrives in what for India must be record-breaking time—something less than a minute. Delivered in a chipped cup and saucer, it is "milk tea," the standard form of the beverage in India—a slightly aromatic blend with lots of milk and sugar already added. Its warmth and sweetness are welcome. I down it in several gulps.

"Another, sir?" Shafi asks, eyeing me solicitously.

"No, I think not. Shall we go?"

Shafi gestures toward the doorway.

Outside, the mist is thick enough to bottle. It occurs to me that it may be the thickest fog I have ever seen. I pause for a moment, turn, and glance up at the castle facade, not very surprised to discover that the upper stories dissolve into nothingness twenty feet above my head. In the courtyard, perhaps ten yards in front of me, I can just make out the pale form of a parked jeep, facing the castle entrance. Shafi walks toward it, circles the back of it, and climbs into the driver's seat. I head along the passenger side and slip into the seat beside him.

"*Very* cold this morning," he says, pulling on a pair of holey gloves he has produced from his jacket pocket.

"Bloody cold," I say, pulling my woolen cap down over my ears and hugging myself. In a tone that is half teasing, I ask, "Do you think we'll see a tiger today?"

"Tiger do what *he* wants," Shafi says with a somewhat nervous smile and a shrug. "Maybe today we are lucky. So many tiger at Ranthambor."

He turns the key in the ignition and the engine roars. He grinds the jeep into gear, releases the clutch, and we roll downhill, the chill fog whipping painfully around the windshield as we pick up speed. At the third or fourth hairpin turn, a small animal darts out in front of us. It lopes along for a second or two, then lunges off into the mist. "Black-naped hare," I hear myself report. I can't help noticing from a corner of my eye that a little smile disturbs Shafi's cold-stiffened features, as though he is thinking *This fellow is getting excited about a hare*?

For a moment it seems that he is about to speak. But in the end he keeps his peace.

Within a few minutes, having traversed the no-man's-land at the foot of the hill we drop down to the paved road over which Raj and I arrived last evening. Shafi turns right onto it, and since the fog has lifted a little, he is able to shift into a higher gear and pick up speed. In less than a quarter mile, however, an unwieldy and strangely flowing tangle of whiteness suddenly looms up in the road in front of us. For a second or two I cannot imagine what it might be. Then it comes to me. Goats. There must be hundreds of them.

Shafi slows the jeep, flashes the headlights as we approach. The goatherd, a vagrant spirit, materializes out of the mist. Black-bearded, with obsidian eyes, he is dressed in a three-quarter-length coat and a saffron-colored turban, as though he were a walking, talking hallucination who has followed the wrong exit sign out of *The Arabian Nights*. Tossing a disdainful glance our way, he urges his charges off to the side, whacking them with his staff, butting them with his knee, making clicking and yodeling noises, cursing them, at last picking up a small stone and bouncing it off the back of a recalcitrant leader.

Shafi moves the jeep cautiously into the surging sea of bleating, confused, flop-eared quadrapeds. The road falls away beneath us, and I feel strangely disoriented, as though suddenly afloat. Breaking out on the opposite side of the flock at last, Shafi immediately shifts gears and we resume speed. Only then do I notice the sour expression that has blossomed on his face. "*Goats,*" he says, almost spitting the word.

Perhaps a mile further on, at an unmarked dirt road, he applies the brakes and turns right. Twisting and turning through a naked landscape in which bare trees jut out of the mist like props from some creaky old expressionist film, we are traversing, I realize, yet another corner of the ghost forest. The terrain begins to steepen and close in on both sides. A nearly dry streambed littered with smooth round stones appears on our left. Though it is difficult to be sure, it would seem that we are headed into a sort of box canyon.

As we round a corner, a fortified stone gate reminiscent of a Roman triumphal arch suddenly appears, straddling the road in front of us. I realize at once that it is a remnant of the Rajput dynasty, which ruled Ranthambhor half a millennium ago. There is an air about it that is definitely threatening, and I can only imagine that foot-weary invaders five hundred years ago must have found it an impressive landmark. And that, of course, was no accident. This is martial architecture, designed to deliver a simple, if double-sided, message: *If you are a friend, enter in peace. If you are an enemy, return whence you came. Here you will only find your death.* I am mildly surprised that after all these centuries the dark magic still works. A unexpected shudder ripples up my spine as Shafi slows the jeep and we cruise under the arch.

Beyond it the road begins to climb. We enter a new sort of landscape, one that, to my pleasure and surprise, is green. Shafi downshifts and we begin to climb through a proper forest with trees and undergrowth, a type of terrain I would have found inconceivable just a mile back. The road levels out. We pass several dry watercourses, Shafi looking deliberately up each one, performing a sort of double take when he thinks he has spotted something, resuming speed instantly when he realizes that his eyes have deceived him. It is obvious that he has seen interesting things here before.

After about five minutes the road swings off in a broad arc to the right, then hooks back left. Straight ahead, in a sort of airy grove with tall, broadly spaced trees, are a turreted guardhouse, an arched gateway, a stretch of crenelated wall—more Rajput fortification. The road we are traveling on leads directly under the arch. Shafi drives right up under it and brings the jeep to a halt. Switching off the ignition, he says, "I must take permit." He swings his legs out of the jeep, walks over to a screened door, and disappears inside.

Directly ahead, the sun showers the road with golden light. The first light of the morning, it looks so inviting, so comforting, I can't resist it. Stepping out of the jeep, I walk under the arch and pass into the ephemeral glow of light and warmth. I close my eyes and just stand there, taking it in.

A raucous chatter starts up somewhere off to my right. Opening my eyes, I look up to the crown of a nearby tree. Two long-tailed tan birds with gray heads and breasts are chasing each other from branch to branch.

"Treepies?" a disembodied voice behind me inquires.

I turn and find myself gazing into the face of a giant of a man. Like some character in a fairytale, everything about him is oversize. Dressed in khaki, face framed by a full, somewhat unkempt black beard, he stands facing me with a ham-sized fist clenched around a steaming cup of liquid, his look demanding but friendly. I find myself wondering who in God's name he might be. Some local warlord? A circus strongman? A disgruntled tenor in flight from La Scala?

"Yes," I reply at last, "treepies."

"They're quite common here, actually," he says, enunciating each word with the liquid precision and purity of one of the better announcers on the BBC. "You're an ornithologist?"

"A naturalist. I lead wildlife tours."

"Tours to India?"

"I've just finished one."

"And you brought your tour to Ranthambor?"

"Unfortunately not."

"Pity. Ranthambor has some of the finest wildlife viewing in India."

"I've heard that. You seem to know the place well."

"Well enough."

I study the giant's face, more convinced with every passing second that I have seen his photograph somewhere very recently. Then it comes to me. "Are you Valmik Thapar?"

"Yes," he says, with a mild look of surprise. "And you?"

"Richard Ives is my name."

"Pleased to meet you," he says.

"It's funny meeting you here," I say, smiling. "I was just reading your book last night up at the Joomar Bhowari. I'm enjoying it."

"You mean *Tiger: Portrait of a Predator,* I take it?"

"Yes."

"They have a copy of the book up there?"

"No, I brought it with me from the States."

"You're staying at the Joomar Bhowari?"

"Yes."

"Rather a dump these days, isn't it?"

"It's not exactly the Ritz. I gather from your book that the tigers here at Ranthambhor are a lot easier to observe than they were, say ten years ago."

"It's like night and day. A few years back, the idea of actually *seeing* a tiger at Ranthambhor was something of a joke. We would go night after night, sometimes for weeks on end, and we would see nothing."

"And since Ranthambhor became a park, the tigers have become more habituated to humans?"

"In a nutshell, yes."

"Have you always been interested in tiger? I mean, do you have a background in biology?"

"Nothing of the sort. I was living in Delhi and I was bored. I read something about Ranthambhor in the newspaper and came down to have a look. I met Fateh Singh. He's the director here. We talked. After that first time, I just kept coming back. I couldn't stay away. It began just like that."

I hear a scuffing sound and turn. Shafi has stuck his head around the corner. From the expression on his face, I know that it is time to go.

"You're riding with Shafi?" Valmik asks.

"Yes."

"Shafi is a good spotter. You might see a tiger."

I try to think of something to say, regretting at the same time that there isn't time to say more. "Well, I'd better get moving."

"Perhaps I'll see you later on," Thapar says.

"I'll look forward to it."

"Have a good drive."

Seven

THREE HOURS LATER, the day has turned sunny and warm; the sky is vivid blue; the air is full of dragonflies. Sheltered in the cool shade of a silk-cotton tree, Shafi and I are parked a few steps from the gently lapping waters of a beautiful lake, having a snack of glucose biscuits and chalky chocolate, washing it down with drafts of warm water from Shafi's canteen. We have spent the entire morning driving the more or less circular route that winds through the heart of the park, a bowl-like valley with several lakes, their shores dotted with ruined, carved stone pavilions as elaborately sensuous as anything imagined in ancient Baghdad. As similar structures do for the Japanese, these must have provided the maharaja and his guests with unique vantages from which to observe the spectacle of the changing seasons, the setting of the sun, the rising of the moon. But in the midday heat their nooks and crannys are cool places—cool places that tigers like to frequent.

Across the lake, half hidden in the vegetation along the shoreline, is a little palazzo, its reflection neatly doubled in the water's mirror stillness. Shafi has explained that like the Joomar Bhowari, it is one of the maharaja's follies—a shooting lodge this time, dating from an era earlier in the century, when Ranthambhor was held to offer some of the best tiger hunting in India. Looming high above it, dwarfing it, dominating the entire scene in that direction, is a sheer cliff on top of which stand the ruins of Ranthambhor Castle, whose crenelated walls straggle along the clifftop for at least a mile.

Against this exaggeratedly romantic backdrop we have seen a great deal of wildlife, far more in a single locale than I have seen anywhere else in Asia. There have been small groups of chital, or spotted deer, and sambar, the Asian equivalent of the American elk. We have had close looks at nilgai, the very strange "four-horned antelope" endemic to India, which for my money has always seemed a hybrid of draft horse and short-necked giraffe. We have come across many chinkara, the sleek little Indian gazelle, every bit as elegant and handsome as its more familiar African cousins. We have even had the good fortune to catch a glimpse of a sloth bear, a species shy and seldom observed; interrupted at its excavation of a termite mound, it bounded off into the woods. There have been, in addition, at least sixty species of birds—vultures, eagles, hawks, geese, and ducks, among many others.

But Shafi is clearly unhappy. Although we have kept patient vigil over half a dozen watering holes, sat in silence studying the mouths of several promising-looking dry gullies, investigated every favored place Shafi knows in this part of the park, not one of the forty-odd tigers said to live at Ranthambhor has deigned to make an appearance—a failure of cooperation that Shafi appears to have interpreted as a personal affront. I have tried to reassure him that I am not the least bit upset, that I have observed tigers elsewhere very recently. But Shafi is inconsolable, it being for him, I suspect, a matter of professional pride. By way of a substitute, he has resorted to a strategy known to empty-handed hunters since the dawn of man. He is telling me a story.

"Do you see that arch there?" he asks, pointing with a piece of chocolate to an arched gateway through which we have driven several times this morning. Its top overgrown with creeping vegetation, it is perhaps a hundred yards up the road from where we sit.

"I see it."

"Last year, in springtime, some English come to Ranthambor. I was their driver. They are city people, from London, who come to see tiger. It was cold morning, very foggy, very quiet, nothing moving. We leave the gate and drive down this way by the lake. We turn up road to the arch. We drive up to the arch and stop. I don't know why, but I stop. Maybe I think I hear something. So I listen. You know what I hear?"

"What?"

"Birds. You know, satbhai?"

"The seven sisters—jungle babblers."

"Yes, the jungle babblers. These jungle babblers very upset, very unhappy, which is very strange because everything is so nice and quiet. Why they so upset? Then I think maybe there is tiger. Not sure, but maybe. So I listen. Then I hear something else."

"What?"

"Treepies. Now it is the satbhai and the treepies. But where? So I look and I find them sitting in the small tree next to the arch." He points to a tree in the distance and says, "That tree there. Do you see it?"

"I see it."

"Well, the jungle babblers and the treepies are in that tree and why they making all that noise? I think there must be tiger on the other side of arch. So I start up jeep, turn it around, and drive through. I look everywhere. No tiger. I can see the birds in the tree. Still upset. I turn jeep around and drive back through arch. Birds still in tree. No tiger anywhere! But I know tiger is there. So I turn around jeep again and drive back through arch four, maybe five times. English think Shafi is crazy. 'What are you doing?' they ask. I cannot explain. Finally, maybe fifth time, when I drive through arch, I look up and I see something."

"What was it?"

"This," he says, holding up the tip of his thumb for inspection. "All black. I see it in crack in the rocks. I stop jeep, back up. I ask one English to borrow his binoculars. I look up at this small black thing. Then I smile, because I know what it is."

"And what was it?"

"Tiger's tail, but tip only! Only tip is showing because tiger is laying in the weeds on top of the arch!"

"Watching you driving back and forth under it."

"Yes. Yes." Shafi laughs. "Watching us! English think Shafi is crazy. Tiger *know* Shafi is crazy!"

Perhaps five minutes later, toward the end of another tale, almost as good, I am aware of a sound—evidently from some distance—which at first I take for a hoarse human cough. Shafi, interrupting himself, sits up straight in a posture of acute attention.

"What was it?" I ask.

Not responding, he sits absolutely rigid, staring up the road. Again the cough comes, louder this time. *"Langurs!"* he cries. "When langur cough like that, he is seeing tiger!"

Without another word, he reaches down, starts the engine. A second later, we are barreling down the road.

After two minutes, Shafi slows the jeep to ordinary speed, then to a crawl, his eyes darting from one side of the road to the other, scanning the trees. Something on his side of the road captures his attention. He applies the brakes sharply and the jeep comes to an abrupt halt. "Look," he says.

I hoist myself up in my seat and gaze down at the soft shoulder of the road. Impressed on the sandy earth, a series of huge, clearly defined pugmarks continues along the road ahead of us, two by two, as far as I can see.

"A male?"

"A *big* male. I know him."

Shafi allows the jeep to putter forward about twenty yards, not taking his eyes off the tracks. Then, with no warning, he stops. I look down. Now the pugmarks are barely recognizable, not resembling footprints so much as hasty whisk marks made with a broom.

"Here he begins to run," Shafi says quietly.

My eyes track the whisk marks up the road to a point thirty feet ahead, where they veer into tall grass. From somewhere off to the right the cough comes again, hoarser and more desperately drawn out this time, as though the cougher is being throttled. Shafi switches off the engine and gazes over the four-foot-tall grass to a tongue of dry woodland, consisting of half a dozen medium-tall trees, which juts out into the meadow. "The langurs," he whispers.

For a moment I haven't a clue what he is talking about. Then I spot them: five pale gray langur monkeys the size of young children, with black faces and tails hanging straight down behind them like slack lengths of rope, clustered in the center of the tree that juts farthest into the meadow. Feeding on ripe red berries, nibbling with quick, nervous bites, allowing the inedible remains, seeds and stems, to fall to the ground, they seem at once utterly concentrated and completely mindless, not unlike a gang of teenage sociopaths lounging around some third-rate coffee bar.

Two of the monkeys, however, seem more aware, and look distinctly uneasy. One in fact is extremely agitated. Obviously the appointed sentinel, he grips the small branch in front of him and stares fixedly at a spot in the grass between his perch and us, not more than twenty-five or thirty feet from where we sit. I raise my binoculars and bring him into focus. At the precise moment I do, he curls back his upper lip, revealing sharp yellowish canine teeth, and delivers a throat-vibrating choked cough of warning.

"Tiger is *there,*" Shafi whispers.

"Where?"

"Where the langur is watching."

Calculating the precise angle of the langur's gaze, my eyes follow the angle to a tuft of high grass, an anonymous clump of rank vegetation, indistinguishable from any other. I turn my binoculars back to the langur. His expression tense and fearful, he stares, eyes fixed on the thing that would subdue him and devour him, given half a chance.

I look back at the clump of vegetation, half aware that the langur's anxiety has been relayed to me. The tiger's form flourishes in my mind's eye like an image on a computer screen. A simple silhouette etches itself on a blankness, contours gradually fill in, and at last the picture is complete. The tiger lies openmouthed, panting, waiting for that perfect moment, when the youngest, the stupidest, the least experienced of the langurs, provoked by sheer nervousness, takes a miscalculated leap and, missing the foreseen grip, plummets earthward. The thought that I could step down from the jeep and wade through the grass to where the tiger is lying in less than twenty seconds provokes a shiver.

"What do we do now?" I whisper at last.

"We wait."

The nearest standing tree is more than fifty yards away, and the sun begins to pound. The minutes ooze by. Beads of sweat burst on my scalp like kernels of popcorn and trickle stingingly into the corners of my eyes. Within minutes, I am silently cursing the fact that I left my hat back in the room.

More minutes pass. Just as my head begins to throb and

(as I imagine) the gray tissues begin to liquefy, I become aware of a shadow passing over us and look up just in time to see a crested serpent eagle swoop down, so close I can hear—or imagine I can hear—the superheated air crackling like hot grease in the splayed tips of its primary feathers. The bird tilts uncertainly, as though its navigational skills have been disordered, circles erratically, glides off in smooth silence over the tops of the trees.

"We have no luck today," Shafi says, apparently reading the bird's vanishing as an omen. Wiping his glistening forehead with the back of his shirtsleeve, he adds, "Tiger so close . . . But he does not move. Only waits for langur to fall. He thinks of nothing else."

"When do we have to be back at the gate?"

"Now."

"Too bad."

Shafi nods in disgusted agreement and looks away, his expression so dejected I feel compelled to console him. "Well," I say, trying to cast a positive light on the situation, "there's always this afternoon."

"Morning time is better."

"I have to leave tomorrow morning. I've made arrangements to meet a friend."

"This afternoon then," Shafi says, setting his jaw. "This afternoon we will see a tiger."

Eight

THE STEEP COBBLED PATHWAY leading up to Ranthambor Castle, broad enough for four horsemen to ride abreast, is girded by sheer stone walls forty feet high. Zigzagging every twenty yards, it leads from bright sunlight to cool shadow. As I walk over the polished cobblestones in the silence, aware of the regularity of my breathing and of my accelerated pulse, I find myself thinking of all the life that once thrived here, of all the human beings for whom this lonely place was once the center of the world. And somehow their uneasy spirits persist. Even in broad daylight it is a paranoid masterpiece.

Arriving at the top, a little winded, I find myself standing at a sort of crossroads at the edge of the castle precincts, and turning around, I look back over the valley. The view is panoramic, the area through which Shafi and I drove this morning laid out before me—the exaggeratedly bowl-like valley with its glistening lakes, bordered by crumbling pavilions half swallowed by dense jungle and patches of forest, the dry hills beyond. Plunking myself down on a large, flat stone, I gaze out at it all, feeling my thoughts rise with the heat in the silence.

Within seconds I am aware of an intruder. Turning my head to the right, I spot, less than thirty feet away, a perky brown bird that has materialized on a low wall and now perches, bobbing up and down like a coil-spring mechanical toy. It is a brown rock chat, a species so fond of human habitations, old forts, and the like and so seldom sighted anywhere else that a better name for it might be ruin chat. Vibrating with nervous energy, it flicks its wings, spreads its tail, jabs its bill at an invisible insect, and flits out of sight.

Realizing that to have a comprehensive view of the ruins I shall have to climb higher, I stand, stretch my legs, and head up one of the nearby cobbled streets, each pavingstone of which has been polished to smoothness by a thousand years of wear. Within a minute I reach an open area which seems to offer a view behind me. I turn and look back. What I expect is a ruined castle. What meets my eye is something more closely approaching a ruined city.

"The site is impressive, isn't it?" a thin voice says.

The speaker is an elderly European, or at least not an Indian, seated in a shadowy alcove nearby. "I apologize for catching you unawares," he says.

Perhaps seventy years old, he is a very good-looking man. Dressed in a striped shirt, suspenders, and light brown trousers, he sits with his jacket neatly folded in his lap. In comparison to my overheated and slightly out-of-breath self, he seems cool and collected. His expression, slightly owlish, is alert and full of inquiring intelligence. But it is his eyes, or rather his eyebrows, that I can't stop staring at. Bushy salt and pepper, they curl up dramatically at his temples like furry wings.

"That's all right," I say. "I don't think I was expecting anyone to be up here at midday."

"Mad dogs and Englishmen. But don't worry. I'm neither English nor hydrophobic."

Suddenly conscious of the fact that his speech is very slightly tinged with an accent that might be Slavic, I ask, "You're up here by yourself?"

"*Tout seul.* Don't I look capable of being left to my own devices?"

"Well . . ."

"Do you know the history of this place?"

"Ranthambor? Only rather sketchily, I'm afraid."

"For me," he says, smiling, "history is everything . . . Well, not everything perhaps. But a sense of history must have been encoded in my genes at birth. Do you care anything for history?"

"Well, yes. Are you a historian, a history teacher?"

"A professor. At least, I was once."

"And where did you profess?"

"Harvard, Oxford, a few other places. But I profess, as you put it, no longer. I have become a wandering albatross, albeit a terrestrial one, a wanderer over the face of the earth."

"A traveler?"

"A traveler."

"And where have you been wandering?"

"China, Japan, Peru, Bolivia, Zimbabwe, Ethiopia . . . I was in eastern Europe last year." He pauses. "I've even been to New Jersey."

"And now Ranthambor."

"Yes, Ranthambor."

"You are American?"

"By adoption only. I was born in Galicia."

"Poland."

"Very good. Most people, if they have ever heard of it, think it is a part of Spain. Yes, Poland. My first university was—and I employ the term in the way that monster

Maxim Gorky understood it—a place called Belzec. You have heard of it?"

"Yes, I know the name. It was a camp, wasn't it?"

"I congratulate you. Yes, a camp, one lacking the cachet of Auschwitz or Belsen or Dachau, but very like them in all the essential dehumanzing effects. You know some history, evidently."

"Some."

"If you are interested and have a few minutes, since you have admitted that you do not know much about the history of this place, I could tell you something about it."

"I am interested."

"Old habits die hard, you see. Once a professor, always a professor. May I suggest, then, that you join me here on this bench? My voice is not what it used to be."

I have not climbed the hill with the expectation of meeting a peripatetic historian on reaching the top. But my curiosity is piqued. I have no pressing engagements. So I walk over to the bench and take a seat next to him.

Once I am settled, he gazes out over the ruins of the city, which are shimmering slightly in the heat, and says, "If you would understand Ranthambor and the extraordinary events that occurred here, it might be useful to enter a sort of mental time machine, if you can, and travel back to the very beginning of the present millennium. It was during that era that the great Norseman Leif Ericson, his ship blown off course, discovered Vineland; then that one of the most refined civilizations ever conceived by the human imagination was gathered around the spectral personage of the emperor in the ancient city of Kyoto; then that most of the world was lost in darkness. Everywhere men ruled or were ruled by the sword. It was at that moment, in the place we now know as Afghanistan, that a charismatic young chieftain strode onto the stage of history. His name was Mahmud, and he meant to conquer the world . . ."

Like a child seated at his father's knee, I sit listening to the old man's voice, following, or attempting to follow, what is without doubt the most lucid and colorful exposition of any subject I have ever heard. His grasp, his command of dates, of social and political influences, the flow of dynasties and empires, the rise and fall of regimes, is mind-boggling. For the first few minutes I struggle to follow him, but within a very short time my mental capacities are defeated. The canvas is too large and complex, too teeming with detail. I find myself content in the end to listen to the sound of this old man's voice making music of the history of the world.

"And so at last we come to Ranthambor," he says after perhaps ten minutes. "As I have explained, Sultan Ala-ud-din-Khalji was no fool. In my opinion, history has scandalously underrated him. He was in fact something of a genius, grasping as any superior tactician would that any future claim to Rajputana depended utterly on the sack of Ranthambor. To that end, in the year 1300, he struck, sweeping in with his forces from the northeast. Ranthambor was invested, and the siege continued for months. This was one engagement that Ala-ud-din-Khalji had no intention of losing. The defenders of Ranthambor, led by the great Rana Hamir Deo Chauhan, fought valiantly. But the sultan's forces were ultimately overwhelming. When at last the people of Ranthambor learned that Chauhan was dead, slain on the field of battle, the news swept through the city in minutes, its significance clear to every inhabitant. Ranthambor was lost. Its defenders could expect no mercy. Only a short time remained before the gates were breached.

"The women of the city were fully aware of what the cosmic responsibilities of their caste demanded—the ritual of *jauhar*. In a clearing, perhaps right here where we sit, they brought together a great mass of firewood, jealously hoarded for months. A bonfire was lit. To avoid dishonor, they would enter the purifying flames. They dosed their children with *bhang*, an infusion of cannabis, and when the children's eyes glazed over, they cast them one by one into the fire, chanting their *puja* as they did. When the last child had gone to its fiery death, the women joined their children, some running wildly, others walking with dignity, their saris igniting as they entered the holocaust."

The professor falters for a moment. He sits, trembling, slightly out of breath, looking out over the ruins. Then, getting a grip on himself, he turns to me with a smile and says, "It would make quite a novel, wouldn't it?"

"Perhaps you should write it."

"At this stage of the game, I think not."

"Are you all right?"

"Quite all right, thank you. There is a good deal more to the story, you know. This city lived for a long time, and it is still living, in a sense. A thing is never quite dead as long as someone speaks of it." The professor glances down at his watch and looks a bit surprised at what it indicates. "Well," he says, sitting up straight, "my driver will be rather upset with me. I am due in Jaipur at five o'clock to see a man about a book, a very old book, probably a fake. But we shall see. We shall continue another time, perhaps?"

"I'd enjoy that."

"Did you learn something?"

"Most definitely."

"Good," he says. Turning, he reaches out for the walking stick that is leaning up against the wall next to him. It is an extraordinarily handsome thing, its ferrule shaped like a dragon's head. "Could I impose on you to help me up?" he says, glancing at me. "When I have been sitting too long, my joints seem to crystallize."

I take him by the forearm and help him to his feet. "Shall I come with you down the hill?" I ask.

"No, no. Thank you very much. Once upright, I am efficiently bipedal. But it is kind of you to offer." Taking one last look out over the ruined city, the professor says, "Ranthambor is every bit as enchanting as I always thought it would be. Do enjoy your visit here."

"I intend to."

"Goodbye, then," he says with a smile.

I sit down on the stone bench and watch him go, my mind awash with the images of the story he has just told me. For a long time I sit listening to the receding *tap tap tap* of his cane on the cobbles, not quite conscious of the precise moment they merge with the silence. Only then does it occur to me that I did not even think to ask him his name.

Nine

AN HOUR LATER, I am sitting on a rickety wooden chair on a narrow porch on the water side of the Joghi Mahal, the little shooting lodge that Shafi pointed out to me this morning from across the lake. Smaller than it appears from a distance, it consists of two compact wings, each possessing a couple of rooms. It has crossed my mind that if the great palazzo-maker Palladio had been born a little further east—in the Punjab, say, instead of Padua—he might easily have produced something like this.

For the past half-hour I have been sitting here in the cool shade daydreaming, looking out over the lagoon, the waters lapping just below the railing at my feet. A few minutes ago, a sudden movement registered at the corner of my eye. Glancing out over the water, I saw a little grebe, a waterbird the size of a small hen, rise up briefly before settling back onto a mass of rotted vegetation anchored to a water hyacinth less than twenty feet away. Her plumage is so cryptic, she and her nest blend so well with their surroundings, that even now, if I take my eyes off her, I have trouble locating her again. As strategies for survival go, this one has much to recommend it. With a little luck, she will be left in peace.

But the lagoon is not all cozy domesticity. Reminding me that this is no mere pond in a big-city park is an eight- or nine-foot-long mugger crocodile, jaws propped open wide in response to the heat. Displaying an impressive set of teeth, it is sunbathing on a rock a few yards beyond the grebe—so close that if I had a pebble or two, I could probably bop it on the head from where I sit. Charming though the lagoon is, it is clearly no place even to consider taking a refreshing dip.

For the last few minutes I have been paging through a book I purchased at a secondhand bookstall on Janpath Road in Delhi last week, *Hints on Tiger Shooting,* by a certain Colonel Kesri Singh. I have discovered, quite by chance, that it contains a good deal of information about Ranthambor during the days of the great tiger shoots. Colonel Singh, I have learned, was responsible for organizing hunts for the maharaja of Jaipur and his guests here at Ranthambor for over thirty years, from the 1930s to the 1960s. At the beginning of his chapter entitled "Shikar Camps at Sawai Madhopur," I have found a neat little description of the building in which I am sitting when it was the haunt of European royalty, famous statesmen, American millionaires, and movie stars.

> The Maharaja of Jaipur is a great sportsman and also has a remarkable taste in decorating his various buildings and palaces. Evidence of this is a romantic Shooting Lodge in the beautiful jungles of Sawai Madhopur. The lodge is a small building, neat and comfortable, having a couple of bedrooms on the first floor. There is a spacious lawn adjoining the house, big enough for croquet and badminton, providing an interesting interlude while the guests are waiting for tiger news. In order to accommodate a large number of guests a camp is laid out consisting of several double and single pole tents, having baths and dressing rooms attached to

each. A big shamiana (canvas pavilion) is pitched in the centre where all assemble before the shoot. The area is enclosed with a six-foot canvas screen to keep away trespassers. Recently six huts have been constructed to lodge the guests and this has done away with the necessity of putting up tents, etc. Inside the enclosure, there is plenty of room for the guests to take their morning exercise on camels. A camel ride before breakfast is a good specific for shaking the liver after a previous hangover.

This must be the most original, and least appealing, cure for the morning after ever devised. I do not find it all that easy to imagine the likes of Lord Mountbatten, millionaire socialite Barbara Hutton, and Jimmy Stewart, all of whom came to Ranthambor to hunt tiger at one time or another, stumbling bleary-eyed out of their tents in the predawn light to have their livers shaken by Colonel Singh and his camels. But if the colonel insists, I am obliged to believe it.

I hear footsteps and look up.

Valmik Thapar appears around the corner and says in his perfect Oxbridge accent, "I thought I might find you here. Am I interrupting something?"

"Nothing that can't wait. Have a seat."

He pulls over one of the wooden chairs and sits down, the chair groaning and creaking under his bulk. "Have you had your lunch yet?" he asks.

"There's a man downstairs who claims to be making me some."

"It'll be along eventually, then. I just ran into Shafi and he told me that you had a tiger cornered this morning."

"It was more the other way around, I'm afraid."

"That happens. I'm not sure I'd like to know how much time I've spent sitting in jeeps waiting for a tiger to make an appearance. It can be very frustrating."

"There's a tiger that lives here, I can't remember its name —the one that ambushes sambar in the water—"

"You're thinking of Genghiz."

"Yes. I saw that film *Land of the Tiger* on TV in the States. The footage of the hunt in the water was incredible."

"Yes, the film was quite good, wasn't it? It was shot here and at Kanha by some friends of mine, wonderful film-makers, the Breedens. They were shooting here at Ranthambor off and on for nearly a year."

"And the tiger's name is Genghiz?"

"Was."

"He's no longer around?"

"Unfortunately not."

"What happened?"

"Nobody knows. We speculated about it endlessly. He simply vanished one day. He was either killed by another tiger or run out of his territory. You know, the law of the jungle and all that."

"There were villages here before Ranthambor became a park, weren't there?"

"Oh yes."

"And were there problems when the government informed the villagers they would have to move?"

"Of course."

"What happened?"

"The villagers turned a bit nasty. I can't say I blame them. The villages had been established here for a long time."

"But the people finally cleared out?"

"Of course. They had to leave. Laws were passed to protect Ranthambor and its tigers, so they had to go. If they hadn't left, you would have seen farmers tilling their fields and herders tending their flocks on your drive around the lakes this morning."

"And where did the villagers go?"

"Out. Several places, I think."

"And the park is well protected now? I mean, if you're American or European and you're talking about a national park, it usually means an area that is fenced, or at least an area that is well defined and patrolled. Except for the gate where the permits are handed out, I haven't see any guards or fences."

"It's all a question of resources. Or rather, a lack of them. In fact, the situation of Ranthambor is not very different from that of any other park in India. It is slowly being nibbled away a leaf, a twig, a branch at a time."

As he says this, I find myself thinking of that terrible area in the foothills around the pink palace where I am staying, that overgrazed wasteland I have come to think of as the ghost forest. "Over where I'm staying, at the Joomar Bhowari," I say, "the whole area looks as though it had been bombed."

"Well, that's just outside the park boundary. But it's all on account of the drought. It has lasted now for more or less seven years, and the villagers in this part of Rajasthan are getting desperate. There are dozens of villages nearby, with thousands of people, not to mention thousands of animals, to be fed. Until the drought ends, and God knows when that may be, the situation will continue to worsen. People will keep driving their flocks into the park and they will keep stripping the vegetation for firewood. I don't think anyone or anything can stop it."

At that moment, from the corner of my eye, I catch the movement of the grebe shifting on her nest. "Have you seen my bird?" I ask.

"Your what?"

"My bird. It's a little grebe." Resting my arm on the stone railing of the balustrade, I point directly at her. Thapar looks, but I can see from his expression that he cannot spot her.

"I take it," he says, "you're pointing at something out in the water?"

"Yes, it's a floating nest. If you aim down my arm, I think you'll be able to see it."

Rising from his seat, he crouches down in back of me and sights down my arm. For several seconds he draws a blank. Then, on an expelled breath, he says, "Ahh, I see it . . . My God, she really blends in, doesn't she?"

As he resumes his seat, I realize that I am still thinking about his comment about overgrazing. "But you do think the park will be protected in the long run, don't you? I mean, if I am lucky enough to come back here in, say, twenty-five years, there will be a park here, won't there?"

Thapar smiles and sniffs the air and says, "Who knows? That's all in the future. The future is an unknown place. This being India, the future is something I try not to think very much about."

Nearly three hours later, just before sunset, on our way back to the Joomar Bhowari, Shafi and I drive across the same series of dry watercourses that Shafi paid such close attention to as we drove into the park this morning. Each time we cross one, he eases his foot off the accelerator and gives the adjacent woodland a brief but definitive inspection. As we come up to an unusually wide streambed and Shafti slows the jeep to cross it, his gaze shoots off right, his eyes for a moment registering nothing. Then, in a perfect double take, they do. "*Tiger!*" he shouts.

Jamming on the brakes, jutting out his arm so I won't crash through the windshield, he brings the jeep to a skidding halt. He yanks the gearshift into reverse, the engine whines, and we lunge backward so violently I am almost thrown out of my seat. We cover the forty feet of ground back to the place where the streambed crosses the road in five seconds. The jeep slams to a halt, and I look to the right. Standing in the middle of the dry streambed, not more than ten yards from where I sit, is a tiger.

"I know this cat," Shafi whispers with a tremendous grin on his face, reaching down and switching off the ignition. "I have seen her here before. Always in the morning. There is a pond at the top of the hill there where she likes to go to drink."

"She seems young," I say.

"She is young. But already she has two litters."

"Why is she just sitting there?"

"Waiting for us."

"Why doesn't she just go around?"

"Why should she? Maybe every evening she comes down this streambed and crosses the road right here. And why not? This is her place."

The young tigress does not move, only stares, with a curious but patient expression on her face. She seems to be in no hurry, as though she realizes that we, being humans, will sooner or later simply lose interest in blocking her path and move on. After a couple of minutes, Shafi reaches down to the key in the ignition. He gives it a twist and the engine roars. The tigress's ears perk up. But she does not move.

Reaching down to the gearshift, Shafi puts the jeep into four-wheel drive, then very slowly releases the clutch, revolving the steering wheel as he does. The jeep edges toward the tigress. I start to object. Then I don't. My experience with Amar Singh has taught me a thing or two. Shafi must know what he is doing.

As the gap between us closes, the expression on the tigress's face does not change. But then, when we are no more than twenty feet from her, it does. Bolting off the track so fast that I cannot follow her movement, she crashes into deep brush. Within a few seconds she breaks onto the road behind us, crosses it in a streak, and bounds up the hill, revealing a flash of orange through branches and leaves as she clears the top. When I turn to Shafi, another broad grin has stretched across his face.

"You see," he says. "I told you we would see a tiger."

Part Two

A Tiger in His Den

Ten

THE AFTERNOON is cloudless, warm, sun-drenched. There is not a breath of air. At the side of the road a bullock lies in a shallow ditch, eyes blank, too-short legs pointing stiffly to the sky, the leathery skin of its abdomen scissored open, laid back in ragged flaps, exposing glistening viscera. There are thousands of flies. Fifty vultures have gathered around the carcass; three or four perch uneasily atop it. One of them, giving no warning, lunges at another, losing its balance and regaining it almost instantly with a shuffling of wings. The birds glare at each other, but they are too nervous, too caught up in the violent moment to feed.

Ten yards away, C and I stand half sheltered from the pounding sun in the mottled penumbra of a spindly shisham tree, studying the birds through binoculars. "There are three species there," I explain to her in my best didactic tone. "The birds squatting on top of the carcass are whitebacks. The whiteback is a close relative of a vulture you may have seen in Africa. The small group of birds to the left are longbills. Their bills are narrower than those of the whitebacks, and their plumage is browner. The pink-headed one off to the left by itself is a king vulture, *Sarcogyps calvus*, literally 'bald flesh vulture.' "

"Fascinating," she says.

"It's the whitebacks and longbills who always turn up first," I continue, ignoring the suggestion of sarcasm in her voice. "They perform the major surgery with those meat-cleaver beaks of theirs. When they've eaten their fill, they allow the much smaller Egyptian vultures to come in to haggle over the remains with the jackals. They're the cleanup patrol. In a few days, there won't be anything left but bones."

"Charming."

"Have you had enough?"

"I think so."

Nearly a week has passed since I left Ranthambor, and it seems longer. As we turn and head back toward the car, it crosses my mind how odd it is for me to be traveling with a woman. Unless I am leading a tour, this is something I seldom do. When I met C in Kathmandu a little over a month ago, we discussed the possibility of her coming down to India to travel for a few weeks sometime after my tour ended. Once I got back to Delhi from Ranthambor, I telephoned her. Getting through to her on the first try seemed altogether extraordinary; hearing that she was ready to join me, had in fact already made arrangements to do so, struck me as little short of miraculous.

She flew down to Lucknow yesterday, and I met her at the airport. I had hired a car and driver, and now here we were on our way to meet one of India's most renowned tiger experts. Unfortunately, in my eagerness to meet "Billy" Arjan Singh, I may have set us up for disaster. Upon making inquiries in Lucknow, I learned from a portly desk clerk at the Carlton Hotel that short of actually driving up there,

there was literally no way to contact Tiger Haven, "Billy" Arjan Singh's farm.

"You mean there's no phone?" I asked, staring at the clerk.

"No phone."

"Can I send them a wire?"

"Yes. But I doubt that they would receive it."

"There must be—"

"Oh, I am very afraid not, sir!" he said, grinning around a mouthful of bright red betel. "No Pony Express in these parts, no *carrier pigeon!*" He laughed out loud at this sally of rapier wit, and as he did, the corner of his mouth overflowed, sending a spurt of blood-red juice cascading down his already soiled shirtfront.

On C's arrival, I rather self-consciously explained our dilemma. The lodge was six or seven hours from Lucknow by car. Since there was absolutely no way to get in touch in advance, for all I knew, we could drive all the way up there only to spend the night huddled up like a couple of refugees in the back seat of the car. C's reaction both surprised and pleased me. "Well," she said, "it looks as though we're going to have an adventure."

Once we are back in the car and our exceptionally close-mouthed driver has pulled onto the road, I steal a glance at C. There is, I realize, very little about her that suggests that she may be even a potential connoisseur of vultures. Fashionably thin and blond, a dedicated urbanite, she is obviously out of her element in this environment—the sort of woman who might harbor the belief that raccoons are dangerously carnivorous. But I like her just the same. Carrion eaters aside, she seems to be enjoying the trip so far.

I turn and gaze out the window. Here in the north of India it is harvest time. Ever since leaving Lucknow this morning, we have been watching tall, almost impenetrable stands of cane being felled by the local folk, the scarecrow-thin men squatting in their dhotis, wielding hand scythes, the women and children gathering the fallen stalks into sheaves and loading them onto oxcarts. C seems to derive special pleasure from the villages we drive through. She seems to enjoy the noisy bicycle-rickshaw-oxcart traffic jams, the swirling crowds, the various wafting odors, some unpleasant, but most of them spicy and alluring. One element that has made the journey a success for me is that our driver is cautious behind the wheel. He does not appear to be overly fond of the game of chicken, and as a result there has been thus far a pleasing minimum of flashing headlights and heart-stopping near-collisions.

The roads in this area, even by Indian standards, are poor. Barely wide enough for a single automobile, they support two-way traffic nevertheless. The accepted protocol here, as everywhere in India, is that when two vehicles meet, both pull halfway off the road and edge cautiously around each other in a studied minuet, like two overly polite, shiny-carapaced beetles meeting head to head on some shadowy forest path. This, needless to say, makes for slow going. But any greater speed would be a risky undertaking. Too many potholes, too many people using the margins of the road as a footpath, too many children, too many wandering cows.

Turning away from the window with a smile, C says, "So tell me about this Billy Singh. What does he do exactly?"

"Well, I think I mentioned to you in Kathmandu that he's a writer and naturalist. He has written a number of books about various wild cats—tiger and leopard, for instance—which he hand-raised and released in the wild. His farm, Tiger Haven, butts up against the boundary of Dudhwa National Park. It seems that he was more or less responsible for getting the government to make Dudhwa a park in the first place. Unfortunately, over the past couple of years particularly, there has been a lot of trouble up there."

"What kind of trouble?"

"Apparently the park has no buffer zone, and—"

"Buffer zone?"

"That's supposed to be an area of forest around a park that shields it from human interference."

"And Dudhwa Park doesn't have one."

"Exactly. It's the same sort of problem that is occurring all over India, and all over the world, with variations. At Dudhwa, the local farmers have been allowed to plant cane right up to the park boundary. But the tigers that live in the park have no interest in boundaries. They leave the forest in the heat of the day to lie in the cane, and when the farmers come to tend their fields . . ."

"They're attacked."

"Right. There have been several hundred killings and maulings in recent years. In revenge, the farmers have taken to killing tigers whenever and however they can."

"And Billy Singh is on the side of the tigers."

"Yes. His stance has pretty much alienated the farmers. One article I read quoted a local thakur, or village headman, as saying that Billy Singh doesn't care about people, he only cares about tigers."

"Sounds like an interesting man."

C is quiet for a moment, then says, "Tell me about tigers. I mean, we're going to visit this world-famous tiger expert, and I realize I don't know a thing about them."

"Well, the first thing you need to know is that they're not really very much like lions. For starters, they spend relatively little time out in the open. They're as secretive as hell, in fact. If you want to observe them, you really have to go where they live."

"Into the forest."

"Right."

"I think I read somewhere . . . aren't they mostly solitary?"

"More or less. Males spend most of their lives alone. They control large territories which encompass the smaller territories of a number of females. They try to dominate as many females as they can—an average might be five or six, but the figure is sometimes higher. They are very protective, very territorial about their females and their patch of real estate. They usually attack any other tiger or leopard they catch wandering into their area."

"Sounds like a rough life."

"It is rough. Anyway, every couple of months a female, provided she is not pregnant or tending cubs, comes into estrus. Hormones are released into her urine, and since, like the male, she makes a habit of marking her territory by pissing on various trees, the local male is soon alerted to the fact that she is ready to mate."

"And if she's ready to mate?"

"Then they mate. Not just once or twice—sometimes a hundred times in the space of twenty-four hours. The interesting thing is that she doesn't ovulate until after mating begins. The whole thing seems to be designed to guarantee that she'll get pregnant. Anyway, she remains receptive for only a few days. Then she drives him off."

"At which point the male, feeling rejected, goes off in search of another female who might be more accommodating?"

"Right."

"Ah, *men* . . ." She smiles. "And if she's pregnant, what happens then?"

"After about three months, she gives birth to two to four cubs. Normally only two survive the first couple of weeks. She nurses the cubs until they are about a year old, by which time they're eating meat. Generally speaking, when the cubs are about two years old, they're out on their own."

"And the cycle begins again."

"I think you've got it."

Eleven

THREE HOURS LATER, when the sun is hovering like a glowing, deliquescent pumpkin over a deep purple silhouette of forest, I am feeling as exhausted and nervous as a testy tomcat left locked in a closet on a sweltering afternoon. Though we have been on this narrow country road for almost seven hours, our driver has yet to offer the slightest indication that we are anywhere near Billy Singh's farm, and the question of where we will end up spending the night has begun to gnaw at me. There was a town not far back. It occurred to me as we passed through it that it must possess some sort of hotel. But it is all too easy to imagine what sort of place it would be—beds with soiled mattresses, fingerprints on the walls, a naked bulb dangling from the ceiling, cockroaches and rodents skittering in the shadows. Just the sort of place for C.

In spite of my anxiety, I feel certain that we must be somewhere near our destination. Over the last half-hour or so, the endless fields of mustard and cane have increasingly given way to patches of forest. These scattered groves of trees, silhouetted against the evening sky, have lent a new element of mystery to the landscape. And I think I know why. With every passing mile, we are leaving the human world behind. We are entering tiger country.

Looking over at C, who seems completely exhausted, I say, "We'll be there soon."

"How soon is *soon?*"

"Soon."

The hum of the engine like a descant over the silence, we watch the great orange ball of the sun sink behind a dark barricade of leaves. The last speck of light is gradually being swallowed up when I feel the driver ease up on the accelerator, tentatively at first, then with greater conviction. From his air of concentration, I can tell that he is watching for something, a landmark perhaps. At last I feel him apply the brakes and the car slowly rolls to a stop.

Following his gaze off to the left, I notice a dirt track that heads downhill toward open woodland before veering right just short of a wall of cane. "Tiger Haven?" I inquire. The driver, as usual, has no comment but with a subtle rocking of his head suggests, Hindu fashion, that this is indeed the entrance to Billy Singh's farm. I breathe an audible sigh of relief. We have made it.

With no further ado, the driver grinds the Ambassador into gear and moves off the pavement onto an array of ruts which, though crusty and hard-edged, appear to have been gooey mud a short time ago. I have been reading in the newspapers about all the unseasonable rain that has fallen in northern India over the last couple of weeks, and it is clear that this area has had its share. With a thump, the car's tires settle into the most deeply incised set of petrified tracks, making it literally unnecessary to steer. But the driver, unwilling to concede control of the expensive automobile with which he has been entrusted, grips the steering wheel and slows to a crawl.

In less than a minute, we are hemmed in on both sides. To

our left stands a dark barrier of cane, leafy stalks undulating against the deepening blue of the sky and so dense it is impossible to stare even a foot into it. To our right is a woodland stream, its banks shrubby jungle. I roll down the window on my side and stick out my head. I take in a deep satisfying breath, rich with the damp odors of evening.

I have no sooner settled back in my seat than we round a bend and a greater coucal struts out onto the track ten yards ahead of us. This mostly ground-dwelling relative of the European cuckoo is a handsome chicken-sized bird with a black head and fuselage and cinnamon-colored wings. Hesitating for a second, stretching its neck to get a grip on who we are, it explodes in a flurry of feathers and nose-dives into the seemingly inpenetrable wall of vegetation. At that precise instant, the driver applies the brakes abruptly and the Ambassador skids to a halt.

"What's the matter?" I ask. But directly ahead, I see what is the matter.

Fifteen yards away, the track descends into a slight hollow, then vanishes into what appears to be a very large muddy pool. I half hope that the driver will react in some way, perhaps offer some kernel of insight. But he does not. He sits utterly impassive, a lump at the wheel.

"Well?" I say at last.

Because the face staring back at me in the rearview mirror is a blank slate, I feel my equanimity begin to crack like old plaster. Intuiting that mere words will be ineffective, and realizing that the world outside is growing darker by the minute, I opt for action. Grasping the door handle, I swing the door open and step out of the car. Slamming the door behind me, I cover the twenty steps to the pool in the exaggerated gait favored by axe-wielding psychopaths.

Seen close at hand in the richness of the fading light, the pool takes on the disturbing proportions of a mini-lake. Though probably not more than thirty-five feet long, certainly nowhere more than a few inches deep, it might as well be Tahoe or Baikal or Titicaca, from the point of view of traversing it without benefit of four-wheel drive. Looking to the right, I see that the earth is soft and falls away from the track into a shallow vegetated gully. To the left of the lake, however, the ground seems more promising. Following the muddy border in that direction, pushing through almost knee-deep grass, I test the ground for firmness as I go. After several seconds, it occurs to me that with just a little luck, we might be able to make it.

Turning back to face the car and employing a bit of elementary sign language, I attempt to communicate my optimistic conclusion. The driver, however, in spite of the fact that his eyes are open, gives the strongest possible impression that he has expired at the wheel. Stirring himself at last, he opens the door, steps out of the car, and ambles toward me. Arriving at my side, he gives the mini-lake a perfunctory visual sweep, casting a glance best described as doubtful at the detour I have indicated.

"We'll go this way," I say, giving the air in front of me a karate chop. In no mood for discussion, much less dissent, I turn, stride back to the car, open the door, climb in, and slam the door behind me.

Only then do I realize that the driver is still standing exactly where I left him. As though reading my mind, he turns and marches sullenly back toward us. He opens the door, climbs in, and closes it firmly. Since it is just dark enough outside now to make the headlights useful, he switches them on.

Grinding the transmission into gear, he eases off the clutch. The Ambassador edges forward. Ten feet. Fifteen feet. Just short of the water, he deftly coaxes the car out of the tracks and pilots it toward the proposed detour. "Good," I hear myself mutter approvingly.

With what at first appears to be surpassing mastery, he

guides the car into the grass. Within seconds the halfway point is passed, and I begin to feel certain that we are, as they say, going to go the distance. But the self-congratulatory monologue fizzles as I become aware that the car has suddenly lost momentum. From somewhere below and behind us a high-pitched whine saws into the silence.

"Stop!"

The driver, responding instantly for once, slides his foot off the accelerator. Opening the door, I step out of the car and slip my foot into wet creamy ooze, which soaks immediately through the fabric of my shoes. "Ugghh," I hear myself mutter with some distaste, as I lower my other foot into the muck.

I step away from the car and take a look. Even at a glance, it is obvious that we are in big trouble. The right rear tire has settled a good three inches into sodden grassy soil. A quiet curse escapes me. I turn and wade around to the back of the car and stand there for a moment scanning the area for anything—a log or a branch—that I might be able to jam under the wheel to provide some traction.

Just visible in the shadows, fifteen feet back in the direction from which we have come, something is lying half concealed in the grass. Either a largish branch or a hungry python. Trudging back to it, I see that it is a limb, much too large for my purposes, with several substantial branches and prickly leaves attached. Bending over, I take hold of one of the branches and attempt to break it off. But the rubbery wood refuses to crack. Suddenly feeling utterly helpless and stupid, I glance around me, wondering by what brilliant stroke of the imagination I contrived to get us into this mess. As no alternative presents itself, I drag the branch toward the car.

After five minutes of tugging, pushing, heaving, and grunting, I manage to jam, or rather half jam, one end of the branch under the wheel, by which time I am soaked with sweat and my hands, shoes, and trousers are smeared with mud the consistency of cake frosting. "All right," I say at last to the driver, who has not budged from his seat. "Let's try it."

He obligingly grinds the Ambassador into gear, revs the engine, and then inadvertently pops the clutch. The sequence of events that happens next occurs not in real time but in gauzy slow motion—the spinning wheel, spitting mud, half surmounting the branch, hovering for a single heroic instant before sliding inexorably, sickeningly, along it toward the mini-lake and me.

"Wait!" I cry.

Deafened by the roar of the engine, the driver pays no heed.

"WAIT!"

He responds.

But too late. The tire has come to rest a full six inches into the muddy ooze. In a state of semishock, I cannot help taking perverse note of the fact that the Ambassador is listing a little now, not unlike an unlucky packet that has taken a torpedo amidships. Gazing at it dumbly, I sigh with the knowledge that now I shall have to face C.

Wading around the back of the car, I open her door and peer inside. In the shadows her very tense gaze meets my own. "We're stuck," I say.

"I'd gathered that. What do we do now?"

"We have a choice. We can spend the night here, or . . . we can walk."

"How far is it?"

"Not sure. Probably not far."

"Does the driver know?"

I glance at the driver in the rearview mirror. He gazes back. I glance at C, who glances at the driver, then back at me.

"Sorry I asked," she says.

We take less than a minute to decide what we will bring with us. A flashlight would be helpful, but of course there is no flashlight. We decide at last to take only the barest essentials: C's shoulder bag, my binoculars, our toothbrushes and jackets. The luggage will be left behind, locked up in the trunk. Once outside, standing in knee-high grass, C looks at me and says, "I just want to ask you one thing. Is it safe to walk here?"

"Of course."

"Didn't you tell me this morning that there are man-eating tigers up here?"

"Oh, but that's only . . . at the edges of the park."

"I see. And that isn't here?"

"No," I say, gesturing vaguely off to my left. "That's way over there."

"I see," C says. "There are man-eaters at the edge of the park, but the edge of the park is way over there. Well, that makes me feel much better." Casting a steely, arched-browed look at me, then at the road winding off into the cane, she squares her shoulders, sighs, and says, "Well, then—shall we be on our way?"

In the gathering darkness the first crystalline stars burn into view. As we walk hand in hand along the treacherously uneven muddy track, enclosed on both sides by walls of cane, I find myself calculating our chances of literally stumbling into a tiger. I halt for a moment and look back.

The driver, hanging well back, obviously knows precisely what he is doing. If C and I do surprise a tiger, it is undoubtedly he who will have the best chance of getting away. I have not the slightest doubt that he would abandon us in a trice to be butchered in the mud. And who in his right mind would blame him?

We trudge on in silence. In the west the silver sliver of a moon appears in a gap in the trees. Rounding a bend, I stub my toe on an unseen clod. Just as I recover I hear C expel a sudden breath as she comes to a halt in the middle of the track. "What's that?" she says.

"What's what?"

"Something crossed the road."

I feel her grip tighten.

"Maybe it was a bird," I say.

"It was bigger than that."

"How big?"

"Big."

I stare, aware of no movement or sound beyond the empty susurrus of faintly rustling cane. I put my arm around her, and in that instant I see the debacle whole. We could be somewhere else right now—sitting in a nice restaurant, deeply engaged in a discussion of something really profound, like wallpaper or professional sports. But no. That would be far too easy. *Much* more intelligent to be wending our way through the middle of a canefield in some lost corner of India, patiently waiting to be ambushed, mauled, and murdered.

"Look," I say, "I'm really sorry about this—"

Just then lightning flashes in the distance. I look heavenward, but the sky is free of cloud. Then I hear it. Not thunder, but the unmistakable sound of an automobile engine.

C and I turn, almost in unison.

Spurts of light erupt over the cane tops as the approaching vehicle traverses the ruts and hollows of the track. Two headlights swerve into view with a roar, and I know instantly from the sound of the engine that the vehicle is a jeep, know also that I shall have a good deal of explaining to do. Suddenly mortally self-conscious, I step off the track, and C follows. Our driver, I notice, has already done so.

The jeep pulls up to us and stops. In the dim reflected glare I can see that it is loaded with passengers. The driver of the jeep is a stocky Indian man, whose steady gaze and bearing give an impression that is, for want of a better word, military. Summoning up my most winning smile, I say, "Good evening. I'm afraid we've gotten stuck."

"We noticed that," he says in English that is without a trace of an Indian accent.

"Is this the way to Tiger Haven?"

"It is."

"Do you live here?"

"Indeed I do."

"Is there any chance you could put us up for the night?"

"Well," he says, after a slight hesitation, "the problem is that we're all going away on holiday, except for Billy, and I don't—"

"Well, we can't leave them out here." A woman's voice rings out from the back of the jeep. It is a voice as clean and sharp as a new piece of cutlery. "The thing to do," it continues, "is to come up to the house and have a cup of tea. We can sort it all out there."

This directive is unchallenged, and I am immediately aware that the passengers have begun to shift to make room.

"Thank you," I say. "That's very kind of you."

As C and I turn to the back of the jeep, I catch a glimpse of her face in the reflected glow of the headlights, and for a single fleeting instant I can read her mind: *We are saved!*

Twelve

OUR DRIVER, C, AND I climb into the jeep and settle into our seats. In the pale reflected glow of the headlights, I notice that we are sitting face to face with an Indian lady, and I realize at once that it is she who has just spoken out on our behalf. Slim, handsome, fiftyish, with enormous dark pools for eyes, all the more striking because of the way she keeps her hair—which is cut in something of a pageboy style, parted on one side and swept across her head—she fixes us with a smile suspended between some inner rigidity and a requisite civility. She introduces herself—I do not catch the name—and demands in turn our names and nationalities.

I am instantly impressed. Her mannerisms, verbal and physical, far from being Indian, are perfect upper-crust London. With her chin slightly elevated to produce vowels that are softened and impossibly elongated, she either half swallows her nouns or brings them strongly to the fore, where they are forged into little hammers for emphasis. I cannot resist a smile. With only her voice to go by, I might easily take her for a duchess bending over a plate of fancy cakes at a fashionable party in Belgravia.

Five minutes ago C appeared to be hanging on at the frayed end of her tether. Now, the presumption that she has been plucked from the jaws of death has apparently provided her a new lease on life. Fielding questions with the easy elegance of a seasoned shortstop, she is obviously as interested in the Indian lady as the Indian lady appears to be in her. For a couple of minutes I am drawn into this feminine feeling-out session, until at last I notice the wavering beams of the headlights playing on the walls of a complex of white buildings which I recognize from photographs I have seen in Billy Singh's books. Tiger Haven.

As the jeep swerves, then lurches to a halt, several servants crowd around to greet us. The Indian lady is instantly out of the jeep and on her feet, delivering several sets of orders in Hindi, and the servants scurry off, our driver in their wake. Turning to the remaining passengers, the Indian lady says, "Now, everyone, go straight into the house."

C and I climb down. It is only when I turn back to the jeep that I note with surprise that another white-skinned person is among the passengers—a woman. The driver douses the headlights, and I see that the buildings we have driven up to stand at the edge of a large clearing. To the front of the buildings are several large trees and beyond them, off to our left, what appears to be a fallow field stretching into the distance. Standing there, I have the strange sensation that beyond the pale emanation of light from the windows of the house, out in that distant field of cane, a tiger is watching us.

"Go right on inside," the Indian lady repeats, dissolving the image. She is now stationed in front of the doorway. "It's too chilly to be standing about out here."

I wipe the muddy soles of my shoes on the threshold and step onto a screened porch dimly lit by a candle burning in a metal dish that has been placed on a wooden table. The Indian lady then urges us through yet another doorway into a sort of oblong sitting room illuminated by the soft glow of several kerosene lamps. A fire is blazing in the hearth.

The room is welcoming. A couch and several chairs are arranged around the fireplace. The opposite end of the room serves as a sort of library; two of its walls are lined with waist-high book cabinets enclosed by glass doors. Beneath a window to our right is a window seat, and beside it a glass-fronted highboy, also filled with books, all the books in this case written by Arjan Singh himself: *Tiger Haven, Prince of Cats, Eelie.*

But it is the photograph-covered wall above the cabinets that captures my attention: Billy, naked to the waist, displaying a handsome physique, smiling paternally at a tiger cub; Billy paddling a canoe, gazing proudly at the full-grown leopard that is posed in front of him, standing at the bow. Atop the cabinets themselves I note a number of objects that are, to say the least, unanticipated—a television, a VCR, and a selection of videotapes. Naively, I have not expected to discover a so-called home entertainment center in a remote corner of the Indian forest.

Turning away from that corner of the room, I find that all the passengers from the jeep have assembled in front of the fire. The European lady is, I judge, in her late forties. Attractive in an unflashy sort of way, she has a pleasant smile and a shy, somewhat vulnerable air. Standing next to her is an attractive young Indian couple and their child, a good-looking, dark-eyed boy of four or five, gripping his mother firmly by the hand. It crosses my mind that they and the European lady are paying guests, having driven up from God knows where for a few days of tiger viewing.

Standing directly to the left of the Indian couple is the driver of the jeep. My first impression of him now seems accurate enough. An inch or two shorter than I, he is powerfully built and has a massive head and hardly any neck, a feature that, combined with his impeccable posture, gives him the air of a slightly rotund obelisk. I would not be surprised in the least to learn that he is a batallion commander in the Indian Army.

But it is the final passenger who interests me most. Standing apart from the group, he is sixty-five or seventy years old. Wearing a pair of eyeglasses that make him look slightly dotty, he appears somewhat diminished and frail, not to mention a good deal older than the person featured in the photographs on the walls. I know, nevertheless, that this is "Billy" Arjan Singh.

"Well then," the Indian lady says, spinning on her heel in the middle of the semicircle we have automatically formed. "It's time for proper introductions, isn't it?" Smiling somewhat stiffly, she introduces C and me to the rest of the passengers. Touching herself lightly on the breast, she then says, "My name is Mira, as I told you before." Then, indicating the European lady, she says, "This is Margaret, an old friend who has come from England on holiday. We're very pleased to have her here." Gesturing in the direction of the burly driver, who seems to stiffen a bit, she says with a great deal of pride, "This is my husband, Balram. Balram is Billy's brother." Pointing to the young Indian couple, she gives their names (hers is Linda, his I do not catch) and explains that they are her daughter-in-law and son. Throwing a fond glance at the little boy, who instantly attempts to conceal himself behind his mother's leg, Mira says, "And this of course is Raj, our own little jewel in the crown." Turning finally to the other man, she smiles pleasantly and says, "And this, as you probably have already guessed, is Billy."

Billy, staring at us blankly, dips his chin in recognition perhaps a sixteenth of an inch.

The formalities complete, Mira announces that supper will be served in an hour. Sidling up next to me, she mentions that this might be an opportune time for me to speak to Balram about "settling up" for our stay. Giving C a radiant smile, she instructs one of the servants to show her up to our room.

Twenty minutes later, perched on a low wooden stool next to a metal tub in a bathroom upstairs, I am witness to an unforgettable scene. We are in a tiny low-ceilinged room which is uncertainly illuminated by the flickering flame of a single candle. C sits half reclined in the painted blue metal tub, eyes shut, knees flexed, skeins of steam drifting up and dissolving in the ever-shifting shadows—an odalisque, parboiled, caught in definitive chiaroscuro. It is only the occasional dousing she gives her washcloth, which she then carries up the contours of her body and squeezes, allowing the warm water to dribble onto her pale skin, that gives any indication that she remains among the living.

"They've just come with the luggage," I say.

"I heard them padding up the stairs."

"We're set for the next two nights. They're all going away tomorrow, except for Billy. Balram, their son and daughter-in-law, and the jewel in the crown will be off tomorrow morning. Mira and Margaret will be taking the train tomorrow night. They're going to Dehra Dun, I think they said, for a family get-together. Anyway, it seems that Billy will show us around tomorrow. And they've sent our driver off to the nearest town to find a room."

"Poor fellow," C says. "A crypt might be more appropriate."

"I'm sorry about everything that happened. I—"

"Don't worry. We're here now, wherever *here* is. Do you think it's conceivable that we've slipped through a reality warp, that we're trapped inside some unpublished Evelyn Waugh novel?"

"I was surprised by Billy."

"Why?"

"He's just so much older than I expected."

"People get old."

"I suppose I'm used to the photographs he likes to use in his books."

"He's been ill."

"How do you know?"

"I just do."

I admire C from head to toe and decide she is a pleasing sight. Taking note of my reconnaisance, she looks me directly in the eye and, giving me a wry smile, says, "If you're thinking what I think you're thinking—and that's extremely hard for me to imagine after what we've been through today—I think you'd better start thinking something else. It wouldn't be polite to be late for supper."

Thirteen

"OH, *THERE* YOU ARE!" Mira exclaims with a broad smile after C and I have entered the drawing room. "I was just about to send up one of the boys to ask you if you'd care to have a drink before supper."

"I hope we haven't kept you waiting," C says.

"Not at all. You're just in time."

The assembled group—Mira and Balram, their son, daughter-in-law, and grandson, plus Margaret—is seated in a rough circle around the fireplace, with Billy hovering somewhat to the side. As we approach, everyone, or almost everyone, rises, and a brief spate of musical chairs ensues as they make room for C and me. Balram, who is seated directly in front of the fire, stands up and very politely offers his seat to C. I spot a footstool nearby and claim it. As Balram finds another seat, I take a quick survey, which informs me that faces have been washed, heads of hair slicked back, shirts changed. Mira, I notice, looks particularly smart in a Shetland sweater and dark slacks.

"Now, what would you like to drink?" she asks. "Whisky, Richard?"

"Yes, thank you."

"A full peg or a half?"

"A full peg—I think I can use it tonight."

"Of course."

"Do you have something nonalcoholic?" C asks.

"A fresh lemon soda perhaps?"

"That would be lovely."

"Sugar?"

"No, thank you."

Mira turns to the rather dour, bespectacled head of the household staff, who is standing nearby, and says, "Ek whisky, sa'b ke liye. Ek lemon soda, memsab ke liye." The servant gives an understanding nod, turns, and heads toward the kitchen. "Well, Richard," Mira says, settling back in her seat, "Balram was explaining to us that you are a naturalist and that you have just led a tour here in India."

"That's right."

"And where did you take your clients?"

"To Bharatpur, Kanha, and Bandhavgarh. Then out to Kaziranga."

"And you led the tour yourself?"

"Not exactly. The company I've been working for hired Raj Singh to take care of arrangements here. Raj's uncle and aunt came along with us. Delightful people and excellent naturalists both. I liked them very much."

"You were in good hands, then."

"I would say so."

"Were you able to show your clients a tiger?"

"Several. We saw a couple of them very close up."

"And where was that?"

"Bandhavgarh."

"I see. And the people on the tour enjoyed it?"

"I think so."

"All of them American?"

"Yes, American."

"And how much does such a tour cost these days?"

"They're expensive. Airfare included, I should think they're not less than about four and a half thousand dollars."

"Oh, that is quite expensive, isn't it?" Mira says with a little purse of the lips. Then, taking a sip of her drink, she adds, "But then, so many of your countrymen are filthy rich."

I barely repress a smile. The comment, intended to be moderately cutting in a very English sort of way, reminds me of nothing so much as a piece of badly written dialogue lifted from some low-calorie boulevard comedy. Feeling suddenly that it would be wisest to move on to another subject, I glance over at Billy and notice that he is holding a large book of photographs in his lap. He appears to be engrossed.

Mira, who never seems to miss anything, notices me noticing him. "There was a young chap here last week," she says, "who claimed to have worked as a game warden in Kenya. Chock full of stories about the animals. But there was something about him, something that was a bit off, and I believe Billy has decided he was a fraud."

"But why would anyone go around claiming to be a game warden?"

"Who knows? People do the strangest things, don't they? Perhaps he could impress Billy in some way. But Billy tends to be quite astute in these matters."

Billy looks up from his book for a moment, but says nothing, seemingly content to allow Mira to speak for him. No one, however, seems much interested in his "fraud."

Catching the eye of Mira and Balram's son, I ask him what he does in Calcutta, having learned from an offhand comment of Balram's that Calcutta is where he and his family live. "I'm in construction," he says, but he does not appear to be especially eager to elaborate, explaining only that he is moving his family to Dubai, in the Gulf States, "where there are better opportunities."

"It's so dreadfully difficult for young people to get ahead in India these days," Mira interjects. "Dubai seems to have ever so much more to offer."

The head of the household staff arrives with our drinks, and raising my glass, I say, "Cheers."

The conversation lapses for a few seconds; then I hear a voice say, "Where did you get those bracelets?" The voice belongs to Billy, who is now standing next to C, looking down at the bracelets on her wrists.

"I bought them in Kenya last year," C says. "They're nice, aren't they? They're carved camel bone."

"They look like ivory," Billy says, fondling one of them.

"Well, they're not," C says. "These two bracelets together cost less than twenty-five American dollars. I'm sure real ivory must be much more expensive than that."

"She wouldn't buy ivory," I pipe up. "She's been to Africa twice and she's very well aware of what's happening to the elephants."

A doubtful expression plays over Billy's face. Turning away abruptly, he says, "Well, they look like ivory to me."

C shoots me a glance of alarm. I look back. But neither of us says a word.

Ten minutes later, the conversation having swirled back to Dubai, past big oil and international finance, I find myself trying to think of something to say, some leading question perhaps, which I can employ to open up a conversation with Billy. For reasons that I am unable to fathom, he has been very rude to C, and I realize that if conditions were somewhat different, I would not hesitate to call him on it. Rude is rude. But we have come a long way to kiss the hem of this world-renowned tiger guru, and I have no intention of being put off so easily. Remembering an article I read in a Lucknow paper just a few days ago about a tiger that had wandered into the environs of the city and was shot as a maneater, I turn to him and ask, "Did you happen to read in the paper about the tiger that was just shot outside of Lucknow?"

"Yes, that was horrible, wasn't it?" Mira says. "That chap at the Forest Department looked quite proud of himself, having killed that lovely animal. Imagine how Billy must feel."

I look at Billy, but he keeps mum. Turning to Mira, I ask, "You don't think the cat had to be shot, in view of the fact that it had killed two people and was still on the loose?"

"Nonsense," Billy suddenly intones, his voice soaked in vitriol. I look into his eyes, which seem to drill into me. "Killing that tiger was completely unnecessary. It had harmed no one."

The bitterness of his reaction fascinates me, and I find myself thinking, *What is the matter with these people?* But I am in no mood to placate him. I ask, "Are you saying the newspaper was lying? It mentioned the names of two victims."

"And which newspaper was that?" Billy asks.

I am suddenly aware that I don't know which of the two English-language newspapers in Lucknow published the article. "I'm afraid I can't remember which paper."

A sour little smile creeps over Billy's face, which seems to communicate that my failure to remember which paper I read the article in completely negates anything I have to say about it. I sit staring at him for several seconds, realizing that the Alice in Wonderland quality of this silent rebuttal has left me breathless. Is it really possible that Arjan Singh makes a habit of treating his guests (and I might add, his *paying* guests) in this fashion? Is this sort of behavior a habit? Or is it only the temporary aberration of a flinty curmudgeon? It occurs to me that there may be a way to find out. Looking directly at him again, I ask, "Do you think that David Hunt was killed by a man-eater?"

Billy gazes at me for a moment, his face pale. If any single event in recent years has stirred up more controversy, rancor, and recrimination in the world of Indian wildlife than David Hunt's death, I am unaware of it. Hunt, an English ornithologist, tour leader, and writer on natural subjects, achieved a degree of posthumous fame far exceeding any he had known in life. Leading a group of birdwatchers along a road in Corbett National Park, some three hundred miles to the west of Tiger Haven, in February 1985, he set off into the forest by himself and was fatally attacked by a tiger. His body was found later on, one leg partially eaten. Hunt is one of the few Europeans to have been killed by a tiger in India since the Second World War, and I have little doubt that Billy will have some definite opinions about the incident. But he says nothing. Then, in a voice laden with disdain, he asks, "What *is* a man-eater?"

It flashes through my mind that this is not very different from having Albert Einstein confront one with the question "What *is* matter?" Nevertheless, having girded myself, I answer. "If I am not mistaken, a man-eater is an animal, a carnivore—a tiger or a leopard, for example—that has been found guilty of taking a human life."

"Found guilty by whom?"

I smile. Epistemology, apparently, is his strong suit.

Before I can reply, Mira throws me a sharp look and says, "May I ask who told you that David Hunt was killed by a so-called man-eater?"

I hesitate a moment, then lie coolly. Unwilling to reveal my source, whose identity is hardly germane to the argument, I substitute the name of a researcher in Nepal of whom I feel sure they have never heard.

"Well, I don't know that fellow. But I can tell you that he is wrong," says Mira.

"Your researcher should know better," Billy says.

"Yes, he should," Mira agrees. "We happen to know that the man-eating version of the story is not true. We know the authorities at Corbett well, and we have it on their authority that the tiger was not a so-called man-eater."

"I see," I say. "Well, perhaps he was mistaken."

"He *was* mistaken," Mira says.

I glance over at C, who has clearly become weary of the conversation. It does not strike me as unlikely that the other guests share her feeling. Though I am intrigued by the rudeness of our hosts, it is obviously time to bail out. "Well," I say at last, "perhaps it was *I* who misunderstood them in the first place."

Less than an hour later, C and I are upstairs, curled up in bed. I am lying on my side watching, fascinated, a brown moth with a wingspan no greater than a fingernail orbit the lighted candle on the nightstand in ever-tightening concentric circles.

"We're going out on an elephant tomorrow morning," I say.

"I know."

"You must be exhausted."

"I don't think I've ever been so tired."

"That was a very strange conversation downstairs, wasn't it?"

"Sad . . . The whole thing was sad."

"What do you mean?"

"I didn't understand what was going on at first. But I think I do now. Their world, the world they've always known, is falling apart. That's why everything is so tense. It's all vanishing in front of their eyes. For them, there's nowhere else to go."

C pauses. I wait for her to say more. Then I become aware that her breathing pattern has changed. I feel her tremble as she drifts down to sleep. I turn over and look at the candle, around which the moth is still circling. I stare into the flame for a moment. Then I blow it out.

Fourteen

LOST AND ADRIFT in curtains of shifting mist, the mahout halts the elephant near a scraggly tree. His breath drifting up white, he gathers his worn blanket around him, fidgets, tugs at the rag wrapped around his head against the cold, gazes out toward a patch of clear horizon where a purple-orange sun has surfaced above a watermark of trees.

"It looks strange, doesn't it?" Margaret says.

"A sun without heat," C comments. "It's like a frozen tangerine on a bed of dry ice."

"I think it's lovely," Mira says. "I do so love the dawn. It's my favorite time of day. Is everyone ready? Shall we push on?"

Mira gives the mahout a nod, and the mahout gives the elephant a nudge with his heels. With a lurch we set off through the high grass, which is everywhere coated with droplets of glistening dew. This morning Mira seems calm, very much at peace with herself. I can see more clearly who she really is. She has taken it on as her task to protect Billy from anyone who would misunderstand him or misrepresent his work. In a sense, that is all she was doing last night —protecting him from the intrusions of a potentially hostile world.

C sits at my back, facing away from me, next to Mira. She seems to have slept well. Once again she seems perky, ready for anything, a fact that leaves me feeling amazed and grateful. Margaret sits next to me, on my left. Although we have had only a few minutes to talk, I realize how much I like her. She seems to me to be the finest sort of Englishwoman, friendly, sensitive, and sincere. From a few things she has said, I take it she has not had an easy life. An art teacher from Kent, she has raised two children on her own. She is smiling now, has been smiling ever since I first saw her this morning, over an hour ago. She seems to be very pleased with the ride so far. She tells me that this is the first time she has ever been on the back of an elephant.

Within a few minutes we come to an opening in the grass, which the mahout urges the elephant to pass through, but she is definitely reluctant. Producing a hardwood stick from the folds of his blanket, the mahout delivers her a very sharp thunk on the head. I can almost feel C cringe, and I make a mental note to tell her that an elephant's skull comes wrapped in a couple of inches of tough, leathery hide. The elephant can feel the blow, which is no doubt uncomfortable, but I seriously doubt that it is very painful. The elephant, heeding the command, places a tentative foot on the almost overgrown trail, hesitates for a moment, and then carries us through the opening and down a steep, slippery embankment, the howdah tipping so acutely that Margaret and I have to hold tight to avoid sliding off. At the foot of the incline, we arrive at the edge of a broad and shallow muddy stream.

If the stream itself is nothing more than an unimpressive meander, the bed over which it flows is extraordinary—a chaotic palimpsest of signs, a record as informative in its own way as the glyphs on a Sumerian deed of sale. I can make out the tracks of birds, the slithering drag mark of a largish python, innumerable signs of wild boar. There are two distinctly different kinds of deer hoofmarks, the smaller belonging to chital, the larger either to sambar or to the very rare swamp deer.

The mahout urges the elephant onward, with a quiet word. She responds, but has traveled less than five steps when he gives the command to stop. Staring fixedly at a patch of mud just to our right, he says something which I cannot make out.

"Tiger pugmarks," Mira says, turning to us.

My eyes search the muddy ground, but it takes me several seconds to spot them. A few yards away, they head away from us, following the course of the stream. Two of the marks are quite distinct; the third is practically effaced. As tiger tracks go, these are not especially large.

"A female?" I ask.

"Probably," Mira says. "One can't always be certain about pugmarks."

"Female," I hear the mahout say under his breath. "From yesterday in the night."

Mira does not dispute him.

Five minutes later we find ourselves halted atop a small rise from which it is possible to see grasslands interspersed with patches of forest, stretching off to the horizon. In the rising warmth and brightness of the sun, struggling now to burn through the mist, every blade of grass is dripping with moisture. The world seems newborn, a world without end.

But at the back of my mind I am perfectly aware that this sense of infinitude is illusory, that not more than a mile away, somewhere beyond that hazy line of trees, there are cultivated fields and families to tend them, villages with children, cows, chickens, dogs, goats—the entire human domestic array. And it is by no means a matter of a few villages bordering the boundary of the park. There are dozens and dozens.

What I know from my reading is that since Billy moved here in the late 1940s, the human and domestic animal populations around the park have grown at an exponential rate. The surrounding forest has been cut down, and Dudhwa has now become an isolated environment, an island of habitat protected only by government fiat from the very large number of land-hungry farmers who live around it and understandably view its uninhabited and uncultivated spaces with considerable envy. Here, as in many national parks in India, this unprecedented situation has brought into play a circumstance more appropriate to the world of fairy tales than to the rationally defined world of the twentieth century: human beings going about their business on one side of an imaginary line, wild animals living out their lives on the other.

Here, as always, the large carnivores, tiger and leopard, lie at the heart of the conflict. It has become common knowledge that any tiger or leopard that broaches the strict confines of Dudhwa is automatically harassed and hounded. If it cannot be driven off, it is invariably trapped, shot, or hacked to death by the local villagers. Though it is easy to pass judgment on this behavior, I do not believe that anyone from the outside world—and in this I include myself—can fully comprehend what it means to spend one's life in one of these villages, in an environment where the western concept of time is little more than a novelty, where each daily activity is governed not by the endlessly mutating figures on the face of a digital watch but by the ineffable cycles of day and night, where there is no telephone (and no one to speak to at the other end of the line), no doctor, no television, no books, the nearest school often miles away. Life may be "good" or "bad," depending on the boon or curse of the changing seasons. More often than not, it simply *is*.

I suspect that if I lived in one of these villages and had never read a book in my life, I might still know somehow that "wildlife" has a certain intrinsic, godlike value. I would understand, as Hindus do by virtue of their religion and culture, that life itself is sacred. Even so, if I were to wake one morning to find a tiger wandering around my garden, threatening my animals, my livelihood, my wife, my children, I know that I would not hesitate to pick up an axe and try to kill it or drive it away. But I am saddened by the thought.

Here, as nowhere else I have visited, it strikes me as obvious that human civilization and wilderness cannot long survive side by side, at least not when predators are part of the equation. For the first time, it occurs to me that in the not-so-distant future, this park will be sacrificed, its trees cut down, its grasses burned, its rich bottomland turned to the plow. I see now that this is Billy's greatest fear—that this patch of wilderness, to which he has devoted his life, will in the end be utterly stripped away.

Mira's words came back to me: *Imagine how Billy must feel.* At last, I think I can imagine it.

Fifteen

BY FOUR O'CLOCK the afternoon light is slanting. There is a chill in the air as we walk out to the jeep. Twenty yards up the road two junglefowl are dusting themselves in a golden shaft of warming sunlight. Billy opens the door on the driver's side and slips into the seat. I offer the passenger seat first to Margaret, then to C, but both insist that I take it. Once they are settled in the back, Billy starts the engine, the roar of it shattering the silence as though it were plate glass, sending the two junglefowl skittering off in a panic. For months I have been thinking about what it might be like to go looking for tiger with Billy Singh. Now that the moment has arrived, my feelings are decidedly mixed.

Billy puts the jeep in gear and we head off down the road. A hundred yards from the main house, four or five chital lying on the ground under the spreading branches of a great tree hardly seem to notice as we roar past. Household pets almost, they look as though they are waiting for Gautama Buddha to come and preach to them.

A minute or two later we come to a place where the road

meets the border of a muddy slough. Billy brings the jeep to a halt. Switching off the ignition, he sits up slightly in his seat and peers through a gap in the dense vegetation. I follow his gaze to a mugger crocodile, perhaps eight feet long, lying on the opposite shore. I raise my hand to point out the croc to Margaret and C, and Billy, as though anticipating the gesture, raises his own hand and physically forces mine down.

Anger flashes through me. I give him an appraising look, almost say something rude. But then I don't. This is a lesson that I learned long ago and ought not to have forgotten. Pointing at predators in the wild from an open jeep can be a dangerously provocative business. Tigers in particular have been known to take offense.

We sit for a moment, I mentally smoothing my ruffled feathers. When both Margaret and C have had a look at the croc, we push on, arriving within a few minutes at the minilake where last evening our Ambassador met its unseemly demise. Shifting into four-wheel drive, Billy drives around it, nodding his head in amusement as he does. A hundred yards or so beyond it we reach the paved road and turn left.

After a short drive we arrive at the headquarters of the park, which consists of a series of bungalows painted a sickly green, a tint chosen, apparently, to allow the buildings to merge with their natural surroundings. But the strategy has failed. The endless applications of color, which have caked and peeled, now lend the place the musty, decrepit air of a dilapidated hospital. Roaming the grounds are several overdressed middle-class Indian families looking uncomfortable and slightly out of their depth—weekend visitors come to offer their children a ride on an elephant and perhaps a glimpse of a tiger.

Billy pulls the jeep to a halt just short of the white-painted barrier that extends across the road. A young man is standing nearby, and Billy, switching off the engine, speaks to him in Hindi. The young man hurries off without a word toward one of the nearby bungalows and returns two minutes later with a slip of paper in his hand, which must be our permit to enter the park. The young man climbs into the back of the jeep with Margaret and C. Another young fellow, who has suddenly materialized from nowhere, lifts the barrier pole high enough for the weighted back end of it to pull it upright. Billy starts the engine and we roar out of the compound, leaving the fellow peering after us, making a sour face in a cloud of blue exhaust.

Twenty minutes later we are parked in a clearing at the end of a little-used track in some obscure part of the forest. The trees around us are tall and stately, their interlocking crowns, bathed in the last of the soft yellow sunlight, forming a nearly seamless canopy far above our heads. But on the forest floor, the light and warmth have fled.

Billy sits perfectly still, lost in a kind of meditative trance, staring straight ahead at the dry but well-vegetated watercourse ten yards away. Since our arrival at the clearing neither he nor anyone else has said a word. There has been no need. We know why we are here. We are waiting to see a tiger.

My eyes searching every space and opening, I find myself thinking about the legendary Tiger Men, people like Valmik Thapar and Billy, and in an odd way, for the first time it feels as though I have begun to understand them. Though perhaps they would insist that in their own lives it is daily contact with the animals themselves that is of paramount importance, I believe there is another issue of much greater significance. Unless I misinterpret them completely, they possess a fragile but vital connection to the ancestral being that survives in all of us. And it is because of this connection that they understand, as relatively few people do, that when tiger, lion, and leopard no longer wander the earth, we human beings will have lost something invaluable that can never be replaced. Having severed our connection with nature itself, we will find ourselves cut loose and adrift, separated from the creatures we essentially are, forever.

Gazing up the hill in the chill dry light, I find myself thinking about this tiger, about the darkness it carries within itself. How, if it appears, will it come? If it descends the hill to the left of the stream, where the terrain is more open, there is every possibility that we will see it early on, when it breaks cover. But if it comes down the hill to the right of the stream, without seeing us or hearing us, without detecting our scent, it could conceivably remain unaware of our presence until it steps clear of the brush altogether, at that open spot directly in front of us, less than twenty feet away. What will happen then? What if in that split second of contrary emotions, it decides to attack? An unexpected tremor of anxiety rolls through me. *Nothing to be afraid of. Nothing . . .*

Time is suspended in the dying light. Then Billy, with no warning, looks away from the stream, and the trance is broken. For a moment he looks puzzled. Without a word of explanation, he reaches down and switches on the ignition. The engine roars, the sound of it ringing through the darkening wood. Grinding the gears, he turns the jeep around and we head back up the lonely road in the direction from which we came.

A few minutes later, having traversed a part of the forest, we arrive at a small lake. Across its still expanse, a wooly-necked stork, illuminated in the last of the golden daylight, skirts the tops of the trees, and the mere sight of it fills me up. Back in the forest everything seemed locked in funereal silence. But this great gawky bird is gloriously, indubitably alive.

Without a word, Billy climbs out of the jeep and sets off down the trail that skirts the edge of the water. We follow.

Ten yards down the path, Billy stops, looks down, and points to a patch of mud. Turning to me, he says, "Look."

At the edge of the muddy patch is part of a tiger pugmark, half effaced by a human footprint. I stare down at it, realizing that at this moment, in this place, the irony of it is almost too perfect.

"The tigress who claims this territory comes here almost every morning," Billy says. "She was here this morning."

Eager to communicate my interest, I study the pugmark. But the gesture is wasted. Billy has already turned and walked on. I follow him.

About twenty yards on, however, he stops again. Indicating the trunk of a slender tree at the edge of the trail, he asks, "Do you know what that is?"

Aware that I am being tested, I glance at the tree. From a point near the ground up almost to eye level, it has been incised vertically in several parallel grooves, as though with a very sharp blade. I have seen trees like it before. "It's a scratch tree," I say.

"Smell it," Billy says.

I bend over and sniff.

"Lower down," he says.

Easing one knee down onto the damp ground, I put my nose almost to the bark.

"What does it smell like?" C asks.

"A kitty litter box," I say, looking up at her. "Want to try it?"

"I think I'll pass."

I get to my feet and brush the mud off my knee, noticing the thinnest suggestion of amusement on Billy's face as I do. He turns and heads up the trail. Again I follow him.

Within a minute the path narrows, dense riparian growth crowding in on both sides. Now it is impossible to see more than ten or fifteen feet ahead of us, and I find myself thinking about the tigress who claims this side of the lake as her territory. What, I wonder, would happen if we were to meet her face to face along this lonely narrow trail?

We enter a small clearing, and a structure reminiscent of a medieval wooden fortress appears in front of us. It is a large and elaborately constructed hide built on stilts—what Americans familiar with hunting refer to as a blind. A steep stairway with a roof of woven fiber leads up eight or nine feet to the observation platform. This, I realize, has been our goal all along. Billy gestures for us to go ahead, and we do, filing up the stairs one by one. Billy brings up the rear.

The observation platform is a rectangular room with square viewing holes cut in the wooden wall. I walk over to one of the holes and peer out. The first thing I notice is a small group of shaggy-looking deer standing up to their hocks in shallow water, about eighty yards away. The deer are very stocky, and one of them has an impressive rack. I know they are not sambar. "Are those barasingha?" I ask, turning to Billy.

"Yes," he says, seemingly surprised by the question.

I have seen swamp deer before in central India, but not this race. Once common in marshy places throughout the subcontinent, the barasingha has been brought to the very brink of extinction, mostly by habitat destruction. Dudwha is one of its last strongholds.

Along the shore are several thousand birds, and they make an extraordinary sight. As I look them over, I automatically begin to sort through them to discover what species are present. I point out various ones to Margaret and C, both of whom are immediately caught up in my enthusiasm. Straight ahead of us are a dozen or so spoonbills, wonderful, white-plumaged, thick-legged creatures, with enormous spatulate bills perfectly adapted for sifting mud in shallow water. There are cormorants and darters, at least four species of heron and a whole flock of bar-headed geese, which breed on the high-altitude lakes of Tibet and migrate south through the high passes of the Himalaya to winter on the plains of India. There are sizable gatherings of greylag, which, because they are the ancestral stock from which domestic geese are derived, look as if they would be perfectly comfortable in a barnyard in England or America. Seven or eight species of ducks—green-winged teal, red-crested pochard, tufted duck . . .

I get so excited that I completely forget that Billy is standing beside me, and I am slightly startled when he says, "Have you spotted the comb ducks?"

"Where?"

"There," he says, jutting his chin, "at the edge of the water by that small island—next to the greylags."

I spot them and point them out to Margaret and C.

"Why are they called comb ducks?" Margaret asks.

"You can't really tell by looking at them this time of year, can you," I say. "But if you were to come back in the spring, it would be obvious. The males develop a horn, or comb, on the top of the bill. Something to do with hormones and making them sexually attractive."

Margaret listens to my explanation, then smiles and says, "A strange business, isn't it?"

Five minutes later, the last yellow speck of the sun has been swallowed up in the shadowy crowns of the trees across the lake. A glance at my watch tells me that the hour is late. Turning to Margaret, I say, "I think we'd better go if you and Mira are going to catch your train."

"Yes," Billy says. "It's time to go."

"Such a beautiful place—so peaceful," Margaret says with a deep sigh, taking one last look over the lake. "I could stay here forever."

Then she turns and heads toward the door, and C follows. As I turn to go, I catch a glimpse of Billy, and I am surprised by the unexpected expression on his face.

He is smiling.

Sixteen

THAT EVENING, after supper and after C has gone to bed, Billy and I are sitting in front of the television watching a video. Although this would not have been my first choice for the evening's entertainment, Billy has made it clear, without really saying so, that he regards it as an important introduction to his work. Knowing that he has appeared in a number of British-made Anglia documentaries, I expect to be treated to a typical piece of TV nature fodder, the sort of thing people the world over use as a kind of visual sedative and antidote to the various ills of modern civilization.

As soon as it begins, however, I see that what he has chosen to show me is very far from that. Not in the strictest sense of the word a film at all, it is a visual record, very professionally turned out, made up of individual still photographs Billy has taken at Tiger Haven over the years, with a voice-over narration delivered by Billy himself. More than half expecting to be bored, I realize after the first couple of minutes that these pictures of flowers, birds, and animals are some of the best photographs of the Indian natural scene I have ever come across.

As the images rise and dissolve on the screen, accompanied by Billy's narration, I begin to realize, somewhat semiconsciously, that they and Billy's commentary are having a hypnotic effect, provoking responses in me that are altogether unexpected. In them I find a sense of depth, of tender irony and mortality, which catches me completely off guard. They are, I realize, in their own way, that perfect melding of precision and passion I had always searched for in Billy's books but never found.

Tara appears on the screen. This is a young tigress born in captivity that an English zoo handed over to Billy to hand-raise, the idea being that she would eventually be released into the wild. Almost instantly Billy's voice modulates in the direction of awe and paternal softness. With the pride of a father eager to demonstrate his daughter's beauty and intelligence, he shows her at the various stages of her development: Tara playing with Billy, standing on her hind legs with her paws on his shoulders as though the two of them were about to take a turn around a ballroom floor, Tara and Billy walking side by side along some lonely forest path in the company of another of Billy's pets, a tame leopard. The tenderness revealed in these photographs, the tenderness that Billy feels for Tara, and she for him, is tangible. At last, and with some force, it comes over me that I am watching something rather more complicated than a simple tale of beast and master. Though Billy may never have come to think of it in such terms, it is clear that in every way beyond the obvious, he and Tara are lovers.

When Billy's recounting of their story reaches the point at which he releases Tara into the forest, it is very evident that his first impulse is joy at the fact that she has been set free. But when he speaks of the days that followed, the tone of his voice changes. A distinct element of sorrow, of regret, of which perhaps he is himself unaware enters into it. Under the pretext of observing her adaptation to her new environment, he tracks her through the forest, sensing sometimes that he is near her but never actually seeing her. At last, when months have passed, he finds her. But she is no longer the pet she once was. She has reverted to a wildness she was not born to.

With a roar, she charges. Billy holds his ground, as though inviting her attack, snapping pictures of her, one after the other, until she is so close the lens of the camera refuses to focus. At the last moment, when she must either attack him or flee, she halts, roars, turns, and lopes away into the forest.

I sit stunned, spellbound, considering the fact that she could have killed him with no trouble at all. Why didn't she? What passed through her mind? What decision had she made?

I turn and gaze at Billy. What was he thinking at that moment? Why had he followed her so obsessively into the forest? Was he looking for an answer? An answer to what? Is it possible that he was searching for his own death?

Five minutes later the film has ended and Billy and I are seated in front of the fire. None of the lamps has been lit. As the twisting shadows of the fire play on the wall, I feel as though I were in the presence of a wizened paleolithic medicine man, sitting in the depths of his cave. Since our outing early this evening, Billy's mood has mellowed so dramatically that for the first time since my arrival, I feel confident enough to ask him a few questions.

"So what has happened to Tara?"

"She is there, in the forest. I saw her about two months ago."

"She has bred now?"

"Twice, I think."

"What do you think will happen to her?"

"I don't know. Each time I see her, it crosses my mind that this might be the last time. This park is no longer a safe place for tigers."

I gaze into the fire for a long moment. Then I ask, "How did you get interested in wildlife in the first place? Was your father a hunter?"

"Not at all. When I was a child, I really had no interest in nature, aside from a taste for Corbett's books. Corbett was a hero of mine. I think it must have been because of his books that I had some idea of becoming a tiger hunter when I grew up."

"Did you ever meet him?"

"I was in the same room with him once, but I was much too shy to speak to him."

"Were you a hunter when you were a child?"

"No, but I did own an air rifle, and if you can believe it, I often took it with me on visits to the zoo."

"The zoo?"

"Yes, the zoo! Can you imagine! I remember one day I stood in front of the flamingo enclosure, and after looking in every direction to make sure no one was watching, I took aim at one of those beautiful birds and fired. The ball struck the poor creature in the leg, and the bird recoiled and cried out in pain. The thing that shocks me now is that I was so *proud.* The leg was broken, and I felt very much the great white hunter as the bird hobbled away. It was one of the few things I have done in my life for which I have never forgiven myself."

An hour slips by, the conversation twisting and turning with no particular logic from one subject to the next, coming around eventually to the subject I have secretly wanted to discuss with him ever since we arrived. "What do you think are the prospects for tiger in India?"

He looks at me evenly and says in a calm, quiet voice,

"The same as everywhere. I do not believe there are any prospects."

For an instant I wonder if what he has said is a joke.

"You mean everything will go?"

"Everything."

This is not what I wanted to hear. I would have preferred a platitude, however absurd. How can he really believe it? How can he accept the fact that his life's work will come to nothing? I want to ask him these questions, almost do. But at that moment the fire settles into itself, sending up a whirling cloud of sparks, shedding yellow light on Billy's sphinx-like face. No words will broach this mask. In the end, he will keep his secrets.

The next morning is one of brilliant sun and a wind so chilling it seems to have whistled down the mountain passes all the way from Tibet. A few wispy clouds race off toward the southeast. Billy stands at the drive, slightly hunched against the cold. He, C, and I are watching our driver load the baggage into the trunk of the Ambassador, which he has cleaned and polished so effectively that the flying tatters of cloud overhead are clearly visible in its mirrorlike sheen.

When the driver has finished, Billy turns to me, his face utterly expressionless, and says, "This is something for you." I take the envelope and gaze at the words that have been typed on the front of it: *Director—Sunderbans Tiger Reserve.*

"I know the director there," Billy says. "If you ever go there, perhaps he can be of help to you."

I look down at it and realize how unsettled, how incomplete all this feels. There is so much I would like to say, but in the end all I can manage is "Thank you."

Billy offers me his hand stiffly, and I shake it. Then he shakes hands with C, who smiles graciously and says in the precise tone she might employ on taking leave of friends in the Connecticut countryside, "Thanks so much. We've really enjoyed it."

The driver opens the door for us and we slide into the back seat, one at a time. Billy closes the door. It crosses my mind that I should roll down the window to thank him one more time for the letter, but just then the driver slides into the front seat, slams the door, and, peering into the mirror, asks, "Lucknow?"

"Yes, Lucknow," I say.

He reaches down and starts the engine. As we pull away, I turn to face Billy. But the space he occupied is vacant. I look back. Dry leaves are tumbling across the road toward the fallow field. It is as though in that brief moment he vanished off the face of the earth.

Part Three

An Informant at Home and Elsewhere

Seventeen

THE RAIN stopped before dawn and the morning light is scintillating. Puddles litter the road like rounded mirror fragments, reflecting clouds racing off to the southeast. The young taxi driver, a Sikh with a straggly beard, looks uncertain as we turn into a featureless residential street in one of Delhi's wealthiest suburbs, territory evidently as strange to him as it is to me. A starved-looking dog, its coat a patchwork of bubblegum-pink mange, wanders out into the road ahead of us. A sad business, it sniffs for a moment at a filthy spot, then continues across at a trot.

I have just seen C to her plane, and feeling none too pleased about seeing her go, I have decided to take up the invitation extended to me by the well-heeled ex–tiger hunter I met in that hotel garden in Calcutta. Though I am certain that at the very least he will be good for a few interesting tiger stories, I am compelled to admit an ulterior motive. Indians, and Indians of his class particularly, are renowned for the warmth of their hospitality. In the wake of our visit to Tiger Haven and C's departure, a little warm hospitality seems to me just what the doctor ordered.

All the same, contacting my prospective host has not proved easy. For the last several days, in fact, I have tried on numerous instances to reach him by phone, only to find myself treated repeatedly to the same passage from some eerie modernist electronic symphony—the Indian phone system, in other words, functioning up to its usual inimitable standard. Last night, however, I did at last manage to get someone named Joseph on the line. Joseph explained that though his employer was out for the evening, he had left instructions that if I happened to call, I ought to be invited to stay. Since the hour was late, Joseph suggested that it might be best if I delayed my arrival until morning.

"Number thirteen, isn't it?" the driver asks, glancing into the rearview mirror.

"Yes," I say, "number thirteen."

The driver eases off the accelerator. We pass one oversize set of doors after another, each belonging to a separate private home. As we come up to a set of large blue doors, he applies the brakes with firmness and brings the taxi to a halt.

I gaze out the window. At eye level, just to the right of the doors, is a small blue plaque with a white stylized "13" at its center. The driver switches off the ignition, opens his door, and climbs out. I do likewise and stand looking up and down the street, which is so deserted and so quietly anonymous it could be a street in a swank neighborhood almost anywhere—or the film set for some science-fiction apocalypse.

"You'd better wait," I say to the driver, who is about to remove my bag from the trunk. "I want to make sure this is the right place."

Walking over to the blue doors, I find, just below the numbered plaque, a button that seems to be a doorbell. I push it once and wait. I wait for several seconds, then push it again. I am on the verge of pushing it a third time when from inside I detect the sound of muffled footsteps. A small viewing port in the right-hand door, which I hadn't noticed before, slides open. From behind a metal grille, a portion of brown face appears. The eyes meet mine for an instant, then dart past me to the driver. The viewing port clacks shut. A large bolt is slipped, and the right-hand door swings open about a foot.

A square-featured Indian man, perhaps in his late fifties or early sixties, dressed in a neatly pressed white tunic and trousers, steps into the breach, glances at me and at the driver, and asks, "You are Mr. Ives?"

"Yes."

"Welcome, sir. I believe we spoke over the telephone. My name is Joseph."

"How do you do."

Joseph turns and speaks quietly to someone behind him. The door opens a little more, and a teenage boy dressed in the same immaculate fashion appears beside him. Smiling shyly, he steps through the doorway and walks toward the taxi. I turn to the taxi driver to ask how much I owe him. The fare is a steep one, which doesn't surprise me. Taking out a large note, I hand it to him and say, "Keep the change."

"Thank you," he says with a smile. Then he turns to the boy, who is struggling unsuccessfully to extract my bag from the trunk. I start to join him.

"You have but a single bag, sir?" Joseph asks.

"Yes."

"The boy will take care of it, then. Please come in."

I look back at the driver, who is just depositing my bag on the ground with a grimace of effort. The bag is crammed with books, books on natural history, mostly—field guides to mammals, birds, trees, plants. I am in no way sure that this stringy lad will be able to handle it. But Joseph steps aside and with a polite gesture bids me enter.

Inside the gate, I stop in my tracks, look around, and smile. Across a great expanse of well-tended lawn is a most un–Indian-looking house, with a sloping roof, huge beams, windows with enormous panes of glass framed by large rough stones—the sort of house that seems to have sprung fully constructed out of the pages of *Architectural Digest.* Outside the taxi pulls away, and I am suddenly aware of the slightly hallucinatory sensation of being marooned in very familiar surroundings.

Teetering slightly under the weight of his burden, the boy steps through the doorway, Joseph right behind him. I almost offer to take the bag, but the boy looks so pleased with himself that I resist the impulse. Closing the door behind him and slipping the bolt, Joseph turns back to me with the mildest suggestion of a smile on his lips. Gesturing in the direction of the curved driveway, which is bordered by a neatly clipped hedge on one side and some rather unsuccessful-looking rosebushes on the other, he says, "Right this way, sir." He takes the lead and I follow. The boy follows me, the expression on his face strained but pleasant.

As we approach the house, I see that it is constructed in a U shape, the interior space occupied by a trellised patio, very much in the California style, the trellis itself covered with a climbing vine. As we come up to the doors of the house, which are fancily carved in a flowing, floral style that looks distinctly Balinese, I expect Joseph to veer off. He does not. He keeps to the drive.

Beyond the patio and the end of the second wing, we head off onto a trail of octagonal steppingstones that leads to a sizable rectangular swimming pool. Running nearly the length of the pool on the opposite side is what I assume to be a guesthouse, with a small bathhouse attached at the far end. Even at this early hour the pool looks most inviting. If I am not mistaken, it is the first pool I have come across in a private residence in India.

Walking up to the nearest door of the guesthouse, Joseph unlatches it, slides it open, steps aside, and gestures for me to enter. I walk into a room that is furnished with a boxy sofa and a couple of chairs gathered around an irregularly shaped low glass table. A large television is perched atop a built-in bar. On one wall behind the bar are two framed prints, the first showing the half-human, half-vegetable form of a mandrake, identified by the words "La Mandragora"; the second—which for a split second I think might be an original—is Dürer's well-known *Rhinoceros.*

"The bathroom, sir," Joseph says, opening a nearby door. I peer inside. Sparklingly equipped with all the modern conveniences, with fluffy fresh towels laid out, it is as inviting a sight as any I have come across in quite some time. I find myself entertaining the fantasy that my first really hot shower in weeks might be in the offing.

Once I have had my look, Joseph closes the door, then turns and walks over to another door, four or five feet to the left of it, and opens it. I join him at the threshold and stand looking in. It is the bedroom. Of medium size and about as characterless as the average hotel room, it has a large picture window which looks out on a small, formal, sunlit, Japanese-style garden that reminds me of the garden of a house in Kyoto where I once lived for a couple of years.

I step into the room to take a closer look, and the moment I do, something hanging on the wall catches my attention. It is a Plexiglas frame, perhaps twelve inches high by nine wide, in which the largest stag beetle I have ever seen has been mounted. I walk over to it and take a closer look.

It is an amazing bug. Essentially black, with wings the color and texture of some fine, light-colored hard wood, it possesses an extraordinary rack of polished jet-black mandibles, which sprout menacingly from its head like scythes, as though it were a miniature alien warrior from some sword-and-sorcery fantasy. A small white paper label dangles from one of its hind legs. Bending so close to the frame that my nose almost touches it, I read *"Hexarthius deyrollei*—June 25, 1973—Chiang Mai, Thailand." The words on the label have been written in blue ink, and I have the sudden intuition that the specimen is not store-bought.

"Who's the bug collector, Joseph?"

"My employer, sir," he says.

"Nice bug."

"Yes. Would you care for some breakfast, sir?"

"Yes," I say, "that would be great."

"You are American, sir?"

"Yes."

"Perhaps, then, you would prefer an American breakfast?"

"Meaning?"

"Ham, eggs, toast, coffee?"

"Sounds great," I say, barely repressing a smile.

"In a half-hour, sir?"

"Perfect."

"Is there anything else I can get for you, sir?"

"Not that I can think of."

"Very good. If you think of something, there is a button on the left side of the front door labeled SERVICE. Push it once and someone will come directly."

"Your employer, I take it, is not here?"

"No, sir. He was called out of town unexpectedly and will not return until late this afternoon. He has asked me to offer his apologies that he was not here to greet you."

"I understand. And his wife?"

Joseph looks at me for a moment, seems to hesitate, then says, "Madam is not in Delhi at the moment, sir."

"I see."

"Will that be all?"

"Yes, thank you, Joseph. That will be all."

Eighteen

LATE THAT AFTERNOON, perhaps an hour before sunset, I am sitting at one of the metal tables by the pool in a borrowed swimsuit, working on a scotch over ice, watching an Indian robin flitting in and out of the climbing vine that has taken over much of the compound wall. For the past few hours, in spite of every effort, I have detected myself sinking gradually into a mood of distraction and black despair. And I think I know why. It is Billy.

When C and I drove up to Tiger Haven, I was not at all sure of what I would find. I had certainly not planned on stumbling into a full-blown tragedy. For me, as for so many others of my generation, the idea that the planet was in deep trouble had assumed an aura of unassailable truth. I accepted without hesitation the proposition that chemicals and nuclear waste were poisoning the earth, that unrestrained population growth and development were decimating the natural world. But nothing, nothing I had ever read or heard, had quite prepared me for the spectacle of India's best-known naturalist being forced to stand by and watch helplessly as the small portion of the natural world he had fought so hard to preserve literally crumbled to dust at his feet.

Yes, of course I could go on and write that book about India's colorful Tiger Men, just as long as I was prepared for the fact that no matter where I went, no matter who I spoke to, the basic message was going to be the same—one redolent of ideals abandoned, horizons dramatically contracted, hopes not so much shattered as simply worn away by the relentless accumulation of hard cold fact. No, it wasn't just Billy. Nor was it only a question of the destruction of India's forest and the extinction of the tiger. Though the idea seemed in its own way quite mad, it was now obvious to me that within a very short time, not more than a couple of decades, the Asian forest and all its most notable wild inhabitants were going to be lost.

Picking up my drink to take a sip, I become aware that someone has appeared from around the wing of the house, someone whom at first glance I take to be Joseph, changed for some reason into casual clothes. Then, a feeble current of recognition flowing through me, I realize that it is not Joseph at all but my host, Kailash, the man whom, for reasons I cannot quite fathom, I have begun to think of as my informant—an informant in the anthropological sense, one who informs an investigator about native customs and practices. All afternoon I have had the odd intuition that I shall learn a great deal from him.

Dressed in a pair of ivory-colored slacks and a black sport shirt, he is carrying what seems to be a notebook binder, the kind college students use to package term papers. He gives a little wave as he comes around the end of the pool, not speaking until he is close enough not to have to raise his voice. "Richard," he says with a smile, "how nice to see you."

I struggle to my feet. "Nice to see you," I say, extending my hand.

He grasps it firmly for something on the order of a second, during which time I study his face, comparing its features with the images I have kept stored away for over a month, certain that the two will neatly match, slightly disconcerted at the discovery that they do not. The face is as handsome as I remembered it. But the eyes are different somehow. On the day we met they reflected only confidence. Now they possess a kind of darting vulnerability.

"You're looking well," he says, pulling over one of the metal chairs and taking a seat, placing the binder facedown on the table as he does.

"Thanks," I say, resuming my seat. "So are you."

"Sorry I wasn't here this morning, when you arrived. I had to go down to Meerut on business last night. Joseph, I take it, has made you comfortable?"

"Very," I say. "He couldn't have been more helpful." Glancing around, I add, "You've got quite a place here. Reminds me a little of California."

"You're from California?"

"I was born there."

"Well, perhaps the resemblance is not entirely accidental. Once upon a time, I lived in California for nearly three years."

"You did? Where?"

"Palo Alto. I did a business course at Stanford."

He turns slightly in his chair so the sun strikes his cheek, and I notice something else that escaped my attention the first time we met: an almost invisible, hair-thin scar running from just below his left cheekbone straight back, ending abruptly in a bunched mass of whitish tissue the size of a matchhead, just short of his ear.

"How was it that you ended up there?" I ask.

"I was young—nineteen, I think. I was under a great deal

of pressure at home. Something happened. I had a kind of break. Stanford, you might say, was part of my therapy. But let's not talk about me. I want to hear about your adventures. Did you succeed in getting out to Sunderbans?"

"No."

"The cyclone? I was afraid of that. I take it, though, you did complete your tour?"

"Yes."

"A success?"

"I think so."

"You were able to show your clients a tiger?"

"Yes."

"And where was that?"

"Bandhavgarh."

"A nice little park, isn't it?"

"Beautiful."

"You've just finished your tour, then?"

"God, no—that seems like ages ago now. No, after the tour finished and I got my clients back on the plane, I tried to get you here, but I couldn't get through. So I made arrangements to drive down to Ranthambor."

"Sorry about the phones. Lately they've been driving us a bit mad."

"It's not a problem."

"How did you like Ranthambor?"

"Loved it. It must be one of the most beautiful places on earth. I was sorry I couldn't stay longer, but I had already made arrangements to meet a friend in Lucknow. We drove up to Billy Singh's place together."

"My God, you have been making tracks."

"It feels like it."

"And what was your impression of Mr. Singh?"

"An interesting man. A great man, in a way. It's a bad situation up there."

"Yes. Tragic."

"Billy doesn't hold out much hope for the future of tigers here in India."

"I can see how he might feel that way."

"What do *you* think?"

"About the future?" he asks, looking away. "Well, I think that the tourists will keep coming to India, as will the documentary filmmakers. They do, after all, have all that television time to fill. I think that publishers in Europe and the United States will continue to produce coffee-table books about the endangered tiger—pretty pictures are, after all, the sort of thing that sells. And I think that within the next quarter century, at the outside, the Asian forest will be utterly destroyed and the tiger will cease to exist as a viable wild animal."

I stare at him, realizing that for the second time in only a few days I have been offered information I might easily have done without.

"I'm sorry," he says at last. "I think I've just shocked you. Let's talk about something else, shall we? How about your book? Any further thoughts on it?"

"Second thoughts."

"Really? Why?"

"Maybe for the reasons you just mentioned. What's the use of writing about an animal that in a few years won't exist anymore?"

"Well, you may have a point. All I can tell you is this. On the day we met in Calcutta, I had a kind of insight that you would eventually write the book we discussed. Don't ask me why."

"I wish I had your confidence."

Joseph appears at the end of the pool, choosing his steps along the path of octagonal stones. On an upraised palm, waiter-style, he is carrying a tray on which a pitcher and two glasses are balanced. Nodding a greeting as he walks up, he lowers the tray, rests it on the side of the table, and removes the glassware.

"I asked Joseph to bring out some water," my informant says, glancing down at my glass. "Would you like something else?"

"Water's just fine."

Looking up at Joseph, he says, "You do remember that we shall have to be off not later than quarter past seven?"

"Yes, sir," Joseph answers with a nod. "Will that be all for the moment, sir?"

"Yes, thank you."

Picking up the tray, Joseph turns and walks off.

Pouring himself a glass of water, my informant says, "I'm sorry, I have a business dinner I have to attend this evening. It's been planned for months, and I'm afraid it's a bit late to bow out."

"No problem. I should have given you more warning."

"Joseph will bring out some supper for you before we go. Will that be all right?"

"Of course."

Sitting there looking at him, I remember for some reason the extraordinary beetle mounted on the wall in my room. Recalling Joseph's comment that Kailash collected it, I ask, "And how is it that the ex–tiger hunter became a bug collector?"

"Joseph showed you the bug room?" he asks with an upraised eyebrow.

"Bug room?"

"Where I keep my collection."

"No."

"Ah . . . Well you must take a look. But then, how . . ."

"The beetle mounted on the wall in my room," I say, gesturing over my shoulder. "*Hexarthius* something or other."

"Ah. I had forgotten all about it."

"How did you become a—"

"An amateur entomologist? I don't know. A psychologist might refer to it as a kind of transference. When circumstances conspired to make me put away my guns forever, maybe I needed something to substitute for hunting. It didn't happen overnight. But gradually, I became quite fascinated with insects."

"You *like* insects?"

"What is there to like—or to dislike? I admire them."

"On what account?"

"Survivors. Inheritors."

"What do they inherit?"

"The planet, eventually. It is the insects that are next up to bat. Believe me, when the last human being on earth breathes his last, there will be an insect waiting and ready not only to step into his shoes but to eat them—and then eat him, too."

"Grim," I say.

"Is it?" my informant says, smiling. "Yes, I suppose it is."

The two of us sit quietly for a moment. Then he says, "When will you be flying back to the States?"

"Saturday."

"It occurred to me, after I heard that you had phoned and said you were coming, that perhaps you would be interested in going up to Corbett to take a look at a tiger. Maybe, though, after all this running around, you would prefer just to stay put."

"Looking at tiger is not something I tend to tire of."

"Then you would be interested?"

"Yes."

"Good. I've already made the necessary arrangements. I'm pleased to see that they won't go to waste. Would it be possible for you to drive up there with me tomorrow morning?"

"Sounds fine to me."

"Can you manage to be up at the kitchen of the main house at, say, quarter to seven tomorrow morning?"

"No problem."

He sits looking at me for a moment with a little smile on his face, then says, "It's odd. You remind me so much of someone I knew long ago."

"Who was that?"

"A friend. He wore glasses and was perhaps more of a purely intellectual type, but there is a resemblance."

"You seem to be speaking in the past tense."

"He died when he was only eighteen." His voice trails off, as though the memory has saddened him. "Well, I must be going," he says, rising suddenly. "Six-forty-five tomorrow morning, then?"

"Right."

Just then, however, his eye falls on the black binder that he brought out with him. "Oh, I almost forgot," he says, reaching down and picking it up. "This is something I wrote about tiger—I thought you might be interested." He hands it to me. On the cover the title has been neatly typed: *A Brief History of Tigers and Men.*

"Looks interesting."

"I hope you find it so."

"I'm sure I will."

"Quarter to seven, then?"

"Yes. I'll be there. Have a nice evening."

"I won't—but it doesn't matter."

With a half-wave of his hand, he turns and walks off.

Nineteen

MY INFORMANT has no sooner disappeared from view than I find myself staring down at *A Brief History of Tigers and Men*. Though not really in the mood to read, I am curious. So I pick it up and begin to page through it. Neatly printed out, slightly over a hundred pages long, it seems at first glance to be a very scholarly sort of work, with lots of italics and numbered footnotes. It strikes me as odd that though we had taken up the subject of writing on the day we met in Calcutta, he had made no mention—or at least, none I can remember—of having an interest in writing himself. Was this, then, as he saw it, the basis of our connection? Was this the reason he had taken a shine to me on such short notice?

Considering all this, I pick up my glass, take a sip, open the binder to the first page, and start to read.

Though paleontology is a science, a branch of geology that deals with life forms of the past, and as such pursues its arguments via rational means, it does not eschew the formidably compelling strategies of myth. Bringing imaginative force to bear on what is often extremely scanty evidence—the fossilized remains of bones, shells, and plants—the paleontologist reconstructs the ancient lineage not only of those species that have passed into extinction but those that have survived into the present era. Though such reconstructions are inevitably fictional, they are fictions of an indispensable sort—the unique means at our disposal by which we can visualize the extraordinary evolutionary processes that occurred on this planet before the Age of Human Beings. The manner in which the paleontologist blends careful observation, logic, and intuition to create such fictions, the "prehistory" of species, may be vividly demonstrated in the case of tiger.

Focusing on evidence no more extensive than several fossilized skulls, paleontologists have concluded that the most likely progenitor of all modern-day tigers was a creature that haunted the woodlands, savannas and river valleys of China some two million years ago. Smaller than the average modern tiger, possessing a flatter, narrower, and therefore perhaps somewhat more doglike profile, this "proto-tiger" seems to have closely resembled its modern-day counterpart in all essential respects. The paleontologist who first unearthed the skull of the animal dubbed it with a certain appropriateness *Felis paleosinensis* (literally, "old Chinese cat").

Though undeniably fascinating as objects, fossils often prove uncooperative witnesses which suggest infinitely more than they actually reveal. The *Felis paleosinensis* skulls, for example, betray nothing of the animal's behavior or outward appearance, refuse to confide whether it hunted from ambush, as modern-day tigers do, or even whether the animal possessed the modern tiger's characteristic stripes. What the skulls do reveal, however, particularly in view of the far-flung sites in which they were found, is that the species was a stunning success, radiating within a couple of hundred thousand years (a blink of an eye in evolutionary terms) as far south as Java—in that distant era probably not an island at all, but part of a broad peninsula attached to the Asian mainland.

From southeast Asia the species advanced westward, generation by generation, colonizing the entirety of southern Asia (with the curious exception of Sri Lanka) all the way to modern-day Turkey before hooking back toward the northeast in the direction of Turkestan. At about the same time this southerly and westerly migration was under way, another segment of the original core population was spreading northward from China, toward coastal Siberia, before veering west, migrating along a series of river systems which then formed a sort of crescent over the Tibetan Plateau, penetrating eventually perhaps as far as Turkestan, in so doing creating an enormous, nearly enclosed range, the shape of a stretched-out doughnut, with the inhospitable Himalayas and the barren Tibetan Plateau as its "hole."

In microscopically minute steps, with the passing millennia, these settlers adapted to the new and extraordinarily diverse environments in which they found themselves, gradually evolving and differentiating into an entirely new species, *Felis bengalensis*—the modern-day tiger. Because of the wildly divergent environments in which they were now established, however, the evolutionary development of the various far-flung populations was not everywhere uniform. Those colonists migrating northward from China into the harsh climate of Siberia, for example, eventually developed dense fur and grew to an average size nearly double that of their ancestors. Their equatorial cousins, those settling in Java, developed by way of contrast relatively thin fur and grew to an average size only fractionally greater. Only when in the twentieth century scientists began a detailed examination of these various tiger populations did they discover differences substantial enough to support the eventual recognition of no less than eight different types or races of tiger which had developed from that unique ancestral stock. The common names given to these various races reflect the areas in which the individual populations were found. They are the Siberian, Chinese, Indochinese, Sumatran, Javan, Balinese, Caspian, and Indian (this last known in circuses as the Bengal or Royal Bengal tiger).

Perhaps the most surprising aspect of this epic of colonization and adaptive radiation is that *Felis paleosinensis,* compared with the other predators that shared its world—the larger, stronger saber-toothed cats, for example—was not particularly imposing. But in nature, size and strength do not count for everything, the ultimate fate of the dinosaurs being a case in point. Very simply, an ecological niche was available, and *Felis paleosinensis* appears to have made the most of it. While the larger, more powerful and impressively fanged cats died out, it and its descendants flourished.

But if the fossil record may be trusted, the innate capacity for adaptation in any species is never infinite. Of the millions and millions of plants and animals that have risen to life on our planet over the past billion years, statistically speaking, nearly all have vanished, their extinctions triggered by drastic changes in the physical environment and/or direct conflict with a stronger and more adaptable competitor. The present dilemma of tiger, a species slated for effective extinction in the wild sometime within the next twenty-five to thirty years, provides an almost perfect model for the way in which such extinctions gradually develop and play themselves out.

In the case of tiger, the seeds for its eventual destruction as a species were present in its environment almost from the very beginning. There is a certain irony in the fact that at the precise prehistoric moment that *Felis paleosinensis* was beginning its radiation outward from China, another predator, also rapidly evolving, was gradually, but in ever-increasing waves, invading its territories from the west—a predator that, arising from a completely different mammalian line, would eventually come into relentless conflict with it.

That predator was, of course, Man.

Interesting stuff. Well presented and fluidly written. My informant is a talented and seemingly practiced writer. Curious now to see where he plans to take all this, I skim several pages, then again begin reading.

In Europe, however, the tiger appears to have remained completely unknown until the era of Alexander the Great. Though it may amount to nothing more than a tall tale that Alexander hunted the animal during his blitzkrieg of India in the years 327–325 B.C., Alexander appears to have been responsible, however indirectly, for the first tiger to be seen in the West. Following his death in 323 B.C., his faithful general Seleucus Nicator, inheritor of the eastern wing of his late master's empire, made the showy gift of a tiger to the citizens of Athens. It is intriguing to imagine it placed on display in some prominent place in the agora, at the foot of the Acropolis, the eager crowd pressing forward to gape at the living, breathing creature of myth. Ironically, the Athenian who might have profited most from viewing the tiger, Aristotle, who had written a book, *A History of Animals,* without mentioning tiger, was no longer in Athens. His close ties with the Macedonian regime (at one time he had been Alexander's teacher) made his continued presence a dangerous proposition, and having no desire to become "another Socrates," he had wisely fled the city in the previous year.

Though in the period following Alexander's death the Greek peripatetic philosopher Theophrastus would mention tiger in passing in his seminal *Enquiry into Plants* and the Greek comic dramatist Philemon would likewise make reference to it in a work now lost, it appears that no other tiger was seen in Europe for the next three centuries.

I look up from the page. Though I have come across some of this information before in my reading, nowhere have I found it treated in such detail. And I find myself pondering the fact that there may be a good reason for this. Lots of people in the world care about wildlife—the success of wildlife shows on TV offers ample evidence of that. But how many of those same people give a hoot what some Greek writer who lived two thousand years ago had to say on the subject? It seems to me obvious that my informant, who is clearly extremely literate and very well informed, must realize this. But if he does realize it, why has he gone to the trouble to write this essay? Suddenly even more curious than before to see where all this is leading, I skip a number of pages and again plunge into the narrative.

Tall tales concerning tiger and other exotic animals had no doubt been filtering back to Europe for several generations when, during the second half of the thirteenth century, the reports suddenly became more substantial. In about the year 1260 two Venetian merchants, Niccolo and Maffeo Polo, completed what was one of the most remarkable journeys ever undertaken by human beings, having traveled overland from Italy to China and back. As if this journey had not provided adventure and hardship enough for ten lifetimes, they set out again in 1271, this time with Niccolo's teenage son Marco in tow. On their arrival in Cathay, the Great Khan of the Mongol dynasty, Kublai, who ruled over an empire as fabulous as that of ancient Rome, readily pressed them into his service, the Polos remaining in his employ for the next twenty years.

In 1292, remarkably, all three Polos returned to Venice, having undertaken their return journey in part by sea. Legend has it that Marco, reappearing in his hometown middle-aged and bearded, was recognized by no one, and his stories were regarded as the ravings of a lunatic until he produced bags of precious stones to back up his claims. What fate befell Niccolo and Maffeo after their return is unknown. But it appears that Marco, for reasons unknown, may have been present at the sea battle of Curzola in 1298, during which he was taken prisoner and flung into prison by the Genoese, then disputing Mediterranean trade routes with the Venetians.

While incarcerated, Marco evidently made the acquaintance of a fellow prisoner, one Rustichello of Pisa, a romance writer of some repute. Whether imprisoned for being a bad writer or for a more significant offense, Rustichello, either while still in prison or shortly after their release, collaborated with Marco on a narrative to which they gave the ambitious title *Divisament dou Monde* ("A Description of the World"). Written in Rustichello's Italianate French—French in those days being the preferred language of all serious authors of romance—this "Description of the World," which in later centuries would come to be known simply as *The Travels of Marco Polo,* includes what appears to be the first account of a tiger written in Europe since Martial. In a passage which in one early version begins *"Encore sachiez qe Le Grant Sire . . . ,"* Marco, speaking through the pen of Rustichello, says,

Know also that the Great Khan has many leopards which are good for hunting and the taking of beasts . . . He has several great lions, larger than those of Babylonia. They have very handsome coats, of beautiful color, striped lengthwise with black, red, and white. They are trained to take wild boar, wild cattle, bears and wild asses, stags, small deer, and other small beasts.

These "lions," striped lengthwise *"noir et vermoil et blanc,"* were of course not lions at all. They were tigers.

Twenty

A KNIFE-EDGED RAY of warm sunlight dancing with motes, squeezing between two wallboards, falls at an angle across the chest of my informant, who sits across from me, his back to the wall. We are sitting on the wooden floor of a hide, or blind—a single room on stilts, which stands ten or fifteen feet above the forest floor. A rectangular window space in one wall allows a view of the forest and the little stream not twenty yards away. Since just past midday we have been keeping a mostly silent vigil, speaking only occasionally, and then only in the lowest whisper, shifting now and then to keep the blood flowing. We are patiently awaiting the arrival of a tigress who on some evenings comes to the stream to drink.

It has been a strange twenty-four hours. Finishing the *Brief History* last night, I felt somewhat more certain of who my informant really is. The drive up to the park this morning, however, demonstrated this to be an illusion. If anything, it has made me realize how difficult it is to get to know anyone whose lifelong habit it has been to wear a mask. My thoughts about all this are all the more complicated on account of what happened last night.

After finishing the *Brief History,* I couldn't sleep. After hours of endless tossing and turning, I got up. A glance at my watch told me it was nearly midnight. Five minutes later I was outside, walking through the moonlight. I am not sure I knew what I was going to do as I made my way around the end of the pool. Or perhaps I did. In any case, when I reached the library door on the other side of the pool and found it unlocked, I did not hesitate. I pushed it open.

For several moments I just stood at the doorway, trying to make up my mind whether I ought to step inside. But it was cold, so at last I did, and quietly closed the door behind me.

The room, dimly illuminated by moonlight, seemed caught in a kind of mortuary stillness—so empty-feeling, so dead, I couldn't throw off the creeping sensation that it was not a place for living things. Almost at once I saw that the walls of the room were lined with bookshelves crammed with books, hundreds of them. Stepping closer to one of the shelves, I could just distinguish in the silvery light a number of titles: Ellison's *H.R.H, The Prince of Wales' Sport in India,* Jepson's *Big Game Encounters, Rowland Ward's Records of Big Game, Thirty-Seven Years of Big Game Shooting* by the Maharajah of Cooch Behar, *Tigers of the World, The Tiger of Mysore,* and so on—all the books I could see having to do with tiger, or hunting, or both.

Making my way along the shelves, I headed toward the closed door at the end of the room, passing a sofa, an armchair, a table with a lamp. Then something on the table, something glowing and ominously shaped, looming in the shadows, caught my attention. It brought me to a complete halt. I stared. It was the mounted skull of a carnivore with very pronounced curved fangs—the skull of a tiger.

Turning away from it, I walked on to the door at the end of the room. I tried the knob. Finding it unlocked, I slowly pulled it open, half expecting as I did an alarm to go off. But there was no alarm. In its place was a faint rush of air which bore the unmistakable odor of mothballs—not mothballs exactly, but the chemical crystals of the same family, used to keep insect predators out of museum specimen collections the world over. At the same moment I became aware of the hum of some sort of mechanized climate control. Groping inside the dark doorway, I located the light switch and flipped it on.

The room was of a peculiar sort but one very familiar to me nevertheless. Devoid of decoration, it was lined with waist-high cedar cabinets with lots of drawers. Turning to the cabinet nearest at hand, I reached down and opened the top drawer. Even in that weak, wavering light, its contents took my breath away. Two or three dozen enormous stag beetles, some of them three or four inches long, stood labeled and suspended on pins, row on row, their variety and subtle coloration completely overshadowed by their huge, bizarre, polished black mandibles.

Closing the drawer, I turned to face the opposite wall and opened another, and again the contents were stunning—in this case, a whole tray of *Morphos*, the metallic blue butterflies with a five-inch wingspan, native to Amazonia, arranged here for no other reason than their innate aesthetic shock value. Closing it, I opened another, this one filled with enormous moths, a number of which were familiar to me—a huge mottled atlas from Burma, a comma-tailed, lime-green luna from Malaysia, a death's-head from Thailand, a somber black witch from Mexico . . . I smiled at the sight of them. My informant was clearly an eccentric of the first order, but an eccentric with an eye.

Just then I became aware of an empty sensation in the pit of my stomach which told me that someone, or something, was standing right behind me. Whirling around, ready to strike, I found Joseph standing in the doorway. Suddenly annoyed, I opened my mouth to scold him, but the words were stillborn as it dawned on me that it was I, not he, who had some explaining to do. Feeling like a child caught with his hand in the cookie jar, I tried to think of something clever to say. I opened my mouth to say it. But that was as far as I got.

"Couldn't sleep, sir?"

"I was—"

"Can I fetch you something? A glass of warm milk perhaps?"

"I was just—"

"I saw the light on. I thought I must have left it on myself."

"I was just about to—"

"No problem at all, sir. But when you are finished, would you kindly make certain that the light is turned off and the door is firmly closed? For the sake of the specimens."

"Of course. I was just about to—"

"And a *very* good idea, sir. It's quite late. I suspect that seven o'clock will come early."

And it did.

Through the open window space of the hide a large wasp enters, hanging suspended in an angling beam of sunlight. It circles the interior once, reconnoitering. Finding nothing to detain it, it zooms back outside in the direction from which it came.

"A hornet?" I whisper.

"Yes."

"What kind?"

"I am no expert on wasps. A *Pompiloidea,* perhaps—the kind that stun spiders to feed their hatching young."

I am about to ask another question when suddenly his head jerks left, and with an upraised hand he cuts me short.

Rigid with attention, he stares at the window. After several seconds he turns to me and whispers, "She's there."

I stare at him. What is he saying? That there is a tigress outside? How can he know that? I turn and look out the window, through which nothing out of the ordinary is audible or visible—just the trees of the canopy glowing in the soft, mottled afternoon light.

I glance back at my informant. Eyes fixed on the window, he places the palms of his hands on the wooden floor. Exerting pressure downward, he shifts his weight and gets to his knees. On all fours, he makes his way to the window, the wooden planks of the floor creaking ever so slightly under his weight. Raising his head slowly at the corner of it, he peers over the edge of the wooden sill, down at the stream. For several seconds his expression registers nothing. Then, with that subtle flex of facial muscles that indicates recognition, he turns to me and gives an almost imperceptible nod.

Heartbeat surging, I get myself up on all fours. Moving as quietly as I can, I make my way to the window. Peering over the sill, I gaze down at the stream, detecting at first nothing out of the ordinary. Then, just to the left of where I am focusing, something moves. My eyes dart to it.

A tiger's face, framed by leaves.

For a second or two she does not move. Then she does. Advancing two steps, emerging silently from the undergrowth, she stops and sniffs. Looking right, she stares downstream, as though expecting an intruder. Turning back to the stream, she takes another step forward, lowers her head to the bright surface of the water, and takes several laps. Swinging her head left, chin dripping, she again gazes downstream.

Something behind her moves. A cub's face appears in the foliage. It moves cautiously around from behind her. For a moment it stands staring blankly at the pool; then it bounces forward to the water's edge. Lowering its muzzle, it too begins to drink.

I watch all this with breathless attention. As I do, I find myself being drawn into a little fantasy in which I see myself sitting as though invisible at the edge of the pool, only a few feet away from the tigress and her cub, studying their every movement, watching them drink. Half turning to my informant, I hear myself whisper, "What do you think would happen if I were to go downstairs right now?"

My informant turns to me and stares, a flash of contempt flickering in his eyes. Or perhaps it is only fear. "She would probably kill you."

For a long moment I stare back at him, glancing at the pool just in time to see the tigress's hindquarters disappear into the undergrowth. My informant watches her go. Then, in a voice that is no longer a whisper, he says, "That's the last we will see of her today. She's very skittish these days, very worried about her offspring. Recently one of the males killed her other cub."

"That's a pity," I say.

"Yes," he says.

I turn and scoot back over the wooden floor to the wall and lean back against it with a smile, reflecting on the fact that sometimes a male tiger will kill cubs, apparently to provoke their mother into coming into estrus. Mating with her then, he can effectively substitute his genes for those of a rival. Ironically, the cubs he murders are sometimes his own offspring.

Glancing at my companion, I say, "That was wonderful."

Turning away from the window with a smile, he sits back against the wall. For a moment I look at him, and then an unexpected thought comes to me.

"But how did you know she was there?"

He looks at me, shrugs, and says, "Maybe I heard her."

"You must have great hearing then. I didn't hear a thing."

"I have always had sharp ears."

I glance outside into the fading daylight and ask, "You come here often?"

"Fairly often."

"You seem to know the animals very well."

"I know this tigress well enough."

"How long have you been observing her?"

"Since she was a cub."

"How long is that?"

"Nearly three years."

"How did you—"

Just then, outside and below us, I hear something crashing through the underbrush. It is our trusty mahout and his elephant, come to fetch us. "Sa'b?" The mahout's voice comes ringing up from below.

"Here!" my informant says. He looks over at me and smiles, seeming relieved, unless I am imagining it, that my line of questioning has been interrupted. He stands, extending his arms and stretching as he does, walks over to me, and offers me a hand up. "Well, I hope you enjoyed seeing her," he says. "It was very short, wasn't it? But we'll have another shot at it tomorrow. Now it's time to go."

Seated in the canteen at park headquarters two hours later, waiting for our supper, we have for the last few minutes been discussing all sorts of things, including the day's events. Because the generator has failed, the room is illuminated by two kerosene lamps and two or three flickering candles. Seated across from me, my informant is his usual dapper self. Hair combed back, neatly dressed, he seems rather out of place in these dingy surroundings.

"So I take it," I say, "that you consider the situation in regard to tiger, the situation in Asia as a whole, as rather hopeless."

"You might say that."

"Do people you know agree with you?"

"I think so."

"Then why don't people just *say* it? Why does everyone keep beating around the bush?"

He gives me a long thoughtful look and says, "Hope is something that people are very reluctant to give up—even those who ought to know better. Take your own countrymen, for example. For most Americans, I suspect, it is nearly impossible to imagine that there are—how shall I put it?—situations in the world for which no rational solutions will ever be found. But such situations do exist. In regard to the forests of Asia, in regard to forests everywhere, we are now entering a sort of threshold era. Once that final threshold has been crossed, everything will be different."

"Meaning?"

"Meaning, simply, that when the last tree is felled, when the last wild place is finally conquered, it will become obvious for the first time in the history of our planet what the human species really amounts to."

"And what is that?"

Looking away, he says, "Something sadder, something infinitely more pathetic, than almost anyone has ever imagined."

I stare at him for a moment.

"What does your wife think of all this? Does she ever come with you when you spend time in the forest?"

"She has no interest in it at all."

"I was looking forward to meeting her."

"I'm afraid that won't be possible," he says, gazing at me. "You see, though I was with her on the day you and I met in that hotel garden in Calcutta, my wife and I have not lived under the same roof for many years." Pausing, as though expecting me to be shocked, he adds, "As you well know, all Hindus marry. But few divorce. So it has been with us."

"I'm sorry."

"It all happened a long time ago. We remain very close friends. I depend on her a great deal—and she on me."

"Did her grandfather finally die, then?"

"Yes."

There follows an awkward lull. More to change the subject than anything else, I say, "I was interested in what you were saying when we were driving up this morning."

"About what?"

"About the walking you've done in the forest."

"What about it?"

"I gathered from what you said that it's something that you do quite a lot."

"Not so much. Not anymore."

"Why is that?"

"I have found . . . other interests."

"The way you were talking about it this morning, it seemed to me that you used it almost as a kind of therapy."

"There's probably something in that." Looking away for a moment, he adds, "The truth is, I'm not quite sure what it was. I was looking for something . . . I was searching for an answer."

"To what?"

"I don't know," he replies. "If you had asked me when I did it, I might have said that I was trying to find out if I was really any longer alive."

"And on those walks you often came across tiger?"

"Not often."

"But you did come across them?"

"Yes."

"And what happened?"

"You want my adventure stories?"

"Sure."

"Well," he says with a smile, looking away, "I remember once years ago, when I was hardly more than a boy and was walking in the forest, I met a tiger on the trail. Realizing that he was going to charge, I climbed a nearby tree. It was a thin little tree, and I was able to climb just high enough to be out of his reach. The tiger was so angry with me, so intent on punishing me for frightening him, that he would not let me climb down for hours. But I didn't mind. You may not believe it, but as I sat there on that branch, I was perhaps as happy as I've ever been."

At that moment the waiter appears, carrying two metal plates full of chicken curry and another plate stacked with chapatis. As he places them on the table in front of us, my informant asks, "Would you like something to drink?"

"No, nothing, thanks."

He says something in Hindi, and the waiter turns and walks off. I pick up my fork and take a bite of curry. My companion puts a chapati on his plate and tears off a piece, which he then carries to his mouth. "What about you?" he says, looking across at me. "What are your plans? You're going back to the States in a few days. What then?"

"I'll have some time, so maybe I'll start the book—not that I have a clue where or how to begin. I have a tour of Thailand and Burma coming up soon. I'll probably stop in Thailand on my way back to California and scout it. Then, in July, I think I'll go to Sumatra."

"Research for the book?"

"Yes."

"You've been there before?"

"A couple of times."

"And what was your impression?"

"A mess. Another lost cause."

My informant gazes at me. Then he says, "I hope you won't mind my saying this, but it seems to me from various things you have said that you have become depressed and quite bitter about the way things are— Am I right about that?"

"Maybe."

"You know, there's really nothing you can do. There's nothing *anyone* can do. It's the way the world is." He sits quietly for a moment, and adds, "I hope you won't take this in the wrong way, but if there is one thing I have learned in my life, it is that you cannot under any circumstances allow bitterness to poison your life. Bitterness is one of the great unrecognized horrors of the world. It can take hold of you, far more easily, far more quickly, than you might think."

"And you're not bitter? From the things you've been saying, you sound it."

"No. I'm *sad.* There's a great deal of difference between the two."

I stare at him and say after a moment, "I think I understand that."

"I'm not at all sure that you do. But you will perhaps—someday."

Twenty-one

TWO DAYS LATER, on one of those afternoons when the sun lacks sufficient intensity to dissipate the lingering fog and the world is clothed in misty light, I am back in Delhi, sitting in the library in the home of my informant. Our return journey took up almost all of yesterday, and I am pleased that today I shall not have to spend any time in an automobile.

For the past couple of hours he has been showing me some of his treasures. Just a while ago, for example, he brought out an early edition of *Hakluytus Posthumous, or Purchas His Pilgrimage,* by Samuel Purchas, published in 1625, a book that contains several of the earliest reports of Europeans encountering tigers in Asia. Even more interesting was a first edition of *A New Account of East India and Persia in Eight Letters,* by Dr. John Fryer, published in 1675 —a really beautiful book, charmingly illustrated and wonderful to hold, containing what must certainly be one of the first accounts of an Englishman killing a tiger. Browsing through it, I got so caught up in the good doctor's web of words that I ended up feeling as though he had settled to earth in some creaky, steam-leaking seventeenth-century time machine and whisked me away.

Over the past few minutes our conversation has moved away from the library and its contents to a more controversial subject: just how many tigers survive in what remains of the Asian wilderness. To emphasize a point, my informant has just returned from the shelves with the Asia volume of the *Times Atlas of the World* and placed it on the table in front of me.

"So from what you've just said," I say, "I take it that you think the official figures are exaggerated?"

"Completely," he replies, opening the atlas to one of the India pages. "Take this country, for example. Official reports state that there are between three thousand and four thousand tigers in India. Regrettably, anyone who has actually taken the trouble to visit the parks knows that this figure cannot possibly be realistic. I have considered the issue very carefully, and I have to say that I do not think that there can be more than about seven hundred tigers left in India, and the figure is probably closer to the five hundred mark. That is heresy, of course. Pure heresy. But I have what I think are very good reasons for believing the figure to be accurate."

"Well," I say, trying to take this in, "if the numbers you have just mentioned are correct, why do all the books keep publishing inaccurate data?"

"It's not so complicated. The only census of the Indian tiger ever carried out was during the Project Tiger era, twenty years ago. Unfortunately, the figures bandied about at the time were never anywhere near accurate."

"Why not?"

"There was simply too much at stake. Project Tiger was financed primarily by international organizations that were willing to go all out to raise funds, provided that positive results could be demonstrated within a reasonable span of time. And the project was a success, of course. But the *degree* of its success was mightily exaggerated."

"It sounds as though you are suggesting that there was some kind of plot."

"Not at all. Nothing like that. It is simply that in each region where censuses were taken, the figures got exaggerated. The people actually doing the counting were trying to shed the best possible light on their own operation. Local officials wanted to impress those to whom they were responsible, and so on."

"But people working with tigers here in India and in Nepal know that the figures are wrong?"

"Of course."

"Then why don't they speak up?"

"They're afraid that if they do, the governments and the international organizations involved will simply write off India as a lost cause."

"In other words, if you call it a success, it's a success. If you call it a failure, it's a failure."

"Isn't that the way the world operates?"

"What about Thailand, then, or Malaysia?"

"The same situation. The figures the governments hand out are all exaggerated one to two hundred percent." Reaching down, he turns the pages of the atlas to one of the Southeast Asia maps and says, "If you have traveled extensively in Thailand, as I have, when you read that the official number for the country as a whole is four to six hundred tigers, you realize that something is wrong. There simply isn't enough forest left to support that many tigers. My own estimate for Thailand at the present time is somewhere in the vicinity of one hundred tigers, and the number, whatever it is, is dwindling by the year."

"Three quarters less than they say they have."

"Yes."

"What about Burma? Indonesia?"

"The same."

"So where does that leave the world in terms of overall tiger numbers? I've read somewhere that the world population is somewhere in the six-to-nine-thousand range. You don't think that's realistic?"

"I don't think there have been nine thousand wild tigers in the world since before the Second World War."

"What do you think *is* an accurate estimate, then?"

"I believe that there cannot possibly be more than two thousand wild tigers alive on this planet today, and the figure may be closer to fifteen hundred."

"A quarter of the lowest official estimate."

"Yes."

I sit for a moment thinking about all this. "So what does that mean? For the future?"

"Merely that even if my estimate is completely mistaken, it is almost certain that within the next ten years, tiger numbers will be reduced by half, and that that figure will in turn be halved in the following ten years, and so on."

"Resulting in effective extinction when?"

"Well, people are always reluctant to admit that the last of anything has vanished for good. But I believe that effective extinction of the tiger, as you phrase it, will occur within the next twenty-five to thirty years—say by the year 2025 at the very latest. But do not misunderstand me. At that time there may still exist a small remnant population here or there. But it won't amount to much. Nor will it survive long."

My informant closes the atlas with a snap and places it to one side. I turn and look out the window at the compound—at the cold sun looming beyond the ever-shifting thicknesses of mist, at a busy hoopoe probing with its curved bill for insects in the middle of the lawn. My host takes a seat on the sofa nearby. After a moment I say, "It's funny we're talking about this."

"Why?"

"I think I've come to a decision."

"Yes?"

"I think I'd like to see a tiger on foot."

Having said it, I realize that ever since seeing that tigress and her cub at Corbett the day before yesterday, I have felt an odd realization settling over me, one that is in its own way completely irresistible. For reasons I have not begun to fathom, it has become obvious to me that unless one has seen a tiger on foot, face to face, on its own ground, one has not really seen it at all.

"It's a stupid idea," my informant says, looking directly at me.

Taken aback by his response, I return his gaze. "Is it?"

"Very stupid."

"It wouldn't be the first one I've had."

"What is it?" he says. "You want to get yourself killed?"

"I don't think so. It's just that . . . I don't know. I think it's something I'd like to do." I add, "I'd like you to help me."

His eyes harden. "You are a man of surprises, aren't you?"

"All you have to say is no."

"And if I do?"

"Then I'll probably do it myself."

"You're mad."

"Why do you say that?"

"Because it's a mad idea."

He looks away for a long time, his expression troubled. He looks away so long that I begin to wonder if he wants to continue the conversation at all. Turning back at last, he says, "I'll have to think about it . . . Perhaps the next time you come to India."

□ □ □

That night, just before midnight, the scene at New Delhi's new international airport is the usual bedlam. I have just checked in. My informant and I are standing in front of the metal detector shaking hands. Reaching down to the folder that he has held clutched under his arm ever since we left the house, he hands it to me and says, "This is for you."

"What is it?"

"You'll see."

"Well," I say, looking down at it, "thanks, for whatever it is. And thanks for everything else too. It's been great."

"My pleasure. Just remember, don't do anything stupid in Southeast Asia, will you?"

"I won't."

I turn and place all the things I am carrying, the folder included, on the conveyor belt of the x-ray machine. I wait a moment until I receive the okay from the guard, then pass through the metal detector. By the time I have retrieved my things and think to look back, he is gone.

Twenty-two

ON A COOL SUNNY MORNING three days after leaving Delhi, I am standing in a tiny forest clearing in Khao Yai National Park in south-central Thailand, looking through my binoculars at a creature poised in the canopy fifty or sixty feet above my head, a creature of such bizarre and extravagant appearance it seems less a living being than the product of some feverish Oriental fantasy. One of the world's great natural treasures and at the same time one of nature's supreme oddities, it is that species of bird to which ornithologists have given the name *Buceros bicornis:* the great hornbill.

Its wings, momentarily outstretched, are huge—over four feet from tip to tip. But it is the bill I can't stop staring at. Nearly two feet long and curved like a two-handed scimitar, it is ornamented at its base with a bony structure resembling nothing so much as the carburetor intake vent of a customized American hot rod. As I look at it, I reflect that it may be a good thing that this refugee from the Mesozoic subsists entirely on fruit, the bounty of the forest, and not, say, on human flesh.

Situated on a once-remote plateau that earlier in the century provided a safe haven for outlaws and other social undesirables and that is, remarkably, only a few hours' drive from the gaudy temples, flashy brothels, nasty traffic, and suffocating pollution of Bangkok, Khao Yai is home to thousands of species of animals, plants, birds, and insects, including Asian elephant, several species of monkeys and apes, leopard, and tiger. On previous visits the birds and the primates had been the attraction for me. This time, however, my agenda is different. According to official estimates, Khao Yai is home to some twenty-five to fifty tigers. In the short time I have available, I would like to find out whether this figure can possibly be accurate and to discover, if I can, what their chances of survival might be.

In this regard, my arrival at the park was marked by a fortuitous meeting. Yesterday evening, as I was eating my supper at one of the open-air noodle shacks near park headquarters, I fell into conversation with one of the park staff—a person I will call Kitti—who was dining at the same establishment. Kitti, a handsome young man, perhaps thirty years old, dressed in pressed official khakis, noticed my binoculars and asked me if I had come to the park to look at birds.

"Not this time," I said. "What I'd really like to see is a tiger."

"Well," he said, smiling that charming, slightly embarrassed, mostly inscrutable smile for which the Thai people are well known, "there are tigers at Khao Yai. But maybe not so many."

"The official figure is twenty-five to fifty."

"Maybe," he says, smiling again.

"You don't think that figure is accurate?"

"I don't think so."

"Why not?"

He takes a bite of his noodles, then says, "Tiger kill the sambar deer to live, yes?"

"Yes."

"At Khao Yai, sambar deer live on the grasslands. Grassland area very small. Cannot support fifty tiger."

"How many do you think it does support, then?"

"Nobody know. Maybe ten, maybe fifteen. No more is possible, I think."

"Then the official figures are completely mistaken?"

"I think so."

"Why?"

"Khao Yai big showplace, especially for government. Government want everybody to think everything okay at Khao Yai. But Khao Yai is island, surrounded by sea of farming. Number of tigers is small. In future, inbreeding will cause problems with the reproduction. In short time, at Khao Yai, tiger will be fine. But later not so good. In the long time, there is no future for tiger here. Too many people. Too many problems."

"What about the other parks in Thailand? You think they will have the same problems?"

"All have the same problem."

"The tigers will simply be surrounded and cut off?"

"Yes."

"The official figure is that there are between four hundred and six hundred tigers in Thailand. Do you think that's possible?"

He smiles and shakes his head. "Six hundred tigers in Thailand? You look at map. You tell me where they could be."

"How about four hundred, then?"

"Too high. Poacher poison them, trap them, you know, for the skin and bones and the body parts. I don't know . . . maybe one hundred in Thailand. Maybe more, maybe less. All I know is they not survive very long."

"How long have you worked here?"

"Five year."

"Have you ever seen a tiger here?"

"No. But one man working here, he kill a tiger—a man-eater."

"When?"

"Six, eight year ago."

"The tiger killed someone?"

"A little girl. At night she standing at the window of her house, not so far from here, with window open. Tiger jump up and grab her and carry her away. Some time later the park ranger shoot the tiger. Sad story for the parents."

"Yes," I agreed, "very sad."

As I remember all this, from somewhere far off in the forest comes a coarse echoing *yawkk*. I look up just in time to see the great hornbill in the tree above me cock its head and broadcast a *yawkk* in reply. Spreading its wings magisterially, it catapults itself out of the crown of the tree and, with a series of powerful downstrokes, each producing a powerful whoosh, flaps out of sight.

That evening, back in my cabin, after taking supper at the small restaurant near the campground, I open the folder my informant thrust into my arms when he dropped me off at Delhi airport. I had sneaked a look as soon as the plane was airborne, and was pleased, if somewhat mystified, to discover that the folder contained not only a copy of his unfinished *Brief History* but a modest pile of typed quotations obviously intended at one time to form the backbone of the completed work. Until this moment I have had neither the time nor the energy to look them over carefully.

Setting the manuscript of the *Brief History* to one side, I take out the pile of neatly printed sheets and place them on the table next to me. Adjusting the light, I pick up the top page and discover on it a series of typed quotations, all concerning tiger, drawn from ancient Greek and Roman writers. Most of the quotations are brief, so brief that I have to read each of them a couple of times before I can grasp exactly what the author is trying to get at.

Typical are a few lines of the Roman poet Horace, written in the late first century B.C.: "On account of such merit, father Bacchus, you were conveyed by tigers bearing yokes on untamed necks." This is fairly incomprehensible until I read the note my informant has appended to it: "A reference to the ancient legend that Bacchus traveled to the East where he taught the Indians the secret of wine-making and was by way of recompense provided tigers to pull his chariot."

Along this same line there are quotations from the Greek poet Philemon; from the *Aeneid;* from Seneca's horrible revenge play, *Thyestes;* from Claudian and Boethius. In none of these, however, does the tiger rate more than a mention.

Underneath the top page are four more pages of quotations from the same era, and what I find striking as I look them over is that they all seem to fall into one of two neat categories. They are either essentially inconsequential, like the one from the Greek writer Strabo's *Geography,* first published probably in the early first century A.D.—

> Megasthenes says that the largest tigers are found among the Prasii [a tribe which inhabited that part of the world now known as Bengal], even twice as large as lions, and so powerful that a tame one, led by four men, seized a mule by the hind leg and by force drew the mule to itself.

—or downright silly, like the quote from Pliny the Elder's *Natural History,* published sometime after the author's death in A.D. 79—

> Hyrcania [the regions lying to the south of the Caspian Sea] and India produce the tiger, an animal of terrific speed, which is most noticeable when the whole of its litter, which is always numerous, is being captured. The litter is taken by a man lying in wait with the swiftest horse obtainable, and is transferred successively to

fresh horses. But when the mother tiger finds her lair empty (for male tigers do not look after their young), she rushes off at headlong speed, tracking them by scent. The captor, when her roar approaches, throws away one of the cubs. She snatches it up in her mouth, and resumes the pursuit at even a faster pace owing to her burden, and so in succession until the hunter has regained the ship, and her ferocity rages vainly on the shore *(". . . ac subinde donec in navem regresso inrita feritas saevit in litore").*

Pliny may have been the first great writer on natural subjects in the western world—he certainly has a reputation for being so—but he seems all the same to have had a very high tolerance for moonshine. To begin with, tigers do not have large litters (Pliny's informant must have had housecats in mind), and this fact alone drives the story over the top into the realm of the nightmare that appears to have inspired it.

Still, among the quotations I do discover a few good stories, which in spite of their brevity could almost stand by themselves. On the page underneath the Pliny, for example, I come across a charming story from Cassius Dio's *Roman History,* published in the late second or early third century A.D. It describes, in a very compressed way, how a tiger was seen by the Romans for the first time, during the reign of the emperor Augustus:

> And Augustus came to Samos, and again passed the winter there . . . and all sorts of embassies came to him; and the Indians who had previously sent messages proclaiming friendship, now sent to make a solemn treaty, with presents, and among other things including tigers, which were now seen for the first time by the Romans, and if I am not mistaken by the Greeks also.

Cassius Dio got it wrong, of course. It appears that he had never gotten wind of General Seleucus's gift to the Athenians.

On the page beneath, I come across a passage from a book I read years ago, Pausanias's *Guide to Greece,* written in the early second century and even today a useful guide to the ancient sites of that country. Pausanias, a physician by profession but a passionate antiquary, included in a general discussion of mythological animals this wonderful aside about tiger:

> I am certain that the monster . . . the Indians call 'martichora' and the Greeks 'man-eater,' is a tiger. But the triple rows of teeth in the upper and lower jaw, and the sting at the tip of the tail, with which it fights at close quarters and shoots arrows at a distance, seem to me a fiction about which the Indians have managed to convince themselves.

I read on for a few minutes, a little disappointed in the end to find that of all the material my informant has located from classical times, he has been able to unearth only a single eyewitness account of tiger. This occurs in a book entitled *On the Spectacles,* written by the poet and epigrammatist Martial in A.D. 80, during the reign of Emperor Titus, to celebrate the inauguration of the Roman Colosseum. The first passage reads, "Tigresses not so many has the robber dreaded in Eastern fields by Ganges' side . . . Thy arena Caesar has surpassed Indian triumphs and the wealth and riches of the victor God: for Bacchus, while he drove beneath the yoke the captive Indians, was content with two tigresses alone." In plain English, this suggests that at the opening festivities at the Colosseum, Martial witnessed an extravagant bit of show business worthy of Cecil B. De Mille: three or more tigers harnessed to chariots, circling the field—an unforgettable sight, no doubt.

The second of the quotations is shorter but even more vivid: "Wont to lick the hand of its fearless master, a tigress . . . savagely tore a fierce lion with maddened fang." A lion and a tiger fighting to the death in the arena—the sort of entertainment that imperial Romans are said to have been excessively fond of. But that is all. Not (in a manner of speaking) a great deal to sink your teeth into.

Eager to see what comes next, I whip on past the quote from Marco Polo that appeared in the *Brief History,* and past a reference from Chaucer's "The Squire's Tale" ("There is no tiger, nor cruel beast") . . . my eye landing at last on a quote from an author I have never heard of, one Josapha Barbaro. According to my informant's accompanying note, Barbaro was a fifteenth-century Venetian merchant who traveled on a commercial and diplomatic mission to the king of Persia just a few years before Columbus set sail to what would come to be known as the New World. While attending a royal reception, Barbaro reports, he witnessed what struck him as an extraordinary natural phenomenon.

> There came certain men from a Prince of India, with certain strange beasts, the first whereof was a lion led by a chain . . . which they call in their language *babureth.* She resembled a lioness, but was red-colored, streaked all over with black stripes: her face was red with certain white and black spots, the belly white, and tailed like a lion, seeming to be a marvelous fierce beast.

Marvelous indeed—the animal, the image, and the prose. It occurs to me that this may be the first account of a European actually *seeing* a tiger since Martial. After all, Marco had said that the Great Khan possessed this and that. What he did not say was "I saw it with my own eyes."

Anxious to discover if there is more material along this line, reflecting on the odd fact that this is precisely where my informant gave up writing his *Brief History,* I immediately stumble across a quotation from the renowned sixteenth-century chronicler of the Portuguese empire João de Barros, "the Portuguese Pliny," describing the tiger-fearing habits of the people living in that part of the world now known as Malaysia.

And indeed most of these wretched people sleep at the top of the highest trees they can find, for up to a height of twenty palms the tigers can seize them at a leap; and if anything saves these poor people from these beasts it is the bonfires they keep burning at night, which the tigers are much afraid of. In fact these are so numerous that many come into the city itself at night in search of prey. And it has happened since we took the place, that a tiger leapt into a garden surrounded by a good high timber fence, and lifted a beam of wood with three slaves who were laid by the heels, and with these made a clean leap over the fence.

Sounds incredible, but it isn't necessarily. Large male tigers are capable of extraordinary feats of strength. There is no reason to doubt that one weighing four to five hundred pounds could carry off three ill-fed and scrawny slaves, even chained together.

I turn the page, thinking that I might skip on, but the very first sentence of the next quoted passage captures my attention: "The hunters, having surprised a tiger in the jungle where it was hiding, informed His Majesty Akbar who went forth to meet it."

Who? What?

Consulting the note at the end of the quotation, I discover that this is a passage from a book entitled *Akbar-nama* ("The History of Akbar's Reign"), written in the late sixteenth century by Sheikh Abul (Fadl) Allami, trusted confidant of the great Mogul emperor Akbar. Also mentioned in the note is the fact that this is probably one of the earliest reasonably full accounts of anyone's actually hunting and killing a tiger. I turn back the page and begin to read.

The hunters, having surprised a tiger in the jungle where it was hiding, informed His Majesty Akbar who went forth to meet it. As His Majesty approached a thicket of bamboo, a great tiger suddenly charged out. The king's attendants, losing control of themselves, shot it full of arrows. Akbar, not appreciative of their lack of discipline, ordered that henceforth on no account should an animal be killed until he had given the order personally.

The king had no more spoken than another tiger, as formidable as the first, came charging toward them. At the sight of it, the hair on the heads of the officers stood up straight in fear, but none dared attack the beast because of the orders Akbar had just given. From horseback Akbar loosed an arrow at the tiger, stopping the animal in its tracks with a roar. Descending calmly from his horse, his officers following suit, Akbar took aim with his arquebus and fired, wounding the tiger in the jaw. He attempted to fire again, but by that time the tiger was running so madly from place to place it was impossible.

Akbar asked Dastam Khan to move ahead to draw the attention of the tiger, so that he could get another shot at it. At that moment, however, another officer, Adil, having advanced toward the tiger, shot an arrow at it. The enraged tiger leapt at him, paws extended, landing full on his chest, knocking him over backwards. Adil, jamming his left arm between the tiger's jaws, attempted at the same moment to draw his knife from his belt. But the knife would not come free and the tiger mangled his arm. The knife free at last, Adil struck the tiger several times, provoking the animal to attack his right arm as well.

The other officers, swords in hand, rushed forward to rescue Adil. But in their frenzy and confusion they wounded Adil himself who, in horrible pain, lost consciousness. Though transported to Agra, it was obvious that Adil had no hope of surviving his multiple injuries.

After enduring months of agony, he died.

Now this is more like it!

Expecting more along this line, I go on. What I find instead is Shakespeare—mentions of tiger from five different plays, in fact. Although Shakespeare very probably never saw a living tiger, he certainly knew what one was. Among the quotations I find what is certainly his best-known line about the animal, the famous "imitate the action of the tiger" reference from Henry's rousing speech before Agincourt in *Henry V.* There are also quotes from *Macbeth* and a couple of the sonnets. But my favorite by far, however, is the one from *Romeo and Juliet,* in which Romeo, threatening Balthasar, says

> By heaven, I will tear thee joint by joint
> And strew this hungry churchyard with thy limbs;
> The time and my intents are savage wild.
> More fierce and more inexorable far
> Than empty tigers or a roaring sea.

Enchanted by the verse, eager for more action, I flip on past a quote from Robert Greene, a contemporary and rival of Shakespeare's, in which he refers to the Bard as having "a tiger's heart wrapped in a player's hide"—an insult, apparently, but one that seems to me very apt—and past a quote from Milton's *Paradise Lost* ("Tygers, Ounces, Pards,/ Gambold before them"), to land at last on a passage from a book bearing the awkward title *A New Account of East India and Persia in Eight Letters.* This book, I have already learned, was first published in 1675, half a century after Shakespeare's death, by Dr. John Fryer, a physician in the employ of the East India Company. My informant showed me a copy of it in his library. I smile as I begin to read the now familiar passage that is perhaps the earliest description on record of an Englishman's killing a tiger.

> For our diversion we had nothing but shooting, in which we spent sometimes a whole week in the woods and river sides; for if we expected flesh, or fowl, we must take pains for it; no beef being to be bought here, though up the country from the moors we could; so that our usual diet was (besides plenty of fish) waterfowl, peacocks, green pigeons, spotted deer, sambar, wild hogs and sometimes wild cows. Going in quest whereof, one of our soldiers, a youth, killed a tiger royal, it was brought here by thirty or forty Combies, the body tied to a long bamboo; the tail extended: so they brought it to the house, where we saw 'twas wounded in

three places, one through the hand with two bullets, another through the body slanting up to the shoulders, a third in the leg; it was a tiger of the biggest and noblest kind, five feet in length beside the tail, three and a half in height, it was of yellow, streaked with black, like a tabby cat, the ears short, with a few bristles about the lips; the visage fierce and majestic, the teeth gnashing, two of which broke against stones for anguish, the shoulders and forelegs thick and well-set, the paw as large as the biggest fist stretched out, the claws thick and strong.

The boy shot it from a chouse, or *estarzo* [a sort of hide], as it came to drink, supposing it to have been a deer; the first shot was that under the shoulder, which made her spring three times to an incredible height, at the last of which she fell into the chouse from which she saw the flash, where with the English boy were a comby, and a comby boy of eight years old, asleep a little on the side; she pawed the straw with her feet, while all but the child asleep fled; but wrung with pain, she soon left the place with a horrible noise that made the woods tremble, all which wakened not the lad, nor had it any harm.

In this interval, the English youth charged again with a couple of slugs, and tracing the blood, as she was making at him, discharged through the brain pan, at which she was quiet, but to make sure, he made another shot at her, which he believed was that in her leg. All this time the moon was obscured a[nd] cloudy; the comby that had left him and his son [returned], at length with many more calling "Fringi," the term they have for Europeans and Franks. The boy was walking about, fearing to venture within reach, till at last laying aside his well-advised suspicion, he approaching found the Terror of the Wood slain.

Twenty-three

A HALF-HOUR later I am still at my seat at the table. Spellbound, I have hardly looked up from the pile of quotations. And I don't think it is just me. It is nearly impossible for me to imagine how anyone, having read the first sentence from the following excerpt from Sir Edward Braddon's *Thirty Years of Shikar*, published in 1895, could get up and walk away from it.

And it was an evil feature in the tigers and panthers of the district that they were very generally, if not universally, man-eaters. I have heard it argued that tigers become man-eaters when, in their old age, their teeth have been worn down and their strength and activity impaired; but this apology could not be made for the Deoghur tigers. Young and old alike, their prey was, on occasion, man or woman: they killed the wretched woodcutters, or the old women who picked up sticks in the jungle; they carried off the wayfarer from the highroad; they broke into the grass huts of the sleeping peasant and carried off the husband from his wife's side; and the panthers emulated the tigers in these evil doings. Every year brought its death-toll of men, women and children killed in this fashion, and one tiger alone, of which more hereafter, was credited with, or discredited by, a hundred victims . . .

I was awakened before dawn by a significant pressure upon my knee—a pressure that called me to wakefulness more emphatically and effectively than human voice or trumpet call. It was a reveille not to be disregarded, and I sat up wide-awake to look into the darkness, and feel the silence once more—and the hush was broken, as I would have chosen, by a roar . . . That roar came from a distance, but pervaded, as it seemed, the whole earth and the black starlit vault above; and another came, this time from a different and somewhat nearer point, and so, at intervals, those roars betrayed the tiger's zigzag course toward my buffalo. The brute was quartering the ground with instinctive skill that would have been creditable to the most perfectly broken pointer, and his leisure was highly impressive.

And as the tiger worked his way towards my tree, I looked for the chance of the dawn preceding his arrival. That, too, was close at hand, as the position of the morning star distinctly told me; but would it come in time? Never did the breaking of an Indian day (generally an abrupt proceeding) seem so tardy; and the tiger was steadily and stealthily coming on. And then, when I made the tiger out to be less than fifty yards off, silence reigned again—a silence of deadly omen to the slumbering buffalo, happily unconscious of its impending fate. For a couple of minutes the deadly still lasted. Then came the noise of the tiger's rush upon the prey, that was killed as it slept, and then only the tiger's movements and sucking of the victim's blood. And still the day had not dawned, and the tiger was hidden from me by an impenetrable gloom. For some few minutes the situation remained as I have described, and then (probably because it had come to know of my presence) the tiger dragged the dead buffalo from my tree into the jungle-road, where, at last, I saw it dimly outlined against the sand. This was a tactical blunder that cost the tiger its life. In the glade below my tree it would have remained for some time veiled from my sight by the shade cast upon the spot by overhanging trees; and from that spot it might have retreated into the jungle from which it emerged, carrying its prey with it. But on the forest-road there was no shade to hide; on the contrary, there was white sand, which caught every gleam of early light, and served as a background to the tiger's silhouette.

As the tiger was evidently making for the jungle across the road, I seized my chance and fired. The thud of the bullet and one sharp roar of pain from the tiger told me that I had not missed; but the disappearance of the tiger told me I had not killed . . .

As soon as I had given the wounded tiger time to settle down somewhere clear of my path, and to forget any wasted views of revenge, my shikari and I descended from our tree, and walked home. After chota hazri [a small breakfast] we were ready with half a dozen elephants to follow the tiger up; and we found it, after beating in close lines backwards and forwards in vain, about a hundred yards from the point where it had been wounded. It was moribund, and not of a mind to fight when we did find it. The coup de grace was given . . . The first of the sacred tigers of Byjanauth!

Nothing like a good hunting story.

Since I know nothing about Braddon, I am particularly pleased to see that my informant has appended the following comment to the text:

Braddon's life was so archetypally Victorian he seems to have sprung full-blown out of the *Boy's Own Paper.* A hero of the Indian Mutiny, he went on to an impressive career of public service; as leader of the House of Assembly in Tasmania and, later on, as senior member of the House of Representatives of the Commonwealth Parliament. He spent, as the title of his memoir indicates, three decades of his life in India.

But that is not all. On the very next page my informant has included an article, it seems to me, of similar fascination, which first appeared in the *Madras Mail* on May 10, 1909:

Particulars are published here of the adventures of a party of surveyors connected with the Survey of India in the Lushai Hills, adjoining Cachar, who were attacked by a tiger in early spring. The tiger had been prowling about the camp for some time and one night seized a *khalasi,* who was washing cooking-pots in a stream not twenty yards from the rest of the party. A *tindal* named Nandu pluckily rushed in and tried to beat off the tiger with a stick, but it was not until the rest of the party came up that the tiger dropped the man and disappeared. It returned a few minutes later and seized Nandu, but was again beaten off, only to return presently and seize a third *khalasi.* The third attempt to provide itself with a meal was frustrated like the others and the party spent the rest of the night shouting and surrounded by fires, and at daybreak moved to Lushai village, carrying two of the injured men, but leaving all else behind. Mr. L. Williams shortly afterwards turned up, having heard of the straits the party were in, and did what he could for the wounded men, one of whom died shortly afterwards. Armed Lushais were then sent to the camp, when they found the bedding, blankets, and bags torn and dragged about and a sight-ruled plane table bearing marks of the tiger's fangs. Colonel Longe mentions the name of the surveyor, Amar Singh, who kept his men together and prevented them from leaving the wounded men. Also that of Nandu Tindal, who is only slowly recovering from his injuries, for courage and good behavior in connection with this affair.

I smile. It would not quite have washed had there been no European to ride to the rescue. Still, the Indians do get to be the heroes of the tale—for once.

A few pages beyond this, I come across another passage that seems to me utterly hypnotic and un-put-downable, from a book also unfamiliar to me, *In Malay Forests,* authored by one Sir George Maxwell in 1907.

Thus we came to a discussion of were-tigers, which are in the Malay Peninsula the counterpart of the were-wolves of Europe. That were-tigers exist no Malay doubts; and the popular belief is that men from the district of Korinchi in Sumatra have the power of assuming the form of a tiger at will, and that in this guise they range the forest, hunting the wild game and occasionally killing mankind.

The Korinchi men, who are mostly pedlars of clothes, naturally resent the imputation, and contend that it is only the men of Chenaku, a sub-district of Korinchi, who have this unholy power. But as the contention admits the existence of the power amongst certain of the suspected class, the Malays of the Peninsula are only strengthened in their opinion, and believe the charge to be true of all Korinchis. To'Kaya told me of a village where, for some months, the fowls had been harried by a tiger or panther, both of which are known to Malays by the same generic term, and where one day a Korinchi man lying sick with a fever in the house of the headman, who had pity on him, had vomited quantities of chicken feathers. I, in my turn, told him a story I had heard in the reaches of the Slim River. There, in an isolated hill-padi clearing, lived a Malay and his wife, and their two children, young boys of the age when they learn to read the Koran. One night came a rap at the door of the house, which, like all Malay dwellings, was built upon posts some ten feet above the ground. In answer to a demand from the father as to who was at the door and what was wanted, a voice replied, "We ask for a light, our torches are extinguished, and we still have some distance to go to the house where we are expected." Now, it is well-known that this is a common device of jins and evil spirits to obtain admission to a house, and one should always beware of opening the door to give light to a stranger who pretends to be belated. Well, the two boys, while their father was questioning the stranger, slipped out of the house by the ladder behind the kitchen. Excited by the visit of a stranger at such an hour, they moved silently along the ground under the bamboo flooring to peep upwards at the threshold. There, on the rung of the ladder below the door, stood a man talking to their father; but even while he spoke a tail striped in black and yellow dropped between his legs, and then up and down his lower limbs ran successive ripples of change and color. The toes became talons, the feet turned into paws, and the knee-joints, already striped with that awful black and yellow, were turning front to back.

And all the time the human face of the creature was giving

specious explanations to the questions of the master of the house. Half in fascination, half in desperation, the two boys seized the tail that dangled before them, and shouted to their father to kill the thing. But before he could reach for his spear, the animal, now nearly a tiger, tore itself away from the puny grasp of the youngsters and fled into the darkness of the forest.

I sit back in my chair for a moment, thinking about all these extracts, and suddenly, in the silence and stillness of the room, I am almost overwhelmed with sadness. It comes to me that these words are precisely what they appear to be: visions from a vanished world, a world so strange and distant it might never have existed at all beyond the confines of someone's imagination. Was that why my informant included them here? Was that in the end the aim of the whole exercise? Was that the point he was trying to make?

Twenty-four

AN HOUR LATER I am standing at the doorway of the cabin listening to the mournfully inquisitive call of a brown hawk owl embroidering the silence and darkness. Around the blinding glow of the lamp outside my door a hundred moths are whirling in desperate fascination. It occurs to me that this might serve as a fitting metaphor for what happened to my informant when he attempted his *Brief History*. Beyond the brilliance of the images from a distant past, he could not help being aware of a reverberating darkness awaiting only the ripeness of time. In an ideal world, his book would have been a kind of celebration. But the exigencies of history denied the possibility. Viewed from this perspective, the eloquent pages with which he intended to end his little book might well serve as a kind of memorial, not only for the tiger but for some irretrievably lost part of ourselves.

Though tigers and human beings have been antagonists from the dawn of humankind, there always existed a balance of power between them which persisted until quite recently. Only at the beginning of the nineteenth century did the rising human tide, abetted by European adventurism, begin to penetrate areas of wilderness heretofore ruled by the tiger alone. The inevitable result of these penetrations was a dramatically heightened level of conflict between the two species. No better example of the nature of this conflict can be found than that which characterized the early colonial history of Singapore.

Singapore, unlike most cities, was not created by a gradual historical process, but by mandate. The British colonial administrator, Stamford Raffles, deciding that the empire required a strategic stronghold somewhere near the halfway point along the sea route between India and China, simply opened a map, placed a finger on an obscure island that lay at the southernmost tip of the Malay Peninsula. And the deed was done.

Following the establishment of a British trading post in 1819, plantations began to blossom in the dense pristine forests of the island's interior. According to E. C. Turnbull in his *History of Singapore,* there were no problems with tigers to speak of until 1831, when two Chinese laborers were attacked just outside the limits of Singapore town. As more and more of the forest was cleared to make room for plantations, the number of tiger attacks began to mount alarmingly. Before long, not merely dozens but hundreds of plantation workers were being killed by tigers every year. By the mid-1840s it was rumored that tigers were carrying off an average of one Chinese laborer a *day.*

As the human population of southern Asia exploded and settlements penetrated ever deeper into the wilderness, tiger-human conflicts understandably increased. Within a few decades the myth of the cold-blooded, man-eating tiger was born, a myth soon so firmly entrenched in the popular imagination that the tiger became the object of a genocidal campaign unparalleled in history.

Among the British rulers of southern Asia, the hunting down and shooting of tigers, those alleged to be man-eaters especially, soon came to be viewed not only as great sport but an activity that demonstrated a keen sense of public service. The tiger-killing ritual assumed the proportions of an open-ended saga to which any stout-hearted fellow with a steady aim could add his own thrilling chapter. Soldiers, civil servants, merchants, and ordinary people did not delay in taking full advantage of the opportunity.

Indian naturalist Kailash Sankhala found that during the seven-year period 1821–28, for example, villagers in the Indian state of Maharashtra shot, trapped, and poisoned over a thousand tigers. During a four-year period in the 1850s a certain Colonel William Rice bagged no fewer than ninety-three tigers, which is to say, nearly a tiger every other week, his success no doubt abetted by the ongoing revolution in firearms which continued thoughout the century. While the eighteenth-century musket was deadly at a range of not more than fifty yards, the innovations of the steel barrel and brass cartridge perfected by the 1870s produced weapons capable of killing a tiger at ranges of half a mile or more. For the first time in history a tiger could be killed by a hunter of whose presence it was entirely unaware.

But to blame the tiger's rapid decline on hunting alone would miss the point entirely. Hunters like Colonel Rice and the villager who trapped and poisoned the tiger to protect his family and livestock had a great deal more in common than may be supposed. From the standpoint of late twentieth-century science it would seem that each was in the unconscious thrall of genetic instructions that require all human beings to act in such a way as to insure the reproductive future of the human group. In carrying out such instructions human beings characteristically subdue any species that opposes human interests in any significant way. History has taught us that species that cannot be subdued are invariably destroyed. Such was the case with the tiger.

The most striking result of this genocidal campaign was that while the tiger began a headlong decline, the human population of southern Asia soared. At the beginning of the nineteenth century, the human population of India stood at about 131 million. By the end of the century that figure had more than doubled, standing at about 284 million in 1901. In the ninety-plus years that have passed since then, the 1901 figure has nearly *quadrupled,* leaving India with a population of nearly 1 billion human beings. Such extraordinary rates of growth have by no means been confined to India. China and Indonesia have demonstrated similar demographic patterns in which booming populations have resulted in the devastation of natural habitats and the ongoing destruction of entire ecosystems.

In light of these developments it is almost suprising that the first of the eight races of tiger to slip into extinction—the Balinese—did not do so until the late 1930s. Once the trend was under way, however, it established itself with ineluctable force. The Caspian race of the tiger was essentially finished by about 1959, the Javan by 1979. The Chinese race of the tiger, which now consists of only a few scattered individuals, will in all probability join its fellows by 1999, thereby completing what appears to be a cyclical series of events—one race of tiger vanishing from the wild every twenty years. When the last Chinese tiger dies a few years from now, an important watershed will have been reached in the two-million-year-old tiger-human relationship. At that moment, half the races of tiger living in the world will have gone swirling down the black drainpipe of extinction within the last half-century.

As one might readily deduce from these facts, all four of the remaining races of tiger are now seriously imperiled. In the 1990s in the Russian far east the Siberian tiger is struggling against a variety of threats. Though it has enjoyed strict protection since the 1930s, there is no reason to believe that the recent dissolution of the Soviet Union will in any way enhance its chances for survival. Paradoxically, it may weaken them. Flat on its back financially, the new Russia is not likely to pass up any opportunity, regardless of the consequences, to transform raw materials into ready cash. If, by some miracle, the new progressive government eventually proves as good a conservator of its tigers as its totalitarian predecessor, the Siberian race may have a chance for survival. Otherwise, the remaining tigers could be wiped out entirely within a very short time.

In Southeast Asia, the Indochinese race of the tiger is fighting an increasingly uphill battle for survival. Since the Second World War much of the Indochinese tiger's range has been a theater of perpetual violence, a situation that has endured to the present day. The endless bombing, booby-trapping, and mining that have ruined or destroyed the lives of so many millions of people have had an equally disastrous effect on the region's wildlife. One of the grislier images to have survived the American phase of the Indochina War is that of tigers feeding on corpses after pitched battles. Ironically, no such scene could be replayed today. The tiger has been virtually eradicated from Vietnam.

Other developments in the region have been just as devastating. By the end of the 1980s, in its headlong race to industrialize, Thailand had destroyed so much of its natural forest cover through unrestricted logging that the country experienced terrible floods, particularly in the south, which not only destroyed a great deal of property but claimed human lives. As a fledgling capitalist powerhouse, Thailand has wholeheartedly endorsed the philosophy that profits come before any other consideration.

If, compared to Thailand, Malaysia has preserved, proportionately speaking, a much larger percentage of its peninsular forest, the phenomenon is quite easily explained. Ever since achieving independence from Britain over thirty years ago, Malaysia has conducted what can only be described as a systematic rape of its offshore states of Sarawak and Sabah, located on the island of Borneo. Working under government license, logging operations have ruthlessly felled thousands of square miles of forest, displacing native peoples and destroying the habitats of thousands of unique animal and plant species—two of which are the now highly endangered orangutan and the Sumatran rhinoceros.

In the 1990s both Thailand and Malaysia are poised to cash in on the wholesale destruction of forests throughout Asia. The remaining forests of Burma, Laos, Cambodia, and Vietnam now await the ready supply of hard currency and the all too effective entrepreneurial skills of both countries. In view of these developments, there is every reason to believe that the Indochinese tiger will find itself genetically isolated sometime within the next two decades, with effective extinction in the wild certain to follow.

The Sumatran tiger now also finds itself braced for a final losing battle with extinction. Save Borneo, Sumatra is the largest island in the Indonesian archipelago and one of the larger islands in the world. Nevertheless, its incredibly rich forests are being overwhelmed by the same destructive forces that have so drastically reduced tiger habitats elsewhere, with the added threat posed by the proposed resettlement of millions of people from nearby Java as the forest is cleared.

In view of the fact that the Indonesian government has done little more than pay lip service to the notion of protecting Indonesia's natural patrimony, its announced plans for a series of reserves intended to protect the Sumatran flora and fauna may be regarded as meaningless. Like Thailand and Malaysia, Indonesia pretends to be a democracy. But it is one in which no dissenting voices are allowed. Illegal logging, involving corruption at the highest levels, is common, the lost logs often going to Japan, which is currently the number-one buyer of Southeast Asian timber.

The Japanese role in the destruction of the Southeast Asian forests deserves a word here. It might be understandable, if not excusable, if the Japanese, in paying for the felling of what are in fact the oldest forests in the world, in endangering the oragutan, the tiger, and countless thousands of other animal and plant species, were satisfying some culturally defined lust for, say, fine wooden furniture. In fact, the overwhelming majority of these literally irreplaceable trees are being used to produce plywood, often discarded after use. By using irreplaceable hardwoods instead of softwoods to produce plywood, as the rest of the world does, the Japanese are able to insulate their very important plywood industry from outside competition. This attitude is very much in line with Japanese attitudes vis-à-vis other aspects of the environment. It may be of interest to note that the Japanese word for foreigner, *gaijin*, means "barbarian." It has become increasingly obvious in recent years that this is a word more appropriately applied to the Japanese themselves. A people without consciousness or conscience, they do not know the meaning of shame.

The last of the surviving races of tiger is the Indian. Of the tigers that continue to roam the forests of Asia, approximately half live in India. Because of this fact and because India is large, being about six times the size of France, or about a third the size of the United States, many tiger experts have suggested that India offers the tiger its best chance for survival in the twenty-first century. Tragically, this premise is built on unrealistic assumptions.

No other "developing" country in the world has so warmly embraced the strategies and ideals of modern conservation as has India. In the 1970s an ambitious program known as Project Tiger managed not only to halt the precipitous decline of the Indian tiger but to reverse it. By the end of the 1980s the number of tigers in India was said to have increased. Unfortunately, an unprejudiced look at India's population figures reveals that these hard-won successes will soon be trampled underfoot by human beings whose only crime will be their all too human desire to survive.

Though India currently enjoys one of the lowest birthrates of any developing country (approximately 2.2%), the extraordinary size of the present population (about 850 million) means that once deaths have been subtracted from births, India has a net growth of over 17 million people each *year,* meaning well over a million new mouths to feed each *month.* The net growth of the human population in India just since 1970 is a figure equal to the *entire present population of the United States.* Computer projections suggest that the human population of India could overtake that of China by, say, 2035: what China's population might conceivably be at that not so distant date is a figure that staggers the imagination.

The inevitably negative social effects of India's exploding population growth are every day becoming more evident. In the 1990s no less than five fiercely determined separatist movements are operating within the country. All espouse violence. At the same time, sectarian violence between Muslims and Hindus has reached a fever pitch unknown since the days of partition. It remains to be seen whether the Indian union, which has endured since 1949, will survive the century. Should it dissolve, even a piece at a time, there can be no doubt that the effect on India's wildlife will be devastating, the Indian tiger surviving, if at all, only as a pathetic remnant.

As the twentieth century draws to a close, an impressively large percentage of the world's most familiar wild animals are facing extinction. The creatures that we introduce our children to at bedtime as a part of their initiation into the world—lion, leopard, rhinoceros, tiger—will soon exist only in zoos and in the wilderness of the imagination.

No human being will know when the last wild tiger meets its death. Perhaps in some remaining bit of hill forest in northern Burma a hunter will level his sights on the animal he has been seeking for months. Or perhaps in what was once a national park in the heart of Sumatra that last tiger, driven by hunger, will come to the poisoned bait hopefully set out for it. Or in northern India or Nepal that last remaining wild tiger, emaciated and starving, will be hacked to death by a group of local villagers. All that can be said with a minimum of certainty is that this last wild tiger is no mere hypothesis. Though perhaps not yet born, it will exist. And in all likelihood, it will die within the next twenty-five to thirty years.

For those human beings possessing the courage to look unflinchingly, the fate overtaking the world's wild animals presents itself with irresistible clarity. When, within the lifetime of many children living today, the last remnants of these creatures are trapped and gathered together for their own safekeeping and "the good of all humanity," that great nineteenth-century innovation, the zoo, will come into its own at last. In these hugely funded, highly polished institutions, veritable temples, where the ambient environment and physiological functions of the "living treasures" are monitored as carefully as rising and falling shares on the stock exchange, the zoo will become what it was destined to be from its inception—a place of pilgrimage where human beings gawk in awed stupefaction at the irreplaceable, literally priceless, living curiosities.

But that era will pass soon enough. Within a certain number of generations the descendants of these last wild animals, weakened, robbed of the riches of their genetic ancestry, will, in spite of every known technological intervention, every genetic advance and development, perish.

But it will be a strangely inconclusive death.

In that not so distant era, on a day like today, a tiger will roam free, stalking its prey with infinite patience through a pristine habitat in which the colors, sights, smells, and sounds are hyperreal and literally perfect. It will crouch, claws set to earth, and charge in a burst of speed, closing in with murderous swiftness for the kill . . .

The most perfect of three-dimensional illusions.

A blur of dancing electrons and shifting shadows.

In the awed silence of a darkened room.

Part Four

The Shadow-Line

Twenty-five

IF, FOR REASONS best known to yourself, you were to imagine purgatory as a spit of desolate wasteland barely elevated above a boiling sea, you would, as a matter of course, find yourself in possession of a not inaccurate picture of the island of Tanjung Pinang, which lies hard on the 104th parallel of longitude east, in Indonesian waters just south of Singapore. Though from time to time one hears a place described as existing "at the edge of nowhere," for those travelers unfortunate enough to have found themselves stranded there, Tanjung Pinang surpasses even this unflattering description. It is nowhere itself.

Almost every afternoon a shiny boat butts up against the dock and a troop of brightly clad day-trippers steps ashore, come presumably to gawk at the open market, the open sewers, the pariah dogs—sights no longer easily come by in the steel and glass tourist mecca to the north. In their defense, it must be admitted that the contrasts are striking. In Singapore one can be jailed for throwing garbage into the street; in Tanjung Pinang there is, strictly speaking, nowhere else to throw it.

At high noon, on a day when the sun is obscured in a caldron of superheated mist a billion miles away, and the air is so stupefyingly still it seems ready to ignite, I am crouched in the damp shade of the customs shack on the dock, staring across the surface of the sea, which at this moment seems less a liquid than a boundless, infinitely pliable metallic skin. With an ever dwindling reserve of patience, I am awaiting the arrival of the *Sempoerna,* a vessel whose alleged mission it is to transport, twice weekly, passengers and cargo from this running scab on the face of the waters to the infinitely greater nowhere of Sumatra, traversing in the process a hundred miles of open water before heading upriver to the oil boomtown of Pekanbaru. The entire journey reportedly never requires less than twenty-four hours. But for a journey to blossom and bear fruit, it must first begin, and the *Sempoerna* is now five hours late.

I reach down to the dock beside me and pick up my canteen and unscrew the lid. I carry it to my lips and allow the last drops of spit-warm water to dribble down my throat. Replacing the cap, disgusted, I sit back and make an effort to resist the mental cataloguing of all my needs, the greatest of which probably is sheer distraction—a flashy drugstore thriller, a slick magazine . . . But the case is hopeless.

I find myself at the moment in uncharacteristic possession of a single book, a paperback copy of August Strindberg's *Inferno,* described on its back cover as "an intensely powerful record" of Strindberg's "mental collapse"—discovered two nights ago under the bed in my room at a cheap Chinese hotel in Singapore. Soiled, dog-eared, with all the juiciest passages underlined, it appears to have already served some hapless traveler as a guidebook to the nether regions of the mind. What I know, having read a few pages, is that old August would have loved Tanjung Pinang; it would have slipped under his skin, coursed through his veins like a virus.

That leaves only the letters. Reaching into my shirt pocket, I remove one of them—the one without an envelope, the one I picked up in Kuala Lumpur four days ago. It is damp with sweat, transparent as a fish's skin. I unfold it carefully and begin to read:

San Martino a Scapeto
Italy

Dear Richard,

Your letter finally caught up with me here just two days ago. Though I was very pleased to hear that you are well, I have to admit that I was disturbed—no other word readily springs to mind—at the chapter of your book you sent me to read. Though wonderfully well written, it is such an unhappy piece of work, so obviously, one might even say brazenly, misanthropic, that I found it nearly impossible to finish. Perhaps this will come as a shock to you. I am sorry if it does. Let me try to explain.

Yes, I agree with you when you suggest that the efforts now being made on behalf of the natural world are at best "pathetic." Yes, I agree that in the end, very little, if any, of what remains will be saved. But to question the motives of those who continue the struggle is, I believe, a seriously mistaken attitude of the first order. What would you have these people do? Fold their tents, go home, and spend the rest of their lives wallowing in self-pity? They are, after all, only people, doing the best they can. That is a cliché, I admit. But clichés have their uses.

I wish that I could say that your letter pleased me more, but I am afraid it did not. I believe that this plan of yours to see a tiger on foot is mad. Nothing more or less. It is almost as though in seeing a tiger on foot you were expecting a shower of illumination, or a burst of insight. This is ridiculous.

What would happen if you were to find a tiger in the forest? It would probably simply walk—or run—away. That is the likelihood. But there is of course another possibility. If surprised, it might kill you on the spot, or maul you so badly you would pray for death. Is *that* what you want, then? Is *that* what you are searching for? Are you really suicidal? Do you for some obscure pathological reason *fancy* the idea of ending up like David Hunt, crying out in horror in a corner of some obscure forest as your life drains away from you? You of all people should know that animals don't care a damn about us. They live in their world, we in ours. The two do not mix. They did once. But no more. Believe me, I understand this better than you know. What I know equally is that my foolish talk about my own experiences in the past (during our trip to Corbett especially) is partly to blame for all this. Believe me when I say that I deeply regret that I ever said a word about them.

I know that all this has been unpleasant to read, and I am truly sorry for that. But I felt that I had to speak to you honestly. It is the responsibility of a friend to do so.

But I would like to end on a more pleasant note. As I write this, it is afternoon, sunny and bright. In the garden bees and butterflies are hovering around the flowers. There are a few hard-edged clouds in the sky which remind me, for some reason, of the work of the painter Mantegna. Bach is on the stereo—the first prelude from *The Well-Tempered Clavier.* At this particular moment of my life—except for, perhaps, my worries about you—the world seems utterly benign. I have not had the opportunity to speak to you of my love for Bach, greatest of all the musical masters. Perhaps, if we can settle all this nonsense, we can get around to him at our next meeting. I am very much looking forward to seeing you on 21 Oct. in Kathmandu.

I hope you will not take all this too badly. I care about you and hope that this letter finds you well. Please take care of yourself in Sumatra. Don't do anything stupid. I will be back in India by the time you receive this. If your plans change, you can contact me there.

Best regards,
Kailash

I fold the letter and slip it back into my pocket, at the same moment aware that someone has invaded my solitude—a European, thirtyish, bearded, a bit scruffy. Turning my way, he stares intently for a moment, offering the sort of desultory nod that recognizes presence but demands nothing in return. Walking directly in front of me, eyes averted to avoid any further contact, he proceeds to the far side of the customs shack, drops his pack onto the dock, and sits down, back to the wall. Staring directly out to sea, he makes it abundantly clear, without saying a word, that he has no wish whatever to be disturbed.

It will be a long journey to Sumatra; it might be nice to have someone to talk to. But this guy does not exactly radiate friendliness. Looking at him, I can't help feeling it might be best on the whole to steer clear of him.

I turn and look out to sea. Suddenly desperate at the prospect of being stranded for days in this steaming equatorial hole, and in need of forgetting where I am, I reach into my pocket and remove the second letter, the one still pocketed in its envelope, the one I have read so many times I have it almost verbatim. It is a letter from C.

New York, N.Y., U.S.A.
August 21

Dear Richard,

Quite a shock to hear from you after so long a time. It was nice to find that you are alive, if not, judging from the tone of your letter, exactly kicking. I have to confess straight off that your letter left me feeling quite confused. You seem to be asking if I think it could be possible to continue our relationship. At least, I *think* that's what you're getting at. If so, I am not certain that I can be reassuring.

I want you to understand that I admire the life you have chosen for yourself. There are few people in the world who have the sheer guts to seize the life they want and hold on for dear life. You are one of these. You have chosen to conduct your life on the edge, and I know that has not always been easy.

But if you are asking me whether I think that you, having made that choice, are capable of sustaining a long-term relationship with a woman, all I can say is perhaps, with someone. But that someone can't be me. I have lived too long, come too far in my own life, to settle for a relationship with a man who "drops in" between trips. A bit too much like having a relationship with a ghost. It would be just as scary. I'm sorry. But that is the way I see it.

As for my own plans, things are moving ahead. I have some exciting news. I am wrapping up my practice here in NYC and am (literally) packing my bags for Paris. Yes, I'm really going to do it. I have spoken to several people and am now more convinced than ever that I will be able to set up a practice there. I plan to be there by Sept. 15.

If you happen to find yourself in a writing mood between chasing tigers and stalking orangutans (or is it the other way around?), you can still reach me at the NYC address. The letter will be forwarded.

In closing, I hope that your tour of S.E. Asia and your upcoming group to Nepal go well. It's funny, but the morning I received your letter I was thinking about our time in Nepal and India. In one way, it seems so recent—in another, it seems about a million years ago.

Take care of yourself.

Love,
C

I fold the letter and slip it back into my shirt pocket, wondering for the umpteenth time why I wrote to her in the first place. Though the time we spent together in Nepal and India was wonderful, it did not escape me even then that we were two very different people, from different backgrounds, with very different dreams. And yet I wrote to her. I was not able to help myself. And now here is her reply, which, for all its denial, seems to offer me a choice I am not prepared to make.

Suddenly, from the corner of my eye, I notice that someone else has just stepped onto the dock. Peering, it seems to me somewhat unsteadily, out to sea, he is in fact a sort of giant. With one arm clasped over a filthy red hard plastic carry-bag overstuffed with cheap toys—pink plastic dolls and pinwheels—along with stale chewing gum, half-melted sweets, and God knows what else, he turns in my direction, belches, then gawks, slackjawed, his face an unpleasant stew of features, neither Malay nor Chinese. I cannot begin to discern what racial grouping he might conceivably belong to. Except perhaps oaf.

Wavering slightly, staring at me absently, he reaches up with his free hand and with a fingernail peels a piece of dirt from one nostril. Rolling the prize between the tips of his fingers, he attempts to flick it away. Failing, he smears it on the leg of his filthy trousers. Somewhat amused by this turn of events, he smiles, showing a mouthful of brown teeth, then staggers toward me. It is only now, with that lurching motion, that I realize he is stone drunk. Drunkenness is a form of behavior I have never before encountered in Indonesia, a nominally Muslim country in which public inebriation, at least, is taboo. But the news seems not to have penetrated to the lower spheres.

"Oh Jesus," I hear myself mutter as he sinks down on his knees in front of me. Instantly aware of a foul odor redolent of ripe garbage, a scent of urine and alcohol floating above it, I try to hold my breath.

"English? You buy something?"

I shake my head and look away. He continues to gawk at me dumbly.

"English?"

I try to pretend he is not there.

"You buy something?"

"No," I say at last, "I don't buy anything. Now piss off."

Taking offense, he frowns and says, "Piss off? I Tanjungpinang. I Indonesia . . . my country. You asshole. *You* piss off."

Concentrating on a point somewhere near the invisible horizon, I clench a fist and, studying him from the corner of my eye, try to calculate exactly where and how hard I will have to hit him to knock him over and make good my escape. Calculations locked in, I am stunned when he struggles to his feet, almost banging me in the head with his swinging plastic bag full of goods as he does so. Without another word he lumbers down the dock in the direction of the European, who, if he is aware at all of what has been going on, gives no demonstration of it but only sits as before, concentratedly writing in what appears to be a diary or notebook.

Nearly stumbling as he slumps in front of the European, heavily enough, it seems to me, to pulverize his kneecaps, the giant takes in his new object of interest. The European, whom I expect to be startled at the very least, doesn't even look up and completely ignores the hulk that has positioned itself between him and the sea.

Staring at the European, leaning toward him until his face is only inches away, the giant sniffs through his alcoholic haze. "You buy something?"

The European does not move. Neither does he give any indication that he has heard the words so pointedly addressed to him. He continues to concentrate on his writing, the scratch of his pen almost audible in the stillness.

Head slightly bobbing, the giant continues to stare. Lips moving to no apparent end, he lowers his gaze to something the European is wearing around his neck—a leather thong decorated with a single piece of pink stone. Leaning closer suddenly, a grin spread across his face, he reaches out, curls his stubby fingers around the thong, and gives it a firm yank.

What happens next happens so fast my eyes do not record it. Releasing a guttural exhalation of surprise, the giant heaves over backward, the back of his head producing a clear sharp crack as it strikes the timbers of the dock. Already on his feet, the European crouches over him, a knee plowed into his chest, one hand grasping the collar of the giant's shirt. With the other he holds a huge black-bladed knife to the giant's throat—the sort of knife hunters use to skin animals—the tip of the blade indenting but not breaking the skin.

The giant releases a groan and tries to rise. But the European, staring into his face, bunching the material of his collar to gain a better grip, gives the knife a vicious little twist, a twist designed to draw blood. It does so. A bright little trickle zigzags down the giant's neck.

Eyes wild, the giant reaches up with his free hand, touches the wetness. The sensation of it on the tips of his fingers induces a shiver, accompanied by a doglike whimper. His whole body stiffening, the fingers of his hand bunching into a fist, he stares up into the face of the European.

But the European is ready for him. Tightening his grasp on the giant's collar, he speaks through a grinning mask. "You will go away now. You will go away now and not come back. If you do, I will cut off your fucking head and throw it into the sea. You understand?"

The giant, not moving, not speaking, stares into the European's face.

"DO YOU UNDERSTAND ME?" the European roars, yanking at the collar so forcefully it snaps the giant's head.

The giant shudders. As though understanding suddenly what is required of him, he nods. But the European does not move. Only after several seconds does he release his grip, retracting the point of the blade from the giant's neck. He steps back.

I am vaguely aware of a rising sense of relief. I will not see a man killed today.

But the sensation is premature. As the giant struggles to his feet, I watch the European step backward in a motion of calculated smoothness, almost a dance step. The hand holding the knife swings out in a wide arc, and strikes the giant full in the face, catapulting him backward. Once again the giant's head strikes the dock with a sickening crack. Certain that the European has driven the knife blade through his skull, I feel a wave of nausea roll through me. Then I realize that the European has struck him with the butt of the knife.

Curled over on one side like some horribly inflated fetus, the giant releases a moan, then slowly turns his head. A blood-red flower has blossomed where his mouth was, the bright slick of it spreading down his chin and onto his filthy shirt. Eyes wandering, glazed, he reaches up and touches his mouth.

The European, cocking his head as though trying to gain perspective, smiles a hard smile. Apparently satisfied, he jerks his head to one side, a mute command to the giant that he rise and be gone. Slowly, painfully, awkwardly pushing himself up on all fours, the giant rises, checking as he does whether he is to be struck again, achieving at last a standing position. He gazes stupidly down at the place between his feet where gouts of blood have begun to puddle. Rotating his body slightly, he surveys the toys and sweets that have been scattered nearby, his eyes focusing at last on a gaily colored pinwheel lying a few feet away. Studying it, glancing cautiously at the European, he bends over to pick it up. But the movement stops when the European steps forward and with a kick sends it whirring over the edge of the dock onto the restless mat of the sea.

The giant stands staring at the European. But no explanation is forthcoming. His expression pouting, stupid, like that of an overgrown bully-child who has inexplicably discovered himself pushed off his tricycle, he turns and looks in my direction. Lips working, he stumbles toward me, muttering something incomprehensible. At the corner of the customs shack he pauses, turns, looks back, and in a pathetic gesture of defiance takes a halfhearted swipe at the air. Then, wiping a broad smear of blood on his ragged shirt sleeve, he ambles off.

The European watches him, the expression on his face strangely blank. Glancing down at his knife, he wipes a droplet of blood off the tip of the blade with his fingers, which he then wipes on his trousers. Opening the front of his shirt, he slides the knife back into its scabbard, strapped around his chest. He glances briefly at me, and for a single elongated second I am certain he is about to speak. But in the end he says nothing, only resumes his place on the dock, where, gathering up his notebook and pen, which have landed nearby, he sweeps the sweets, dolls, and pinwheels aside and without another word or gesture resumes his writing, as calmly as if he had just returned from a brief visit to the card catalogue—perfectly calm and cool. And this seems odd to me, since I know that something is shaking. Only when I look down at my hands do I realize that it is myself.

Twenty-six

NEARLY AN HOUR later, across a great expanse of dead water, I become aware of a craft, toylike in the distance, trailing a cocktail of black exhaust which hangs nearly motionless against the gray blankness of the sky—a fata morgana in three dimensions. Studying it as though it were some unknown life form dredged up from the bottom of the sea, I discern that it is neither ship nor boat but one of those worm-eaten hulks that are both mainstay and lowest form of transport among these islands. Flat-roofed except for the slightly elevated wheelhouse, perhaps forty feet in length, battered and scarred from stem to stern, its fittings gnawed with corrosion, irregularly shaped patches of paint frizzily exfoliating, it slows twenty yards out and comes about, revealing via an amateurish scrawl on the port bow the name by which it is known: *Sempoerna*.

Black fatality rises inside me like a case of indigestion. I slump back against the wall of the shack and give an exasperated moan. Only after several seconds do I turn my attention to the dock, where, seemingly out of the very heat and stillness, a small crowd of potential voyagers has congealed, as though summoned by the blast of some archangel's silvery trumpet—perhaps twenty men, women, and children, chattering, smiling, and loafing amid a nearly indescribable flotsam of swollen plastic bags, enormous trussed-to-the-bursting-point cardboard boxes, and homemade wicker cages containing panting, eager-looking chickens and ducks, whose final hours on this earth have no doubt already been carefully calculated. The frayed, too-small hawser is flung dockside and secured by one of the men at the front of the crowd, and the gangplank is dropped into place with a thud as an unbelievable number of people come swarming up from below, like fleas abandoning a cooling carcass.

Sweeping the vessel with a critical gaze, I realize that—from the perspective of modern nautical practice, at least—a few essential details appear to be lacking. No lifejackets or fire extinguishers are in evidence. No lifeboat. In this context, the presence of a chart or compass on board would amount to a blessing, that of a shortwave radio to a heavenly dispensation. Casting an eye over the little group of pilgrims who, along with me, are about to entrust their lives to the seaworthiness of this dented sieve, I hear myself posing a fateful question. Have I survived all these years, come all this way, only to end up a bleached, jellified cadaver floating face down in a warm sea?

When the last of the passengers—an old woman dragging a huge plastic-wrapped parcel behind her—steps clear of the plank, the crowd on the dock begins to hustle aboard. Having gathered up my things and melted into the edge of the crowd, I am surprised to note a young Japanese standing just in front of me, the huge bright blue pack on his back sufficient for an expedition up Mount Everest. Holding a bamboo flute in one hand, he is standing to one side, politely waiting his turn to board, looking mildly amused at the hurly-burly. Glancing back, he catches my eye, and I am about to say something to him when suddenly I am aware of the European looming up behind him, staring directly at me. Something in his gaze tells me that he has been watching me for some time—an observation that leaves me feeling slightly nauseated.

Three minutes later, below deck, in the low-ceilinged single cabin that makes up the passenger quarters, I am struggling over piles of obstructing parcels, squeezing past gymnastically contorted, strongly scented bodies. On each side of the aisle are continuous wooden platforms a couple of feet above the floor, which run the length of the cabin. Each platform is divided into sections; each section is further divided by a mark painted lengthwise down its center to indicate two sleeping spaces; each sleeping space is just large enough for one person to recline on rather intimate terms with a berthmate.

Locating, halfway back, section 9, the number printed in seeping ink on my ticket, I am relieved to find that my berth adjoins a sort of window, or rather the place where a window once was, the lower edge of it exactly parallel to the narrow walkway running along the gunnels topside. Good news. Or bad, depending on the way you look at it. In a calm crossing, the flow of cool fresh air, flushing away the miasma of unwashed bodies, would be a definite plus. If, however, the crossing turned rough, I could with no trouble at all end up drowned in my bed.

Flopping pack, sleeping bag, and tent squarely down on number 9, I hear the idling engine rev up with a roar, sending a whirling cloud of unbreathable blue exhaust between the cracks of the floorboards. I gasp for breath. Almost gagging, I spin around to find myself staring into the face of the European.

"You are number nine?" he asks with a smile, in an accent too uninflected to be American, too flat to be English.

"Yes."

"Then we are berthmates," he says, holding out his paper ticket, on which a 10 has been blurrily stamped. I gaze down at it, wondering what evil conjunction of planets could possibly have provoked this unfortunate coincidence.

"So it seems," I say.

Glancing at my stuff, wondering if the man is as much a thief as he is a bully, and deciding in the following instant that at this particular moment in time I couldn't care less if he took it all, I slip past him and struggle toward the stairs.

Twenty-seven

AN HOUR after leaving the dock I am seated, back to the splintery wheelhouse bulkhead, in the bows of the *Sempoerna,* wind-stunned, bathed in warmth, scanning the horizon for birds. Off the port bow, five yards out, I spot from the corner of my eye a flat bulky thing shearing a bright slick. *Driftwood,* I think. Then, *Turtle.* Leaping from my seat, nearly catapulting myself over the railing, I peer at the creature as it rolls over like an overburdened aircraft and glides down into turquoise depths.

"Beautiful," a voice says behind me.

A shadow has fallen over the face of the sun. When I turn, I find the European, a pair of expensive binoculars dangling around his neck over the precise spot where he keeps his knife. Flushing with annoyance and the knowledge that I am not in the mood to entertain, or to be entertained, I say nothing, only glance back at the receding spot where the turtle descended.

"You know the species, don't you?" he asks.

"Species?" I say stupidly. It crosses my mind that if I

cared what species it was—and I don't, particularly—there is no one on the planet I am less interested in discussing the matter with than he. What I really would like is for him to crawl back into whatever hole he shimmied out of. But in the interest of keeping him off my back until I can escape, I decide to humor him. "A loggerhead maybe."

"Why do you say that?"

"Why?" I say, suddenly regretting that I did not simply walk away when he appeared. "Size."

"That's irrelevant. It was a green, more likely."

"Really?" I say with mock interest, wondering what can have possessed this maniac to believe that he knows something about turtles. "What makes you think so?"

"The greens use Ujong Kulong on the western tip of Java, as a hatching station. It's only a couple of hundred miles from here. Have you heard of it?"

"Yes, I've heard of it," I say, bored with the geography lesson. Eager nevertheless to demonstrate that I know something about turtles as well, I say, "Wasn't it a bit on the small side for a green?"

"A *young* one," he says simply.

The thought sinks in. I feel myself blush. He's right, of course. No one with a whiff of experience with turtles would attempt to identify one at sea purely on the basis of size, unless it happened to be about six feet long, which would, by a process of elimination, make it a leatherback.

"You have an interest in turtles?" the European asks.

"I'm a naturalist," I reply, realizing that I would feel more comfortable confessing to be a mailman.

"In what sense are you a naturalist? A biologist?"

"A field naturalist. I lead tours to India and Nepal and to Southeast Asia."

"Ahhh," he says, "a *field* naturalist." Looking around in a stagey sort of way, as though expecting clients to come oozing out of the woodwork, he says, "You are, I take it, not leading a tour now?"

"No," I say. "My next tour is in a couple of months."

"Where to?"

"Nepal."

"Ah yes, Nepal. Then for the moment you are on a little reconnaisance of your own?"

"You could put it that way."

"Well, that's very interesting. I too am, as you put it, a field naturalist. I have just come from South America. I spent two years there."

"Doing what?"

"Looking."

"At what?"

"Birds, animals—everything."

"And how was South America?"

"South America?" he says with a bitter little smile, looking away. "South America is *fucked.* They are cutting down the forest everywhere, and either corrupting or slaughtering the native peoples. All in all, I would say it's another triumph for the human beings. They are turning the whole continent into a smoldering garbage heap."

"You sound bitter."

"If you had seen the things I have seen, perhaps you too would be bitter. If I had the power, I would kill every city-living human fucker who lives there."

"Violence is really your thing, isn't it?"

"Violence is *everybody's* thing. It's not an aberration. It's encoded in our genes. I always find it amusing when I hear people pandering to the idea that it is nasty old violence that has reduced the world to its present miserable state. It's the great taboo in polite society, isn't it? Never mind that that sort of thinking is simplistic bullshit." He smiles and looks away. Then he says, "What people don't seem to understand is that it isn't violence but cold calculation that is destroying everything. Not that it matters much to me—I have resigned from the logical program. Now I'm on the other side."

I stare at him. I blink. It crosses my mind that this guy may be even crazier than I thought.

Perhaps sensing my unease, he looks back at me and says, "But let's talk about something else. What has brought you to this delightful toilet of a country?"

"Research."

"What kind of research?"

"For a book. Maybe."

"Ah, a *naturalist* who wishes to write a *book*. Sounds dangerous. What sort of book?"

"About tiger."

"You've come to Sumatra to study tiger?" he asks, smiling.

"Yes."

"You're wasting your time."

"Why do you say that?"

"Because in Sumatra there are only a few tigers left."

"The books say that there are four or five hundred."

"That's bullshit."

"Bullshit is a subject you seem to know a lot about."

He smiles and looks away, his expression amused.

But I am rather pissed off now and do not feel much inclined to let the matter drop. "What're you saying?" I say at last. "Are you saying that the studies are wrong and you're right? How'd *you* get to be such an expert?"

"Oh," he replies, "I'm not saying the studies have been faulty. I'm saying they're *lying*. Don't misunderstand me. There are still a few tigers prowling around here and there. But they're going fast. The Indonesian government doesn't want them. Never did. The best tiger reserve in Sumatra was a place called Kerumantan, in Riau province, here on the north coast. Ever heard of it? It was made a reserve sometime in the 1960s and the government promised to protect it. They lied. They never had even the slightest intention of doing so. They wanted it destroyed. Oil, you see. How very inconvenient to have tigers roaming around, chewing on the drillers. For officials in this country, the truth is unknown territory. They lie about *everything*. They recognize but one power on earth, and that is the almighty dollar." He pauses for a moment. Then he says, "Where were you planning to find all these wonderful tigers, anyway?"

"Kerinci-Seblat, Gunung Leuser, maybe Berbak."

"You have been to those places before?"

"Only to Leuser."

"When you were at Leuser you saw a tiger?"

"No. But then I wasn't looking particularly."

"Perhaps in the back country of Leuser Park there are a few tigers left. Maybe the local poachers have not managed to kill them all yet."

At that moment the Japanese boy I sighted on the dock appears with a smile on his face, hand raised in the wavering karate chop that in Japanese body language announces that he would like to pass. I rise from my seat so he can squeeze by. "Ekskyoos me," he says, still smiling, and dipping his head as he does.

He is no sooner out of sight than the European says, "I hate the fucking Japs."

"Anybody you don't hate?" I say, throwing a glance in the direction of the departing kid to see if he has overheard.

"During the Second World War they murdered, raped, and burned their way through Southeast Asia. They left scars that will never heal. Don't believe me? Ask the Filipinos what *they* think of the Japs. Ask the Malays. Or the Burmese."

"What's your point? That you'd like to wipe them out too?"

"The world would be a better place," he says. "But you

know, in truth the Japanese are the perfect human beings. They play the game better than anyone else. They are the most amoral people on earth, and yet they are not afraid to be who they are. They pay cold hard cash for the oldest forests in the world to be cut down. They slaughter whales and dolphins by the hundreds of thousands, without a thought. They fish the seas until they are deader than the Sahara. It makes not the slightest difference to them. They have no interest in soft liberal distinctions. They are the conquerers, you see—the superhuman beings."

Sensing that this conversation has soared into the ozone and realizing that I had better bail out before this guy tries to convince me that he is the Messiah, I gaze off to starboard. About fifty yards out, a pair of terns are headed toward us. I lift up my binoculars. But just as I get the birds in focus, they veer off.

"Greater crested," I say, succumbing to the birdwatcher's instinct to identify, or attempt to identify, any passing bird.

"No," the European says, "*Sterna bengalensis.*"

"Lesser crested?"

"Yes."

"How do you know? You didn't even look at them."

"I looked."

"How can you be so sure they were lessers?"

"Jizz. The flight of those birds was not heavy enough to be greater. The profile was too slight. That is very obvious when you see the two species side by side."

"Where have you seen them that way?"

"Off Columbo, Sri Lanka, five years ago."

Taking a step or two toward the railing, I raise my binoculars and look after the retreating birds. Remembering the description in the field guide, I sense, to my chagrin, that he is right. Turning back to the European and again feeling somewhat one-upped, I say without thinking, "That man today on the dock—would you have cut his throat if he had resisted you?"

The European gives me a surprised look. Then he smiles, and says, "I think it is safe to say that that piece of dirt is lucky to be alive."

Three hours later, just as the sun is setting, the *Sempoerna* arrives at one of the narrow channels of the river's mouth, where a nearly impenetrable barrier of trees and vegetation crowds in on both sides. To the west, in front of us, the melding waters have taken on a brilliant glow of shimmering gold. To the back of us, a few deep rose clouds stand painted against the darkening sky. As we round a bend, four hornbills, cardboard cutout pterodactyls, slide silently across our bow. We are in another time.

I have learned over these past few hours that my companion's name is Werther. I have also learned that he is either one of the world's greatest travelers or one of the world's greatest liars. It does not seem inconceivable that he is both.

He seems to have been everywhere. The names of legendary destinations drip off his lips like jewels—Machu Picchu, Beagle Channel, Okavango, the Atherton Tablelands, Kilimanjaro, Monteverde, the Tepui Highlands, the Namib, the Nile, Ellesmere, the Falklands . . . places I have dreamed about since I was a child. Though his stories sometimes seem fabulous, his knowledge is so detailed that it seems improbable that he could speak about them as he does without having actually visited them. According to him, our paths have almost crossed at least once, in Point Barrow, Alaska, in July 1984. I missed him, apparently, by only a week.

As I surmised, he is not American, though most of his education took place there. His parents are Swiss, his father a career diplomat. He claims that he despises his parents, says that they think he is dead, which is fine with him. Since dropping out of university in the mid-seventies, he has spent his life on the road, moving from continent to continent, working at every conceivable sort of job—digging ditches, washing dishes, crewing on fishing boats, teaching English and German, occasionally taking an unpaid volunteer post at a bird observatory or animal research station.

According to him, he has never had a goal in life other than seeing as many of the world's wild creatures as he can and recording his observations in his notebooks, running now, according to him, to eleven volumes—his true life's work, it would seem. Each sighting is written down in the sort of minute spidery handwriting I have always associated with mental patients. In the final analysis, of course, there is no way to tell how many of his stories are true. He is a brilliant storyteller.

Though the incident on the dock has left no doubt in my mind that he is capable of murder, I have discovered that there is another aspect to him. He is essentially an orphan, a lost soul, much more likely to do damage to himself than to harm others. Oddly, it has occurred to me that perhaps in him I see a version of myself—the person I might have been, the person I might yet become.

As the last golden fleck of sun slips below the black maze of tree branches, I turn to him and ask, "Have you always felt the way you do now—that life is just . . . empty?"

He replies, "When I was a kid in New York, my mother never stopped talking about art and literature and music. She was a real European. All that stuff was her life. From the time I was a baby she did everything she could to jam all that crap down my throat. Shakespeare, Goethe, Mozart—even when I was a kid, I knew it was bullshit. I can't tell you what a relief it was when it finally dawned on me that we human beings are not the center of anything, that we are nothing more than a tribe of carnivorous apes that came down from the trees a couple of million years ago. There was an opportunity, an ecological niche. We seized it. But we could not face what we are, so since that time we have elected some among us to lie, flatter, make up a whole brilliant scenario . . . The truth is, we don't know *anything*. We don't know why we're here. We don't know where we've come from. We don't know where we're going. All this talk about the greatness of humanity." Facing me, he says with what strikes me as amazing bitterness, "You tell me what's so fucking great about it."

I stare at him. But I can think of no reply. At last, for want of something better to say, I ask, "What about science? You don't believe in that?"

He smiles. "It's just the modern religion—more stories, more bullshit concocted to convince us that we are at the center of everything."

"You don't believe in science? All that prehistory stuff you've been talking about sounds like science to me."

"Science is good for one thing—measuring and classifying. That's as far as it goes. At the bottom of every scientific theory, there is always glorification. There is always the hidden presumption that because a human being has given a thing a name or come up with a new theory, that in itself is sufficient cause for us to believe that we are separate from the rest of nature and above it. It's so pathetic. People can't bear the truth. The old myths die and fall by the wayside. What do people do? They swallow new ones. But in the end the two amount to the same thing—more flattery about our supposedly glorious destiny, more lies . . ." He pauses for a moment, staring at the tangled bank. "The truth, the truth that people can't accept, is that we're not really human beings. That's just a label somebody made up. We're all just helpless little animals. Deep down, we're all afraid of the dark."

For perhaps a minute I sit, reflecting on all of this. At last I say, "So where does that leave you?"

A thin little smile plays across his features, and in a voice that is hardly more than a whisper he says, "I don't know. Maybe nowhere."

Twenty-eight

Ketambe
Gunung Leuser N.P.
Sumatra

First time I have touched this book for days.

I must be mad to have gotten myself mixed up with Werther. He is brilliant, very probably the finest naturalist I have ever met. At times his virtuosity is exhausting. It is always breathtaking. The other morning in a patch of forest up in Aceh we came across a feeding flock of birds and he began identifying them, rattling off their names, using their scientific names only—Pycnonotus squamatus, Malacopteron magnum, Malacopteron magnirostre, Stachyris maculata, *and so on, faster than I could even spot them, a performance fit for the stage.*

I understand him more and more. I have even come to like him. What I do not understand, what I cannot understand, is how he can go on living with all that bitterness. Whenever he speaks of a certain wild place he has been, whether it is in Africa or in South America or Asia, he can-

not help appending some comment as to how it is being degraded or destroyed or how many years (usually few) remain until it and its inhabitants will vanish altogether. Sometimes the very mention of a place is sufficient to work him up into a towering rage. Then it is all blackness. The list of people who disgust him, whom he hates, whom he would like to kill (or who he predicts will be killed), is seemingly endless.

At the same time, or rather at different times, he can be calm and strangely gentle. This inevitably occurs when he has found something in nature to look at. I have seldom come across anyone so able to turn his entire concentration on a single object.

The other morning at Brastagi we were up on the edge of the volcano. It was early morning, and as is usual at that hour, we were out birdwatching. We had been working the trail for about half an hour without much success when he either heard or saw something moving in the very top of a tree we were approaching. Flipping up his binoculars, he was able to focus on the bird immediately and point it out to me. "Get on that bird quick!"

I was already on it. It was a thrush-size bird, entirely cobalt blue, with a noticeably long tail and a dark bill. "A whistling thrush?" I asked.

"Something better than that." He smiled.

"You don't mean the cochoa?"

"Yes, that is exactly what I mean."

"Are you sure?"

"Yes, a moment ago it was perched on a branch in good light and I could see the forehead very clearly."

I looked back at the bird, hopping from branch to branch, feeding on berries. I could not see the forehead because the bird was now in a shadowy part of the tree's crown, an area dappled with shadows. Nevertheless, I knew that he was right. It was Cochoa azurea, *known in the En-*

glish-language guides as Malaysian cochoa—one of the rarest and least known birds of Southeast Asia.

I looked back at Werther and he was beaming. It was as though just then all his cares and hatreds and excesses had fallen away. It was as though he had not simply sighted a rare bird but rather had seen something infinitely more precious, perhaps an angel.

Twenty-nine

IN A COIL of choking dust the bus rounds a bend of the road. The town heaves into view, and I am pleased. The three-hour journey from Brastagi has not been pleasant. To begin with, when the bus arrived packed to overflowing, the only available seats were at the very back. An hour out of Brastagi, one of the tires went flat, a situation that required the better part of an hour to remedy. That problem had just been solved when the feverish-looking young woman, not more sixteen or seventeen, seated next to me with her baby began throwing up, splattering my shoes in the process. The odor of vomit is so strong, it is only because the windows of the bus are open, admitting a current of fresh air, that I have managed not to become ill myself. Werther, seated to my right, is not upset in the least. If anything, he appears to be amused by the whole spectacle.

As we pass a line of wooden storefronts, one of them sporting an enormous Coca-Cola sign, the next selling huge fruit bats, hung up by their pierced wings, for food, the bus slows. A typical Sumatran town, this place reminds me of nothing so much as a film set for a spaghetti western—barring the fact, that is, that in spaghetti westerns you do not typically find ragged children, naked except for filthy T-shirts, playing in the dirt at the side of the road.

We pass a large wooden building, which seems to be the most important building in town. A crowd of fifty or sixty people is gathered outside it, spilling into the road. The driver slows the bus to a crawl to allow the outermost members of the crowd to drift to one side so we can pass.

Fifty yards farther on, the bus lurches to a halt at a restaurant shack, the sort of place that has tea, sticky sweets, and warm soft drinks for sale. The stocky driver, looking so exhausted he is almost cross-eyed, stands and makes an announcement. When he has finished, I ask Werther what he has said. Werther reports that we will be stopping for fifteen minutes.

The passengers pile out of the bus. Pleased to be away from the filthy splat on the floor, glad to stretch my legs and get a breath of fresh air not laced with dust and the smell of vomit, I sit down on a nearby wooden bench and order tea. Werther joins me and does the same. The bus driver stands a few yards from us staring down the road at the crowd, and then heads off in that direction.

When the proprietor of the shack, a sad-eyed fortyish man who looks as though he must have some Chinese blood, comes out with our glasses of tea, Werther glances at the crowd and asks him what is going on. The proprietor shakes his head sadly and offers an explanation, of which I understand nothing. As he speaks, I cannot help noticing that Werther stiffens. His face drops. Once the proprietor has finished and walked off, I ask, "What's going on?"

"A little girl has been killed."

"Who killed her?"

"A tiger."

I sit for a moment. "Where?"

"Here—in this town."

"When?"

"This morning. The child's mother sent her out to fetch some water. The tiger attacked her at the well and carried her off. The mother heard her screams and ran outside just in time to see the tiger carrying her away. The neighbors heard the screams. Some men grabbed their pangas and followed up the blood trail. They found the tiger and managed to drive it off. Then they found what remained of the little girl's body."

As he says this, I become aware of the wailing, a sound that at first is so unexpected, so strange, that I cannot identify it. Then I know that it is a sound made by a human being, coming from the direction of the crowd up the street. Beginning deep and low, it winds up to a high pitch, bursting at last into incoherent babbling. Without saying a word, Werther stands, throws a few coins on the tabletop, and heads up the street toward the crowd.

"Where are you going?" I ask. But if he has heard me, he gives no evidence of it.

I sit thinking to myself that this is none of my business, that I had better keep clear of it. Then, impelled by curiosity and challenged, as always, by Werther's recklessness, I follow him.

Arriving at the edge of the crowd, I feel very awkward and conspicuous, sensitive to the fact that some of the looks I am receiving may be of the "This is none of your business" variety. But the crowd as a whole is so transfixed by what is going on inside the building that no one seems to care that I am a stranger.

The wailing starts up again.

I sense that Werther, who is standing a few feet in front of me, will not be content to remain at the edge of the crowd, where little, if anything, can be seen. And I am right. Gradually, in small, discreet movements, he begins to insinuate himself through the ranks, edging himself toward the door. This goes against my grain. At the same time, without even thinking about it, I know that I am going to follow him.

The wailing winds up, much louder now, and breaks as before into formless babbling. Suddenly I feel foolish and guilty. It crosses my mind that I ought to go away, go back to my glass of tea, leave these people to their business, leave this woman, whoever she is, to her grief. But the moment to retreat has already passed. Now I am in the thick of it.

Gradually, receiving a few nasty glances, I work my way toward the doorway. Close enough at last to see into it, over several rows of heads, I can at first distinguish nothing in the shadows. Then, as one person standing near the door moves to the side, I do.

Looming out of the darkness, something wrapped in a tattered blanket is lying on a table just inside the door. The blanket is stained with dark irregular patches. Someone standing almost in front of the table shifts to one side, and in that instant I catch sight of something so bizarre that at first my mind refuses to register what it is: a tiny human foot, barely visible among the riddled folds, on which blood has trickled between the toes and branched in an intricate random pattern.

From somewhere inside the wailing starts up again. I listen to that voice, and a strange, overwhelming sense of horror and sadness settles over me. There is a mute scuffling in the shadows. The blanket shivers. The unseen woman wails, and suddenly I have had enough. As I turn away, half suffocated, and began to thread my way back through the crowd, the wail rises again and the woman begins to babble in that strange language understood perhaps only by the dead.

By the time Werther returns, the bus is just about to leave. He struggles over the parcel-filled aisle to his place next to me in the back seat. There is a bitterly ironic smile on his lips, the sort of smile I have seen on his face before. But it is only when the bus has pulled away and cleared the limits of the town that he says, "You know what she was saying, don't you?"

"No."

"She was screaming at the men. I didn't get the word at first. Then I did. She was calling them cowards. She was telling them that if they were real men, they would go into the forest and kill all the tigers." For perhaps thirty seconds he is silent. Then he says, "She's right, of course. That's what they'll do in the end. They're going to kill them all."

Thirty

ON A SANDY SHORE littered with smooth stones, with the roaring waters of the Alas River a few yards away, I am staring into the fire. Beyond the great black wall of the forest dense clouds hang over the hills, illuminated occasionally from within by electric flashes. The sky overhead is clear, the stars are brilliant, the air is cool and clean-smelling. The wood, damp from the last downpour, was not easy to light. I was on my knees for ten minutes, urging the flame to life.

Something catches my eye off to the left—the beam of a flashlight up near the camp, thirty yards away, raking the darkness. The holder of the flashlight, unsure of himself, apparently unfamiliar with the terrain, wavers. It could be Werther. But somehow I don't think so. Hesitating, half stumbling, the figure trots down the sandy embankment toward me and the fire. It crosses my mind that it could be Sengli, the guide who is supposed to take us into the forest tomorrow. But Sengli, I know, lives in town. Besides, the shape is too large.

Only when the figure is within twenty feet do I recognize

it as Steve, the young biologist Werther and I met this morning—a tall, rangy American kid from Bloomfield Hills, Michigan, fresh out of graduate school. Having forgotten until this moment his suggestion that he might stop by later, I am pleased, if somewhat surprised, to see him.

"Some drencher," he says.

"Get caught in it?"

"Started just after I left. Almost aborted the mission. But what the hell. How are you doing?" he says, pulling his poncho over his head and dropping it onto the sand. Picking one of the flat rocks I have arranged, he sits down on it and stares into the fire. Holding his outstretched palms toward the flames, he says, "Cozy."

"I was in the mood."

"Must've been a bitch to start."

"It was."

"Where's your partner?"

"Dunno."

"Not up at the camp?"

"Dunno."

"Caught out in the rain?"

"Maybe."

"*Weird* guy," Steve says. "You think maybe he's a little, you know . . . nuts?"

"What makes you say that?"

"Well, this morning, after you left, we were up at the cabin and got to talking. We got onto the subject of Central America, where he's been traveling this last couple of years, ya know? Well, we're talking, and out of nowhere his expression just *changes* and he gets real moody. Starts raving on about this place in Venezuela or Guatemala or someplace —this marsh he visited the first time a couple of years ago. A really great place, I guess, with, you know, about a zillion birds. Anyway, he tells me how when he visited there he found this really rare bird, some kind of waterbird—a rail, or something, I think he said. Anyway, a bird so rare it's only been recorded about five times in history or something. I guess seeing it just blew him away. He told me it was one of the great moments of his life." Steve pauses, shakes his head. "Anyway, he gets back to the place last year, and guess what."

"What?"

"It was *gone,* man."

"The bird?"

"No, the fucking *place.* Somebody had just drained it dry. It was a *cornfield.* Can you believe it?" Steve pauses and nods his head again. "Just about drove the dude over the edge. You know what he told me?"

"What?"

"Told me he'd like to take the people who killed the marsh and killed all the birds and drill fucking holes in their skulls and watch their brains ooze out. I mean, the guy is a *case,* wanting to drill holes in people's heads and shit like that."

"He's got a list."

"A what?"

"A list of people he'd like to kill."

"Crazy." Steve stares, then adds, "I mean, *out* there."

Reaching down and picking up a bottle of scotch nestled in the sand at my feet, I offer it to Steve. "No thanks," he says. He reaches into his pocket and removes a thin-rolled joint and a box of matches. Removing a match from the box, he strikes it and lights the joint, shaking his head distractedly as he does. "Drilling holes in people's heads . . ." He takes a long drag and offers it to me.

"No," I say. "I don't do that anymore."

He nods, holding the smoke in, then allowing it to curl out of his nostrils. Choking suddenly, he coughs.

"Local?" I ask.

"Yeah," he says, wiping his nose on his shirtsleeve.

"So . . . what do you do over at the research station?" I ask.

"Work with the leaf monkeys."

"Doing a study?"

"Allegedly."

"You like monkeys?"

"Hate the little fucks."

"Why'd you take the job?"

"Get away from home. My old man is one of your all-American self-made-man types. Just before I finished school, he announced that the money cow had run dry. Permanently. So, you know, it was either this"—Steve smiles—"or get a real job."

"And this was more interesting."

"*Anything* was more interesting."

"How many people are over at the station now?"

"Five, including me."

"How are they?"

"There's a French couple. The guy thinks he's Louis Pasteur or somebody. Real prick. But his wife and the two others are okay."

"You sound pretty fed up."

"Just tired." He laughs. "Got a little jungle fever, I guess. Oh, maybe I'm going a little stir crazy. Dunno. Maybe what I need is some of my mother's pancakes. Or maybe I need to get laid. Or maybe all I *really* need is a fucking Big Mac and fries." He smiles, shakes his head, and adds, "That's the thing about the forest. Great place. Just like they say in the *Geographic,* 'world's greatest repository of living things.' What they don't tell you, the part nobody likes to talk about, is that it's also just about the loneliest, most *boring* place on earth. Spend enough time out here and you'll go right out of your gourd."

He takes a hit of the joint. Then, as though the conversation had drifted into a zone too personal for comfort, he looks at the fire and says, "So what're *you* doing here?"

"Research."

"About what?"

"Tiger."

"Here?"

"Yeah."

"Don't you think you'd do better in, like, you know—India?"

"I've been to India."

"You studied tigers there?"

"No. But I saw some."

"Well," Steve says, "around here, I think you're going to need some luck."

"Why?"

"They've all been shot or trapped out. That's what I hear."

"Who told you that?"

"Sumatran guys who work for the park. Told me there are professional hunters working the park who shoot or trap whatever they can get. Dig pit traps along the trails up in the hills for the rhinos. Bait the tigers and shoot them. I hear the Chinese merchants in Medan pay good money for whatever they can come up with."

"And the park officials do nothing?"

"Nothing much they can do."

"What about the cops?"

"Turns out the hunters *are* the cops."

"That's too bad."

"I think so too. Way I figure it," he says, looking around, "this place is good for another ten, fifteen years, if that. You seen the LANDSAT studies?"

"No."

"They kinda sum it up."

"Meaning?"

"Meaning the park was laid out with a buffer zone."

"Yeah. So?"

"This one's *gone.* Eaten up in twenty years. Farmers around here are cutting down the forest as fast as they can."

"Nobody's stopping them?"

"Not that I can see. Who's gonna stop 'em?"

Over Steve's shoulder, I notice a waving flashlight beam up near the camp—someone standing at the foot of the steps of the cabin built on stilts where Werther and I are staying. All our valuables, including the provisions we have purchased to take into the mountains with us, are in the cabin, the door of which is secured by a padlock you could probably break with your teeth. The light lingers, and I am just at the point of rising to investigate when whoever it is turns and heads down the riverbank toward us, his approach unhurried and slightly wavering. Only when he is within ten yards of us do I make out that it is Werther.

"I was beginning to worry about you," I say as he steps into the glow of the fire. "Get caught in the rain?"

"Yeah."

"What'd you do?"

"Stood under a tree."

I look at his shirt; the shoulders are stained with patches of moisture. "You got wet anyway."

"Yeah."

"How's it going?" Steve says, looking up, taking another hit of his joint.

Werther stares at him blankly, as though he had never laid eyes on him before. Then, without a word, he sits down on a flat rock between the two of us. Only then do I notice that he is grinning, and the grin is unsettling. I cannot imagine what has inspired it.

"So it's tiger hunting tomorrow, eh?" Steve says, glancing over at Werther.

"Right," Werther replies rather dreamily, staring into the

fire. His eyes have a strange unfocused look. His speech seems a little slurred. It crosses my mind that he might be drunk, which would be a strange circumstance, since he has never once accepted a drink from me.

Taking a puff of his joint, Steve looks at Werther critically and says, "I hope you won't take this personally, but, ah . . . you *really* look like shit."

Werther returns the look, his face fully illuminated by the fire. I see that Steve is right. He looks like shit.

"Tired," he says with a weary smile, running the palm of his hand over his face. "Rest. I just need some rest."

Off to the west, lightning boils through black clouds, followed by a peal of rolling thunder. Taking a final puff of his joint, flinging it onto the sand, Steve says, "It's going to start again. 'Course, like a dimwit, I walked over without my trusty umbrella." Grabbing his poncho and getting to his feet, he says to Werther, "You better take it easy." Then, glancing back at me, he adds, "Come on over when you get back. Don't worry yourself about the permit. When you coming back, anyway?"

"Five days," I say.

"Major league. Who knows? Maybe you will see a tiger." Looking up at the sky, he says, "Well, better hit the road."

"Hope you don't get soaked."

"Even if I do," Steve says with a smile, his eyes now quite glazed, "I'll be a happy camper. Hey, take care of yourselves."

"You too," I say.

He turns and plods off across the sand. Werther, staring into the fire as though unaware of his departure, says nothing.

Steve has no more mounted the embankment than a flash of lightning breaks above the forest, for a split second illuminating him perfectly. It is instantly followed by an explosive crack of thunder. I look up. The stars above my head have been swallowed completely. "It's going to start any minute," I say, turning to Werther. "We'd better go up."

Werther doesn't move or react in any way, just sits staring into the fire. For a moment I wonder if he has heard me. Then he stirs and repeats, "We'd better go up."

The cabin is a typical Sumatran forest dwelling, built on stilts ten feet above the ground. The moment we reach the foot of the stairs, a flashbulb x-rays us and a ten-megaton bomb explodes above our heads. There is a sudden gust of wind and the rain falls in a sheet, soaking us to the skin even as we scuttle to the top. I unlock the padlock on the door, flip back the hasp, and swing the door open.

Entering, I feel my way through the darkness to the space between the two beds and find the table. Groping blindly but with great care, I locate the kerosene lamp, remove its globe, and place it gently on the table. Picking up the box of matches, I remove a match, strike it, and hold it to the wick until it lights. I adjust the flame.

The rain hammering on the sheet-metal roof is deafening. I scan the ceiling for leaks and find none. I pull off my wet shirt, wipe down my torso and arms with it, then hang it on the nail in the wall. I remove my moneybelt and place it under my pillow. Then I remove my trousers and start to climb into bed.

Only then do I realize that Werther is sitting hunched up at the head of his bed, back to the wall. He has removed his trousers but has kept on his wet shirt. He is shivering.

"You got a fever?" I ask.

"No."

"Why don't you take off that wet shirt?"

"It's fine."

"You're going to sleep like that?"

"It's not so wet."

"It's soaked. Haven't you got a dry one? I've got one if you want it."

"It's fine, I tell you."

I stare. "You going to be all right for tomorrow?"

"Yes."

"You sure?"

"I'm sure."

I am tempted to say something else about the shirt. Maybe he isn't sick now; after sleeping in that shirt he will be. But I am in no mood to argue. I have already learned that you cannot argue with a stone. If he wants to come down with a fever, that's his business. As I climb into my sleeping bag, the rain comes harder, pounding the roof as though it means to knock it down and sink us into the mud. Leaning over, I cup my hand around the light to blow it out.

"Leave it on," Werther says. "I might . . . like to read."

He never reads. Besides, he doesn't look capable of doing anything beyond sitting in his wet shirt and shivering.

"Sure."

I lie down, turned away from him. I pull the bag up around my shoulders. Outside there is a crack of thunder. The wind howls, rattling the flimsy building as though hell itself were opening up. I listen to the hammering rain—to the relentless strength and steadiness of it. I close my eyes. Then I feel myself dissolving into it, drifting weightlessly down and down into some bottomless black well of sleep.

Thirty-one

IN THE SHADOWED STILLNESS of late afternoon the air of the forest, shimmering with heat, is impossible to breathe, as though all but the inert gases had been leached out of it. Every crevice and pore of my body is coated with perspiration. But it admits no cooling function. The air itself is sweat.

Knee jammed in dense leaf litter to brace myself at the foot of a small hill, I am peering up through airy space to a break in the canopy twenty yards above my head, at a fat-jowled, red-bearded old man balanced in the crotch of two ascending limbs. Hesitant, curious, his face strikes me at this moment as being more human by far than any I have ever seen in a mirror. With no trouble at all, I can imagine our situations reversed—he standing here in my shoes, absurdly clothed, full of judgments and presumptions, I standing up there stark naked, enjoying at least a trace of a breeze. More than once I have read that the genetic makeup of orangutans is essentially identical to that of human beings. Now I believe it. Put this fellow in a Brooks Brothers suit and give him a seat on the stock exchange. Stick a flower in his lapel and invite him to lunch.

"An old man," Sengli says. "All alone now, waiting to die."

This strikes me as an odd thing to say. But then, Sengli is in the habit of saying odd things. Just this morning he told me that he is a Minangkabau, one of that tribe of central Sumatra who possess the ability to lure tigers out of the forest by singing songs—a talent that I have a great interest in seeing demonstrated.

High up in the canopy, the orangutan grunts, turns, and with a heavy leap goes crashing off through tree branches until he is lost to sight. I turn and look back up the trail just in time to see our three porters, teenage boys, emerge from behind a dense clump of vegetation about twenty yards back. All three look overheated and exhausted, their expressions reminding me that we should have reached our camp an hour ago. Catching sight of us, they stop, each of them finding a tree to lean against while we wait for Werther to catch up.

Sengli speaks to them and I hear Werther's name mentioned. In response, one of the boys, the one who always speaks, answers in English that when he last looked, Werther was just behind them. Sengli turns to me and says, "Werther fall back again."

"Yes," I say.

"Werther sick man. I see it in his eyes."

"I know."

"We must go back."

"If you can get him to turn around, I'll be happy to. You know he won't."

"I know," Sengli says a little dreamily. "I go find him now. Wait here, please. This place sometimes danger place. Very danger."

"All right."

I watch him go, realizing how angry I am at Werther for prolonging this fiasco. When he was sick beside the trail this morning, I asked him to turn around. He wouldn't. From that point on he insisted on bringing up the rear. When I asked him why, he said, "Because I want to be *alone.*"

Sengli disappears down the trail. I cast around for a place to sit. The trail here is damp and well shaded. Leeches are a certainty. At noon, when I sat down to rest, I removed my shoe and found the toe of my sock soaked with blood. Removing the sock, I discovered a swollen black leech the size of a fat garden slug curled up between my toes. The words of a medical doctor friend came back to me: *Leeches don't cause infections. They don't have to. They bleed you dry.*

Unwilling to sit, I turn and gaze up the hill where it skirts the edge of a ravine full of vegetation. The summit of the hill, perhaps eighty or ninety feet higher than where I am now standing, seems infinitely distant. At least up there there would be a breath of air.

I look back down the trail. No Sengli, no Werther. No way to predict how far back Werther might have fallen. Could be five minutes, could be half an hour, depending. The idea of just standing here waiting for them for God knows how long is unbearable. They could meet me at the top of the hill. It would take me, and them, less than ten minutes to reach it. Sengli told me specifically to wait. But I do not feel like waiting.

After hesitating a moment, I turn and step over a fallen, half-decomposed log that is lying across the trail. Even the small movement helps. Much better to be moving. The boys can wait for Sengli and Werther. They will tell them that I have gone ahead.

The trail that mounts the hill is narrow, densely vegetated on both sides, with many roots crossing, intertwining like knobby, grotesquely elongated, cancerous fingers, slippery and offering no foothold. There is no way of determining whether a krait or a cobra is lurking under the vegetation.

I move cautiously over the gnarled roots, aware that at any moment I could slip and tumble down into the invisible ravine to my right. I creep along slowly, arriving at last at an exceptionally large root whose skin has been polished to brightness by the passage of four-footed animals. I pause for a moment, half aware of some lingering ripe deadness in the air. The trail is so narrow here that if I am to step over the root, I shall have to place my right foot where my left foot should be, then push myself to an upright position with nothing to hold on to. Hesitating, calculating carefully, I make the move. Halfway through it, I realize that the earth has given way beneath my feet. I am falling.

I land hard and begin to slide. I twist and try to flex my knees, but it is no good. The trail disappears above my head. I flail wildly in an attempt to grasp something, anything. Twisting onto my stomach, I try to stop the slide. Something rips my face. My mouth fills with soil and leaves. My foot plows into something hard, which stops me dead. Clinging to the base of a bush with one hand, I cough and spit and clear my eyes. I test the foothold, whatever it is, and look around.

Less than a foot away is a sharpened bamboo stake planted in the ground, pointed at an angle uphill. Nearly two inches in diameter, the bamboo has been whittled to a razor-sharp point. It is only through sheer luck that I have not been impaled on it. I twist around and look to my left. There is an identical sharpened stake less than a foot away. I have slid right between them, and my slide has been broken by my foot jamming on the base of another.

I become aware of a wetness on my chest and stomach. I am sure I am bleeding, which is odd, because though I know my face has been cut, I am aware of no profound wound. A nauseating odor rises to my nostrils. I push myself up and look down. My chest is covered with dozens of grains of white rice, vibrating, writhing, dancing to some soundless music.

Maggots.

The odor gags me. I fight down the urge to vomit. Bracing myself, I sweep at the maggots frantically, breaking and smearing them across my shirtfront trying at the same time to pull myself up and away from them. But I can't find a foothold. I do not wish to end up impaled on one of the bamboo stakes.

Somewhere above me someone calls out my name. It is Sengli.

"Richard! I have rope! I am coming! Don't move!"

A few seconds later, the underbrush above me moves and I see Sengli edging down the hill backward, gripping a length of nylon rope. Lowering himself until he is next to me, he reaches out so that I can grab his arm. He cries out something in Bahasa, and the rope, in the hands of someone above, begins to ascend. Grappling and climbing as well as we can, we make our way up through the vegetation. Within a minute we are back on the trail.

As soon as I can stand upright, I reach up and touch my forehead. It is bleeding, but not too seriously. Sengli and one of the porters are sweeping my shirtfront, sweeping away the rest of the maggots and filth. The shirt is soaked through; the odor is so strong that I retch.

Throwing my daypack aside, I rip off the shirt, popping the buttons as I do. I turn and gaze at Sengli. The barest suggestion of a smile is drawn on his face. It is the sort of look all Asians have when they are more than mildly distressed but cannot allow themselves to show it.

"Rhino trap," he says quietly. "Something die here maybe four, five day ago."

I turn and gaze down the hill. Werther is standing ten feet away. His face is ashen and covered with perspiration. He moves his lips as if to speak, but they produce no sound. I look at him, then at Sengli, then at the porters, my heart pounding so hard that for a moment I am sure it will burst.

Two hours later, at the camp we have made atop a hillock five minutes' walk from a trickling stream, I put down my plate. I had not thought that I was hungry. I had no appetite. But I have eaten three plates of rice covered with canned fish and drunk two cups of tea. The fall obviously took it out of me.

Sengli sits directly across the fire from me, and three porters are busying themselves cleaning up the dishes. Werther has not made an appearance at dinner. For all I know, he is sleeping in his tent, the blue dome affair pitched on the hillock, twenty yards from where we sit. But there is a light shining inside it, so I am sure that he is awake.

"You have enough to eat, Richard?" Sengli asks.

"Yes, I'm fine."

"Werther will not eat?"

"I don't know. Maybe I'd better go and ask."

I stand and walk past the first three tents, then mount the hillock to Werther's. When I arrive at it, without thinking I fall to my knees, pull back the flap, and peer inside.

Werther lies reclined on his side, left sleeve rolled up, a short length of rubber tubing fixed above the elbow. Just below the tubing is a blue-purple bruise. At the lower edge of it he has placed a needle, which after a second or two he removes. He places the syringe on his sleeping bag. A droplet of purple blood escapes from the wound, but he pays no attention to it. Nor does he look up at me.

For a moment the absurd thought that he is a diabetic skips through my mind. Then the truth settles over me.

Picking at the tourniquet with his free hand, he loosens it, looks up at me, and grins. "So shocked? Don't be. It's just my candy. It always makes me feel so much better."

I stare at him, struggling to think of something to say. But just then his gaze loses its focus, his pupils dilate, and his eyes half roll back in their sockets. He looks away. His whole body seems to relax. Already he is somewhere else.

In the fading light the path down to the stream is steep and unsure. When I reach the bottom, I squat next to the trickling water and stare into it. For a long time I just crouch there in the silence, and at last the ghostly thought settles over me that I know in a way quite unlike the way I have known anything before what this stream is, why its exists, how it works—I see a thousand million tiny rivulets seeping under the thick leaf litter of the forest floor, all connected, all dependent on each other, all answering the same implacable appeal of a perfect endless flowing.

Suddenly, somewhere, a single insect voice begins. A moment or two later, another and another enter the music, sawing, screaming, vibrating, joining, as if each leaf and branch in this green labyrinth had found a voice to protest the night. Then somehow it ends. I look through a space in the canopy at a pale sprinkling of stars. I turn and glance downstream.

It is then that I see it. In the dying light, perhaps twenty-five yards away, at the edge of a clearing next to the water, a tiger is standing, staring directly at me. For a long moment it does not move. Then, without a sound, it is gone.

I blink. Without thinking, I leap to my feet and plunge downstream, splashing water in every direction. Something trips me up in the streambed. I reach out to save myself, I fall. I rise, soaked and dripping, and plunge on.

At the place where the tiger stood, I stand in the lowering darkness, heart pounding, breath racing, feeling the water drip away from me, gazing down at the small stretch of gray sandy shore. The sand is smooth, untouched, without mark or trace. I look all around me. Except for the whispering of the stream, there is no movement or sound. I stand there in the silence, wondering if I have imagined it. Then I close my eyes and know that what I saw was no phantom. It was *there*.

Part Five

Forests of the Night

Thirty-two

THROUGH the scratched Plexiglas windows of a Twin Otter aircraft, vaulting upward in a great circle above the broad Kathmandu Valley, the snow-capped Himalaya seems to girdle the earth, to embrace it from horizon to horizon. Bending forward in my seat, I do what is expected of me and point out the various subranges and summits I can recognize. Far to the west lies the great Annapurna massif, an area through which I have walked a number of times almost to the border of Tibet. Nearer at hand is the Ganesh Himal, named for the elephant-headed Hindu god of wisdom and good fortune. A bit to the east are the rugged peaks of Langtang, whose dense forests harbor the legendary red panda, and a hundred miles farther on, there is the seemingly unimpressive pyramid that is the highest point on planet Earth—Sagarmatha or Chomolungma, or, as it has always been known to Europeans and Americans, Everest.

The Otter banks sharply and adopts a southwest heading. Within minutes we are soaring over steep hills and deep river valleys, the hilltops crowned with villages made up of two-story earth-colored houses. I find myself asking what I am doing here, why I have chosen to repeat the well-known role of road manager, camp counselor, cheerleader, soother of lonely women, general factotum.

My clients aim their cameras and snap pictures eagerly. I do not think they would be amused to hear that the life that is passing below us is by no means as idyllic as it may appear from this angelic height; that in Nepal most families live on what the average American middle-class household spends on its pets; that in the monsoon the picturesque terraces often collapse in a flow of mud that sweeps entire villages and their inhabitants downhill to their deaths; that most of the inhabitants of these villages live out their lives in a darkness of poverty and illness that is unfathomable to the western mind. But I am empty of any desire to meddle with their illusions. My most compelling wish at the moment, the most contrary imaginable for one purportedly leading a tour, is simply to be left alone.

Already we have left the hill country behind. We are coming up just now on a broad expanse of forest punctuated by stretches of grassland and braided streams, glittering belts of gold in the sunlight—one of the last great chunks of this type of habitat remaining in the world. Even today, within its confines, it is so whole, so perfect, it is possible to allow oneself to believe that this lushness forms, as it did in the past, an unbroken unity extending from Pakistan, far to the west, across the whole of the north of India and Nepal, to Burma and beyond. Most of it has vanished now, cut down to meet the needs of human beings. But this small remaining patch is pristine.

The wing tilts sharply and we begin to descend. Somewhere below and ahead of us lies the grass landing strip at Meghauli. The engines throttle back. With a grinding moan the landing gear swings down, locks into place. We drift lower and lower, to the level of the trees. The balloon tires screech as they touch earth, sending up a storm of whirling reddish dust. The landing is perfect. The passengers, not used to flying in small aircraft, offer a round of applause to the pilots. The plane rolls to a halt in front of a simple wooden hut where a faded banner draped over the doorway announces, simply, TIGER TOPS.

The hatch sprung, we file out of the aircraft and are greeted at the bottom of the ramp by a good-looking Nepalese dressed in khaki, Devi Gurung, whom I met on my last visit here. Devi tells us that the four jeeps waiting nearby will transport us to the lodge and that the baggage will be delivered later on. We head over to the jeeps, and when, after a few minutes, everyone is settled, we head off down a dirt road, first through a grove of dusty trees, then past dry paddy fields cut back to winter stubble.

Except for the hazy barrage of trees in the distance, stubble fields stretch off in every direction, the uniformity relieved by occasional mud-and-wattle settlements. Women walk along the road, some carrying bundles of fodder, others balancing earthenware jugs on their heads. Some stop and turn to look, holding the hems of their saris over their faces against the rolling cloud of fine powder boiling up behind us. Bright-eyed, grinning adolescents carrying small children in their arms or on their backs cry out "Hello, mister!" as we speed past.

Another quarter-mile or so and the jeeps slow and swerve down a gentle incline onto the sandy beach of a sluggish river, brown with topsoil washed down from the mountains. I gaze across the water to the opposite shore. It offers the sharpest contrast to the dusty moonscape through which we have just driven—a wall of grass, dense and rank, in places ten or fifteen feet high, breached by a single double-rutted track leading into the forest beyond. It is a path to a different world.

Thirty-three

NEARLY AN HOUR LATER, having crossed another river by boat and walked perhaps half a mile through the jungle, we enter the tented camp. Designed along the lines of similar establishments in East Africa, this is the fanciest tented camp in Nepal—simple enough to give clients the illusion that they are roughing it a bit, luxurious enough for them to leave the illusion behind when the mood warrants. There are solar-heated showers, immaculate pit toilets, and a full bar, not to mention an open-air circular roofed dining area, which commands a panoramic view of the river. Devi assigns us to our tents, tells everyone that dinner will be served at five o'clock, and makes a point of asking everyone not to walk beyond the confines of the camp without a guide. "It is not the tiger but the rhinoceros that is most dangerous here," he says. "If you wish to walk on your own during your stay, a guide will be assigned to you. By the way, walking at night is strictly against the rules. That's all."

The clients disperse, nervous chuckles and jokes about man-eating tigers and mad rhinos erupting here and there, and head off toward their tents. The great red bulge of the sun, poised just over the tops of the trees on the opposite side of the river, sheds a golden light so rich that I cannot bear the thought of going inside. Instead I sidle up to the bar. I am no sooner seated than Bess, a client from Mobile, Alabama, suddenly appears from around the corner, hair combed, lipstick freshly applied.

Bess has been on a trip with me before, and we have become friends. I like her very much and find her about a hundred times more interesting than most women who turn up on these tours. Like a few other southern women I have known, she enjoys pretending that she is some sort of good ol' gal, as though her favorite pastime were sitting on the stoop and sipping corn liquor from a Mason jar. In fact she holds a master's degree in English from Yale and has told me that the reason she signed up for another trip with me was that unlike most members of my profession, I give the impression of "having a mind"—which I take as a compliment.

She has quite a mind herself. An autodidact of extraordinary ambition, she has laid plans to read all the great books of the western world in the original languages. On the last trip, I noticed that she was plowing through *Tristram Shandy,* reading a few pages aloud to herself at bedtime. This time she has brought along *À l'Ombre des jeunes filles en fleurs,* and is working her way through it with the aid of a paperback French-English dictionary. None of which, oddly enough, prevents her from calling people she is fond of "Bubba."

"So, Bubba," she says, taking the stool next to me with a smile, "from that hangdog look of yours, I'd say you might be gettin' the least bit tired of this Hemingway shit."

"Could be."

"Gangrene got ya? Hyenas circlin' your tent?"

"Could be."

"That bad? Hey, what's the matter? Got woman trouble? You look like you could use a drink." Spinning around on the stool and facing the bar, she says, "Name your poison. I'm buyin'."

"No bartender."

"Where the hell is he?"

"Beats me."

"Well, gotta be patient, I guess." Giving me an appraising look, she asks, "When this little episode is done, what exotic destination you off to next?"

"Dunno. Bulgaria might be nice."

"Jesus, you *are* depressed."

Just then another client appears from around the corner of the bar—the CPA from Phoenix, decked out in a shopping-mall safari outfit. This would not be so bad in itself, if it did not serve to accentuate the fact that he is a nonstop grinner, the sort of guy who plays handball during his lunch hour and thinks of himself as a hard-ass.

"Disturbing something?" he asks.

"Not yet," Bess says, throwing me a wink.

"Just wanted to ask you, Richard. About seeing a tiger—how would you rate our chances? Good? Great? Inevitable?"

"Good."

"Just good?"

"Here you have as good a chance as you would anywhere —on short notice, that is."

"God, I hope so. I booked this tour months ago. You know, all my friends told me that I ought to go to Africa. But Africa has been . . . you know . . . *done*. Anyway, none of my friends have been to Nepal or India. So I thought I'd give it a shot."

"I don't think you'll be disappointed. But it is possible to miss, even here."

"Well," he says, "guess I'll just have to keep my fingers crossed. All right if I take a little walk down to the river?"

"No problem as long as you stay in sight. Just watch out for the muggers."

"Muggers?" he says, his expression darkening.

"Crocodiles."

"Ah," he says, "I thought you . . ." But the explanation trails off with a sigh. "Well," he says, "hope we do see a tiger. Expensive trip to go home empty-handed."

"Chances are good."

"Okay. Well . . . guess I'll leave you two young lovers to yourselves."

With a wave, he strides across the dining area to the head of the trail that leads down the bank. Bess watches him go, and as soon as he is out of earshot, she says, "Nothing wrong with that boy. Just your ordinary, run-of-the-mill, Oedipally complexed, anal-retentive, sadomasochistic, manic-depressive, all-American ass-hole. I know about ten thousand guys just like him." She adds, "But hey, I don't want to talk about him. How's that book coming along?"

"Gone the way of the dodo."

"How come?"

"Long story."

"Well now, that's too bad. Sort've had the idea you might turn out to be a pretty good writer." She sits quietly for a moment, then says, "Hey, there's something I wanted to ask you about. You know that little guardhouse we passed drivin' in here?"

"Yeah."

"What's that for? They got soldiers guardin' this place?"

"Sure."

"What're they protecting?"

"The park."

"From what?"

"People who live around it."

"The farmers?"

"Yes."

"They don't let the farmers come into the park?"

"Once a year. They let them come in to cut grass for fodder and building material."

"Not otherwise?"

"Not otherwise."

"Doesn't sound too democratic to me."

"I don't think we're talking democracy here."

"Bet they sneak in and cut grass anyway."

"Sure they do. Devi told me the last time I was here, about an old woman who had just been killed at the edge of the park. She waded across the river in the morning, found a quiet spot, and began to cut grass for fodder with her hand scythe. She worked all morning and managed to clear a considerable area. When she had almost finished she took a last swath and a tiger that had been lying up watching her all morning sprang out and killed her."

"Hold on here—how could they *know* that? How could they know the tiger was waiting for her all that time?"

"The grass was all mashed down where it had been lying. It was just a few feet from where she'd been working."

"Wow," Bess says, obviously impressed. "Now *that* story gives me the willies. I don't know about you, but I need a drink. Where's that bartender?"

An hour or so later, after dinner, I am sitting in front of a roaring fire in the dining area, a glass of scotch balanced on my knee. For the past few minutes I have found myself thinking about Werther. At odd moments all day long stray thoughts about him have been coming back to me. For some reason I keep remembering the last time I saw him, how he looked standing there that misty morning on that lonely forest road, watching as I climbed onto an impossibly crowded bus headed for Padang. The last words he spoke as

I clambered aboard were "Take care of yourself," as though I were the one who needed taking care of. It was only when I looked back at him as the bus was pulling away that I noticed an odd look on his face. It was the sort of look one might expect to discover on the face of a lost child.

Suddenly, from the corner of my eye, I notice a young man dressed in green khaki—one of the camp staff—appear from the shadows. Approaching Devi hesitantly, he gets his attention, then walks over to him and whispers something in his ear. Devi nods, takes a last bite of curry, wipes his mouth with his napkin, and rises and walks over to me. "Richard," he says quietly, "there is a tiger at the bait. We'd better go now."

Rising from my seat, I pass the word to my clients, and they are all on their feet in seconds. They gather round Devi, who announces that they have three minutes to fetch their jackets, empty their bladders, or do whatever else they need to do before meeting back here. Responding to his instructions, they hustle off.

Three minutes later they are back, the CPA at the head of the line. I groan inwardly when I see him. He has more photographic equipment hung around his neck than the average paparazzo. In one hand he is holding a huge flash attachment. Devi gazes at him and says in a tone of genuine regret, "Sorry, no flash photography is allowed. The flash would frighten away the tiger."

The CPA looks at Devi. He blinks. "You mean . . ." But he doesn't finish the sentence. Turning to me, his perpetual grin now a rictus of anger, he says, "Why didn't you tell me that, Richard?"

"Didn't know you were interested in taking nighttime pictures."

He gawks, his expression that of a bullied schoolboy about to rush off to speak to the "proper authorities." But Devi is the proper authority here, and there is no court of appeal. At last, looking infinitely disgusted and mumbling something unpleasant under his breath, the CPA turns on his heel and strides toward his tent. Devi looks at me. I look back. But there is really nothing to say.

The moon is shattered silver through the black branches of the trees. As we walk along the sandy path, nightjars are calling all around us, their calls uncannily like the sound of a dull axe striking a hollow log: *Choink! Choink! Choink!* Devi leads the way, flashlight probing the darkness. A small furry creature with ruby-red eyes appears on the trail and pauses for a moment before slinking off into the underbrush.

"What was that?" somebody behind me whispers.

"A mongoose," I whisper back.

After about five minutes, Devi pauses next to a low wooden shelf that someone has placed next to the trail. Turning to face us, he whispers that we must remove our shoes, explaining that the hide, the place from which we will view the tiger, is not far off, and that from this point on we must maintain absolute silence. When all the shoes have been removed and placed on the shelf, we walk on, the sand cool against the soles of our feet.

Within a minute or two we arrive at the long thatched corridor that is the entrance to the hide. Flashlight pointed to the ground, Devi leads us in. At the end of the dark corridor, where it opens out into an even darker room, he takes each of us by the arm and escorts us one by one to an opening in the wall. There are perhaps eight such openings, each a window without glass, beyond which nothing is visible in the darkness.

Moving back and forth behind us, Devi takes perhaps three minutes to be satisfied that everyone is well situated. Then, taking up his customary position at the opening in the wall farthest to the right, he aims his flashlight into the blackness and switches it on.

About ten yards away, on a small area of swept earth, a dead bullock lies on its side, mouth open, squarish teeth exposed, head unnaturally twisted, the length of rope that held it fast at the moment of its death taut about its neck. Dead eyes reflect the light like brilliant topazes. Its belly has been sliced open; the blue intestines have been dragged out in a pile. A large portion of its rump is missing, as if blown away by some small but efficient explosive device. The pink crater of exposed flesh is licked clean like meat in a butcher-shop window. Reclining at the foot of her kill, the tigress gazes unperturbed into the beam of the flashlight. It poses no threat. She has seen it dozens and dozens of times before, even on the darkest nights.

I raise my binoculars to take a look. In the weak, diffused, yellowish glow of the flashlight, the view is astonishing. Her muzzle is soaked with blood. Fat droplets of it cling to the tips of her whiskers. She turns her head, looks directly at me. I can feel her eyes. I stare back at her. Suddenly I have the overwhelming impression that she is looking not *at* me but *through* me. I stare into her eyes, and the walls seem to melt away. Not expecting it, I begin to tremble.

Then I realize that the person standing next to me is trembling as well. Peering into the darkness, I know somehow that it is the CPA. Releasing a sigh or perhaps a quiet moan, he turns away from the window and gropes toward the passageway. I hesitate for several seconds, unable to decide whether I should follow him. Then it crosses my mind that here, in this place, he cannot be left alone. I follow him.

No more than half a minute later, I find him standing at the edge of the trail in the mottled moonlight, peering into the darkness of the forest. Walking up behind him, clearing my voice quietly so that he will not be startled, I ask, "Are you all right?"

Whirling to face me and holding out a stiffened hand as though to ward me off, he says, "Leave me alone." He turns away. As though struck by an invisible hand, his jaw juts forward, he groans, and a wad of vomit arches from his mouth.

He stands gasping, slightly bent over, hands braced on his knees, staring at the ground. His body is gripped by a spasm, and another wad erupts. I stand there, waiting and watching, not knowing what I ought to do or say. At last he straightens up and turns to face me, a drooping, silvery thread of saliva suspended between the tip of his nose and his cheek. Wiping it away with the back of his hand, he says in a trembling voice, "It's weird . . . I didn't think it was going to be like that." His eyes are bright.

For an instant, I almost succumb to the impulse to put my arm around his shoulder to comfort him. Then I become aware of an equally powerful sensation of revulsion. And to my shame, I cannot bring myself to touch him.

Thirty-four

FOUR DAYS LATER, black clouds cloak the tops of the hills just outside town as I open the screen door of KC's restaurant, in the Thamel section of Kathmandu. In a city noted for the variety and virulence of its intestinal parasites, KC's is a sort of refuge, a safe haven, one of the few eateries where one can entertain the reasonable expectation of dining without taking home some nasty, debilitating microorganism. The restaurant is almost always packed. I am surprised to find it almost empty.

I step inside and take a seat by the window, then gaze out at the street, at the young touts sidling up to tourists with the two immortal questions ("Want to change money? Want to buy good shit?"), at the bored shopkeepers slouched in doorways, engaging passersby with brief but trenchant disquisitions on the unique virtues of their poor-quality carpets, fake bronze Buddhas, and prayer beads, which the foreigners, far from ignoring, obligingly cart home by the hundredweight.

Looking at all of it, I realize just how much things have changed. To anyone who knew Kathmandu twenty years ago, the city is nearly unrecognizable. In those days, in every essential respect, it remained a medieval town. Automobiles were few. Bicycles and pony carts were the accepted modes of transportation, and even these seldom ventured into the narrow, shadowy back streets where a one-on-one dispute with a wallowing pig was almost a dead certainty. The choice of entertainments was limited—only the temples to visit and the mountains. If smoking dope and hanging out was your main interest—and for many visitors it was—you could, after getting high on what was certainly the cheapest and most potent hashish in the world, park yourself in one of the pie shops and munch chocolate cake until you popped. Between satisfying bites, gazing red-eyed at the pigs outside, rooting in the muddy alley, you could sagely note, as though no one could possibly have been clever enough to have remarked on it before, how it was all "just like the Middle Ages."

But that Kathmandu, that little corner of Shangri-la that will always endure in my mind, is no more. A million people now live in the Kathmandu Valley, and tourism has become very big business. The narrow streets of the capital are jammed with Japanese cars, which make the air quality so poor that for days on end the snowy peaks just outside of town are reduced to hazy alpine silhouettes. Because the vastly wealthy dynasty that rules the country has never seen the wisdom of providing the inhabitants of the valley with a supply of clean drinking water, thousands of people, children and the elderly especially, die each year from illnesses medical students in the West know only from textbooks. I am fond of the Nepalese, have always been fond of them, but I do not want to think about what the next few decades will mean for them.

The door of the restaurant swings open. My informant steps inside.

Nattily dressed as always, in a pair of slacks and a jacket

over a pullover sweater, he stands scanning the room until our eyes meet. Smiling, walking over to me, he says, "Richard, how nice to see you."

"Nice to see you too," I say, and, gesturing to the chair across from me. "Have a seat."

He does so. "Been waiting long?" he asks.

"Just a few minutes."

"How have you been?"

"I've been better."

He gives me a long appraising look, sighs, and says, "Are you all right? You don't seem yourself. I have to say that I've been worried about you."

"Why?"

"That letter you sent from Sumatra—I couldn't get much out of it. That story you told me about seeing the tiger . . . Did you or did you not see it?"

"I thought I did. But when I followed it up, I couldn't find anything. No pugmarks, nothing."

"Maybe what you saw was a ghost."

"I don't believe in ghosts."

"Maybe you should," he says. Then, after a moment, he asks, "I don't mean to pry, but has something . . . happened?"

"Nothing worth talking about."

"Are you ill?"

"I'm not sick."

"You don't look well. Maybe you should see a doctor."

I am just about to say in a very annoyed tone of voice that I have no interest whatsoever in visiting a doctor when the waiter, a harried-looking young Nepalese, suddenly appears. Glancing first at my informant, then at me, he attempts a smile and says, "What can I get for you?"

"A white coffee," I say.

"The same," my informant adds.

The waiter nods and walks off.

"In your letter," my informant says, "you didn't say anything about where you'd been. Did you make it to Thailand?"

"I was there—for a couple of weeks."

"What did you find out?"

"About what I expected."

"Meaning?"

"Meaning a mess. I met a guy at Khao Yai who told me that there are people working inside the park who trap the tigers and sell the meat to a restaurant just outside Bangkok that specializes in serving exotic game to rich big-time weirdos. He says they're doing a bang-up business."

My informant stares at me across the table and sighs. "Richard, I hope that you won't take this in the wrong way. But I think you're in trouble."

"What do you mean?"

"You're taking this conservation business, this tiger business, far too personally."

"Think so?"

"Yes."

"Why shouldn't I? It's my world, isn't it? It's personal."

"You're just so angry. Sooner or later you'll just have to accept what's happening. Don't you see that there's really nothing you can do? Are you so naive as to believe that you can start some holy crusade to save the tiger? Do you really think that in a world where human beings are starving and being butchered and being blown up every day of the year, anyone is going to turn the world upside down to save a mere animal? That's not realistic."

"I'm fed up with people sticking their heads in the sand," I say.

"That's just it. That's exactly it—that's the part you don't get. That's what people do. That's what people do to survive."

The waiter arrives and places the two milk coffees in front

of us. My informant picks up his cup, blows at the steam rising from it, and takes a sip. He puts it down and says, "Know where I went this morning?"

"Not much telling."

"To Daxinkali. Have you been out there?"

"Not for a long time."

"Well, I myself had not been there for many years. I had completely forgotten what the place is like. Anyway, I went this morning, and for a long time I stood there at the little temple enclosure, watching the priest slit the throats of the chickens and spew the blood onto the Kali idols. The priest was a very unattractive man with pockmarked skin. There he stood, barefoot, on that floor covered with blood. But there was something about him that was very appealing. Before he killed each chicken he would hold it close to him and stroke it with his fingers. As I watched him, I had the oddest sensation that he really did understand the responsibility of what he was doing, that he understood that taking a life, *any* life, is a matter of utmost seriousness. For the first time in a long while it crossed my mind that there are certain matters in this world that we must have reverence for—and leave untouched."

I stare at him and say, "How very Hindu."

He stares back, then looks away uneasily, his expression pained. "Yes," he says, "I suppose it is."

For perhaps a minute neither of us says anything. Then he says, "Richard, I just want you to know something."

"What is that?"

"I want you to know that though we disagree on some things, I regard you as a friend."

"You're not anybody's friend. You've got too much to hide."

"What do you mean?" he says, his gaze suddenly focused.

"You understand perfectly well what I mean." I stare at

him again. "What happened to you? What's the big secret that you can't bring yourself to talk about?"

"That is my own private affair."

"Precisely."

He pauses. Then he says, "Look, this is getting us nowhere. What do you propose to do now?"

"Get on with it."

"Meaning?"

"See it out—finish it."

"This tiger plan of yours."

"Yes."

"You're mad. It's you who may end up finished."

"Then that's the way it'll go."

He looks away, a bitter expression on his face. After a moment he looks back and says, "You know what your problem is?"

"Why don't you tell me?"

"You can't forgive yourself for being human, like the rest of us."

Pushing back my chair, I stand up from the table. I pick up my jacket and slip it on.

"Are you leaving?"

"What's it look like?"

"Richard, sit down. Don't go like this."

"Sorry."

"Richard—"

But by that time I have already crossed the short space to the door. Without looking back, I open it, step outside, and melt into the passing crowd.

Thirty-five

THE ANCIENT TOWN of Pokhara, situated at the southern extremity of what was once the greatest of the salt routes through the central Himalaya, lies some two hundred miles to the west of Kathmandu. Though the journey by air requires only about forty-five minutes, traveling there by road can take a day or a week, depending on how much of the road has been washed away by the monsoon rains.

Two mornings after my meeting with my informant, having made the journey overland in a dilapidated bus, I am sitting in a teashop near the end of the bazaar that adjoins Shining Hospital, the usual jumping-off place for trekkers headed into the Annapurnas. With pack, bedroll, and tent at my feet, I am gazing out at the parade of humanity passing by—Tibetans, with their weathered Mongol features, coming to market; schoolchildren carrying tattered out-of-date textbooks; porters half bent over, their faces showing the strain of their heavy loads. There are trekking groups, some faces among them looking exhilarated, others exhausted, disappointed perhaps that they have been foolish enough to pay thousands of dollars and fly halfway around the world only to end up feeling abused. And as always there are trains of ponies decked out in faded pink plumes and bells which can be heard a mile away—the true and original sound of these mountains.

For the past few minutes I have been thinking about what happened in Kathmandu. I was very rude to Kailash, and I am sorry that it had to happen. But I did have my reasons. Although I have stayed with him on four separate occasions, have exchanged letters and phone calls with him, and have benefited from his generosity in any number of ways, there has been on my part a growing sense of frustration at his inability to speak frankly, to trust me, or anyone. Increasingly, in his presence I have found myself cast in the role of impetuous fool, while he remains content to stand back and play that of the all-knowing guru. In fact he is the far from all-knowing, and the subject he knows least about is himself. Because of this, because in my opinion he has so much to hide, he invariably resorts to a game of hide-and-seek. But I have grown weary of the game. I have lived too long, come too far to indulge in this sort of nonsense with anyone. As far as I am concerned, if that means that our relationship has come to an end, then so be it.

Suddenly, I find myself staring at a particular group of trekkers approaching along the dusty road—five suntanned faces, half my age, walking next to their Sherpa guide. I have to look twice at the Sherpa's face before I realize that it belongs to my old friend Norbu, the man who outfitted the very first trek I ever organized in Nepal. He glances at me as he passes, but nothing registers on his face until I say, "Norbu!"

He halts, turns, looks in my direction. At first he does not recognize me. Then his face, a face that could have belonged to one of Genghis Khan's lieutenants, breaks into a smile and he says, "Richard!" Glancing at his clients, who have halted beside him, he says politely, "Please go ahead. You will find Pisang just down the road at the first street. Wait for me there. I will follow in a few minutes."

The young sunburned faces look ever so slightly annoyed at having their Sherpa waylaid at the very end of their trek, but they do not protest. Turning back to the road, the trekkers walk on. Norbu comes over to me, extends his hand, and says, "Two years, I think, since I see you. Too long."

"How have you been?"

"Working. Always working." He smiles. Then the smile vanishes and he says, "Mary left me, you know."

There is sadness in his voice. When I last saw him, he seemed very content with his Australian girl. The three of us shared a meal together one evening in Kathmandu. For a moment it seems odd that this confession should be the first thing he has chosen to say to me after two years. But that is the way of Sherpa people. Like their cousins the Tibetans, they speak from the heart.

"What happened?"

"She missed Australia—the big rock. She go back." He is silent for a moment. "And you? You have been leading?"

"Yes."

"Where?"

"India, Thailand, Indonesia, here."

"You are tired of the business?"

"Maybe. And you?"

"Sometimes I want to change. Sometimes I am tired of walking. But what else can I do?" He smiles. "A man cannot live without money." He glances down at the pack on the dirt floor next to me and says, "Trekking?"

"Yes."

"Alone?"

"Yes."

"You must beware of the tiger."

"What tiger?"

"Past two months tiger has killed thirteen people in valley between Naudanda and Dhampus."

"A tiger? Here? You sure?"

"Yes, a tiger."

If true, this strikes me as a very odd circumstance. I can easily imagine a rogue leopard wandering the hills, taking a goat or a donkey, or the occasional farmer or trekker, for a meal. But a *tiger?* It just doesn't seem possible.

"It has been seen?" I say. "It has stripes, not spots?"

"Yes, a tiger. Last week it kill an old grandma who live in a house all alone, not so far from Dhampus. During night tiger come, scratch at her door, and scratch and scratch, maybe all night long, grandma pushing back on the other side. But tiger too strong and he finally push in door. He kill her, carry her off. Two days later, they find some part of her body."

"What's a tiger doing here?"

"Nobody know. Come up from Chitwan, maybe."

"What's the government doing?"

"Shikari from Kathmandu is here. He try to bait it two nights ago near Sarankot. Tiger very clever and he stay away. He is renegade, man-eater. You camp at night by yourself, you must be careful."

"Always am."

"Specially careful, then. You hear about German boy?"

"What German boy?"

"Two weeks ago, German boy sleeping outside next to trail near Ghandrung—murdered."

"Murdered?"

"Someone smash his face with a rock, take his money. *Very* bad," he adds, shaking his head from side to side. "Nepal changing now very fast. So fast." He sits for a moment, then says, "Well, I must go. Clients waiting." Rising from his seat, he smiles and says, "You look tired. Maybe you need a rest."

"Maybe."

"You come to the office when you back in Kathmandu? We drink some beer."

"I look forward to it."

"All right," he says, again offering me his hand, which I shake. Then he gives a little wave of the hand and says, "See you."

I hate to see him go. I wish that he were coming with me. For some reason I realize that at this moment, I have no desire to be alone.

In the evening, just as the dying light has turned the snow-capped 22,000-foot peak of Machupuchare into a pyramid of warm pinkish gold, I am sitting in front of my tent in the field adjoining the lodge in the village of Dhampus. Dhampus, which offers one of the most scenic views to be found in all of Nepal, is the place where trekking groups headed into the Annapurnas from Pokhara usually spend their first night. But this evening there is no group and the field is deserted. The trail leading past the houses is empty, and the village is literally as quiet as a tomb.

The scenery is dramatic. Across the broad valley that faces me from the north, across tilled fields and a couple of ranges of rolling hills, a dark cloud begins its passage over the face of the great mountain—Machupuchare, the holy mountain. As I watch it, I have the overwhelming impression that I have never in my life been more alone.

I turn and look back to the hilltop behind me, which is lost in blackish descending cloud. The sky above me is darkening. The rain is on its way. The thought has no more passed through my mind than a drop splatters on my forehead.

After taking a final sip of tea, I empty the last of it onto the stubbly ground. I reach down and begin to untie the laces of my muddy shoes. By the time I am done, the rain has begun to fall.

Unzipping the mosquito-net flap, I slide my shoes inside. I slip through the net myself, twist around, and zip the flies shut behind me. As I do the world outside goes dark. Lightning flashes in the distance, followed by rolling thunder. I lie back on my sleeping bag, listening to the steady *tap tap tap* on the roof of my tent.

Another flash of lightning, an explosion of thunder. The temperature drops precipitously. I unzip my bag and crawl deep inside it. In the rising darkness, the rain begins to pound. Suddenly I picture the tiger, the man-eater, somewhere out there, shivering, soaked to the skin, lying in wait at the edge of some obscure trail, waiting for some careless child, some helpless old wood-gatherer. I find myself thinking of Billy, and of my informant, and it comes to me that in some odd way we are all renegades, caught in the grip of a darkness greater than ourselves.

On a bright warm afternoon two weeks later, I find myself standing in a grubby little office near the maidan in Kathmandu, passport in hand, waiting to check my mail. I hand the clerk my passport, and I am mildly surprised when, after checking the slot lettered I, he turns to me with an envelope that has my name printed neatly on the front. No stamps, no postmark. It is not a letter but a message. I rip off the end of the envelope and remove the single sheet of Yak and Yeti Hotel stationery. The message is a short one.

Dear Richard,

I am leaving this before going back to Delhi. I have been reconsidering our conversation vis-à-vis you seeing a tiger on foot. Perhaps I understand something now that I didn't understand before. It may be also that you need a lesson in matters that you do not understand yourself. If you will give me a call and come down to India, reluctant though I remain, I shall try to help you.

Sincerely,
K.

Twenty-five minutes later I am in a telephone booth at the post office. The thin-faced man behind the desk nods to me, signaling that the call has gone through. I pick up the receiver. For a moment there is only roaring white noise, littered with snippets of conversation from several crossed lines. Rising out of the chaos, my informant's voice says, "Richard? Is that you?"

"Yes."

"You got my message? Are you . . ." The voice fades.

"Fine. Yes, I'm fine."

". . . relieved . . . changed my mind . . . can't do this alone . . . dangerous . . . come down . . . help you . . . I know a place."

"I can barely make out what you are saying. You want me to come down to India?"

"Bharatpur . . ."

"Bharatpur?"

"Yes."

"All right."

"Can you hear me?"

"Bharatpur. Next Friday."

"Hello? I can't . . . Hello? Can you hear me? Are you there? Are you—"

And in that instant comes a roar like a ton of gravel tumbling down a chute. The line goes dead.

Thirty-six

ON A CHILL GRAY MORNING four days later, in a world blanketed and steeped in mist, I am sitting at the foot of a shisham tree on the shore of a distant levee in Keoladeo National Park, completely alone, watching three Siberian cranes feeding in shallow water not twenty yards from where I sit. Nearly five feet tall entirely white except for their blood-red faces, these birds possess an angular elegance and beauty that defies any attempt at description. Having fled the winter barrenness of their breeding grounds in the Russian tundra and migrated down through the high passes of the Himalaya, they seem to me at this moment unearthly beings, inhabiting that liminal space where mist meets water in a boundless confusion. Aquatic ghosts. Perfect for this place.

This evening, when my informant arrives, I shall have other things to think about, but for now I am content to amuse myself with the thought that Bharatpur, like almost everything in India, is the product of some fundamental illusion. If peace exists here now, it is a peace hard won. I know that because I am a student of its history, a history so bizarre, so bound up in madness, murder, and intrigue, that Dostoevski or Faulkner would have been at pains to invent it.

What I know of it is this: In the last decade of the nineteenth century, possibly after acceding to the throne in 1893, Ram Singh, jat maharaja of Bharatpur, paid a visit to England. It seems likely that he was on his best behavior there and offered little evidence of the sudden shifts of mood, the violent rages, that would bring his reign to a sordid conclusion some seven years later. Feted wherever he went according to his princely rank, he was as a matter of course drawn into the sporting life of the aristocracy, a milieu then dominated in no uncertain terms by the tastes and passions of Queen Victoria's son, His Royal Highness the Prince of Wales. The prince was a renowned sporting man, and it was his affection for one sport in particular—wing-shooting—that created the vogue among gentlemen for striking out into the countryside dressed in tweed jacket, waistcoat, and knee breeches, accompanied by a well-trained cohort of dogs, in pursuit of grouse, partridge, or pheasant. It is said that the young maharaja was so impressed with the stylish spectacle of this sport that he decided that he would recreate this very English world back home in the midst of the semiarid Rajasthan countryside. The idea appealed to his naturally grandiose nature. It was a project truly fit for a prince.

Returning to India, he immediately began to develop and improve a system already in place, built in part by order of his father, to control the floodwaters of the Chambal River. Laying out a system of dikes, some of them hundreds of yards long, he enclosed huge rectangular spaces. The work proceeded very slowly, all of it being performed by hand, there being no mechanical means to achieve it.

As the years passed and the great rectilinear forms took shape, the essential nature of their creator became increasingly evident. There were extended bouts of sleeplessness, nervous attacks, horrible dreams, which left Ram Singh nearly paralyzed. To those nearest him, it was obvious that somewhere deep inside him, a black reservoir of insanity was insecurely blocked up. Inevitably, perhaps, the dam burst, carrying everything before it. Confronted with a misbehaving servant, Ram Singh lashed out. When the spasm had passed, the servant lay sprawled, quite dead, at his feet.

In June of the year 1900, just seven months before his idol, the Prince of Wales, acceded to the British throne as Edward VII, Ram Singh was stripped of his powers by order of Lord Curzon, viceroy of India, and locked away so that he might live the madness of his days out of the sight of ordinary men. Having deposed him, Curzon decreed that the maharaja's son, Kishan, then less than a year old, would, on reaching his majority, succeed his father. Curzon further instructed that until that time, the child's mother, acting under the guidance of an English dewan—a representative of the paramount power in Delhi—would guide the affairs of the state of Bharatpur.

Under the benevolent eye of the European dewan, the massive earthworks were completed the following year and the waters of the Chambal diverted into them. Trees were planted to provide cover, and a wildfowler's paradise was born. Curzon himself came to inaugurate it.

In his early years, the young heir apparent was educated in the palace by an English tutor. But in 1908 the decision was made to send him to England, where two years later, as fate would have it, he was invited to take part in the funeral services of King Edward, who had reigned a mere nine years. Returning to India at the end of that year, the young prince was enrolled at Mayo College in Ajmer ("the Eton of India," whose coat of arms had been drawn up by Rudyard Kipling's father) to continue his education. Though virtually no written testimony survives by which to judge the young prince's personality at the time, it seems likely that even then he must have exhibited certain traits, no doubt inherited from his father—the sudden bursts of energy and violent shifts of mood that observers in later years would find so characteristic of him.

No sooner had the boy reached puberty than, following a custom that extended back to time immemorial, renowned astrologers were consulted to determine the most propitious moment for a marriage. That moment having been decided, the young prince was wed to the sister of the maharaja of Faridkot in 1913, when he was thirteen years old. Among common people and royalty alike, child marriages were not at all uncommon in those days. Actual cohabitation was often delayed for a number of years; such was the case with the young Kishan and his bride. Directly after the wedding ceremony, he was taken back to England to pursue his education at Wellington College. She, naturally, stayed at home.

At the outbreak of hostilities in July 1914, the young prince, no doubt compelled by childish ambitions of gaining glory on the field of battle, fighting for the British as fervently as his ancestors had fought against them, was eager to volunteer. But his age and station were against him, and his appeal fell on deaf ears. In lieu of actual service, he took part in forming a fighting unit known as the Bharatpur Service Infantry, members of which would eventually see service in German East Africa, Palestine, and elsewhere.

So transported was the prince by patriotism and jingoistic fervor, he insisted on returning to India, where he might personally supervise recruiting operations. And his good works in support of the war effort did not go unnoticed. He was so highly regarded by officials of the paramount power that at the cessation of hostilities he was invested almost immediately as the new maharaja of Bharatpur, with full authority to guide the destinies of his half-million subjects.

In the beginning, officials of His Majesty's Government

seem to have felt confident that the young ruler possessed in good measure the virtues they believed themselves to embody—wisdom, a sense of justice, prudence—and there cannot be the slightest doubt that in those early years the young maharaja did everything he could to live up to their expectations. But there was a problem. In his eyes, with the war and its hum of excitement having come to an end, the future revealed itself as a boundlessly flat and featureless plain, a barren stage on which he would be obliged to pursue a meaningless round of formal inanities and day-to-day rituals which would inevitably lead to madness and death. Kishan, goaded by the image of his father, disgraced and banished into his own interior castle, accepted the imperative of keeping his mind occupied, of keeping himself amused at all costs, lest the dark waters roll over him.

Accordingly, he began to fill up his calendar for months in advance. Many hours each day were spent engaging in sports appropriate to his princely station. He entertained lavishly. At Simla, the hill town to which the government resorted in the hot summer season, invitations to the young maharaja's "polo gymkhana teas" became highly sought-after. At home at Bharatpur, the annual hunt at the great reserve his father had created soon became known far and wide as a gloriously elaborate social occasion, built round the best waterfowling in Asia. Within a very short time the hunts at Bharatpur achieved legendary status, and the general lust among the representatives of the paramount power for an invitation to shoot there soon became acute.

It was in fact a hunter's paradise. The geometrical design of the reserve made it possible for teams of beaters to drive great hordes of geese and ducks from one side of it to the other, forcing the birds past the best butts, or shooting stations, manned invariably by His Highness's most highly esteemed guests. Many a colonial administrator went to his grave believing that for a day or two at least, he had lived the life of a great sportsman. Other, more sensitive souls went on record later on as saying how disgusted they were by the piles of putrefying feathered flesh, hauled off by the wagonload.

The lavish banquets that accompanied these slaughters were from the beginning marked by the sort of taste and attention to detail that gave Kishan a reputation for possessing that elusive quality known as style. Though advised that if he continued on this course his state would soon be bankrupt, he brushed all quibbles aside. He was, after all, maharaja, the Great Raja. Was it not his right by birth to do as he wished?

Thereafter Kishan's expenditures assumed a dreamlike quality of extravagance. One year, having developed a sudden passion for Rolls-Royce automobiles, he promptly ordered six, with specially designed leather interiors, which in cow-worshipping India was sure to provoke a scandal. So pleased was he with the cars on their arrival that he proclaimed that henceforth every vehicle in royal service, whether delivery van or limousine, had to be a Rolls. In that same year he purchased six of the best Arab ponies and fitted them out with the entire stock of tack on hand at the Army and Navy Stores.

Soon, as though Kishan had adopted William Blake's famous dictum "Sooner murder an infant in its cradle than nurse unacted desires" as a personal motto, no whim went unappeased. He imported lions from Africa and jaguars from South America to release in his forests, so that he could hunt them. He ordered for his sole use an expensive canoe powered by batteries, so that he could stalk the waterfowl of his reserve in silence. He eventually became the proud possessor of the finest collection of Purdy shotguns in India. He kept a jazz band on permanent retainer. And why should he not? Was he not himself a great prince?

When the treasury was depleted, Kishan soon found himself in the company of persons he had never had dealings with before: professional moneylenders. And he must have found their company congenial, in the beginning at least. He simply signed the notes they handed him, and the next day the money arrived. Unfortunately, since the notes were scaled at an enormous rate of interest, the money was often spent even before it arrived. But he didn't care. Why should he? He was king.

At last his advisers confronted him with the distressing news that his state had, for all practical intents and purposes, ceased to exist. The great system of dikes and levees had fallen into a state of disrepair and disastrous floods had occurred, resulting in great loss of human life and property. The once renowned shooting reserve was a wreck; the roads of the kingdom were in such a poor state as to be nearly unusable. Worst of all, someone had leaked information to the paramount power in Delhi that monies intended for flood relief had gone to the maharaja's creditors, who threatened to expose his maniacal extravagance if he failed to satisfy them.

Kishan listened patiently to his advisers, then sacked them all, replacing them with men who would not insult his intelligence and his office with this endless barrage of depressing news. His new appointments were, however, men of a different class. One of them, a certain Raja Kishan, he seems to have embraced almost as a brother, as though he had discovered right under his nose a monstrously wicked personification of his own darkest self. Raja Kishan, a bugler in the state forces, became his chief of staff.

In the aftermath of the flood-relief money scandal, the viceroy became convinced that a British dewan must be installed to regularize the ongoing disaster at Bharatpur. The maharaja, trapped in his hall of mirrors, finally realized how much was at stake and pleaded with government officials to give him a chance to mend his ways. The paramount power, having no interest in provoking a scandal and knowing full well that anything revealed about the maharaja's behavior would rebound on them, was at the point of agreeing when fate ruled otherwise.

In May 1927 the maharaja's chief of staff, Raja Kishan, was arrested for homicide. In the warrant he was accused of murdering a female acquaintance, burning her corpse, and dumping the remains down an abandoned well. The maharaja, not doubting that Raja Kishan had it in his power to do him great damage, instigated, or at least colluded, in a cover-up. During his short tenure as chief of staff, however, Raja Kishan had made many enemies, and his crimes were too outrageous to remain long concealed. Eventually he was found guilty not of murder, a crime for which he would undoubtedly have been hanged, but of a number of lesser offenses—extortion, kidnapping, rape, and buggery—for which he received a sentence of seven years.

This was precisely the sort of affair the paramount power had worked so assiduously to avoid, and once everything was out in the open, the viceroy could see no alternative but to act decisively. In an extraordinary measure, he banished the maharaja from his own kingdom, ordering him to reside at least one hundred miles from its borders. He furthermore ordered that the maharaja, under pain of prosecution, must take no part whatsoever in the internal affairs of the Bharatpur state. The maharaja and his wife were removed to Delhi, where six months later, no doubt with the knowledge that the curse of his father's blood had come full circle, he died, broken and embittered. He was twenty-nine years old.

Just before sunset, I am sitting at a table on the terrace at the back of the lodge when my informant arrives. He pauses at the door, sees me, walks over. Looking exhausted, he neither smiles nor extends his hand but simply stops, looks directly at me, and says, as though he were continuing a conversation left off five minutes ago, "I only hope I am doing the right thing. Are you ready to go?"

"Now?"

"Joseph is waiting in the car outside. It's a long drive. We'd better get started."

Thirty-seven

It isn't a dream.

Standing at the edge of the dark wood, I can see her in a clearing not far off. Silhouetted against silvery light, her hair flowing to the ground, she belongs to this place. But I know that she will not guide me. Then I am running, out of breath, trying to escape the thing that is only a few steps behind me. I glance over my shoulder. My foot catches on an upturned root, and I fall . . . Rising, the thing explodes on my back, blasting the breath out of me. I strike the ground, my face pressed into soft earth, and twist away. Fangs sink into my neck, holding me. I try to scream. My mouth is full of blood. No one can help me now. Darkness rises and—

I wake with a start, face pressed to the chill window glass. Drawing myself up in my seat, wiping my face with the palm of my hand, I gaze out into the rising light. I look at my watch. Almost seven. I have been asleep since just before midnight, when we stopped so that I could relieve myself at the side of the road.

I turn and look at my informant. Gazing out the window on his side, he has not noticed that I am awake. I can see that he has not slept. He said very little after picking me up last night, confining his comments to absolute essentials. There is so much now that I would like to speak to him about. But everything has shifted. The old contract, whatever it was in his eyes, has been ruptured. Whatever simple amity existed between us has been lost. It is I who have upset the balance of it, blasted it apart. None of this has been necessary, perhaps. Now it is too late to make amends.

Gaining speed as we head down a small incline, the car crosses a bridge over a dry streambed. Joseph removes his foot from the accelerator, slows the car to a crawl. Beyond a large spreading tree resembling a European oak, he turns right onto a narrow dirt track. The track descends through light woodland, reducing the sun to a flashing blur through the trees. We cross another bridge, and the track begins to climb through denser forest.

We follow the winding track for about ten minutes, until at last we enter a clearing, where it veers sharply left past a couple of ill-maintained whitewashed bungalows lost in cool shadow. Joseph brings the car to a halt in front of one of them, switches off the ignition. Reaching down, he opens his door and steps out. He opens the door of my informant, who gets out and stands next to him, whispering.

The screen door of the bungalow swings open. An Indian dressed in a dhoti and thin sandals, with a gray blanket thrown over his shoulders, steps out, smiling. He comes forward to greet my informant. They shake hands and stand there speaking Hindi, apparently discussing our accommodations. After a few moments, my informant nods and walks to the back door of the car, on the side where I am sitting. He opens it, bends over, and looks inside.

"You will be staying in the bungalow across the way," he

says. "The manager says the rooms are ready. Can you come?"

"Sure."

I half notice that a new person has appeared and is standing just outside. I step out, glancing briefly at this Indian boy as I do. But my eye has recorded something, and I look back instantly. The boy does not have a face. Or rather, he possesses half a face. Although one side of it is completely normal, the other looks as though the skin has run like hot wax. The eye on that side is nothing more than a slit in which a dull pearl has been lodged, the ear but a tattered shred.

The boy stands mutely staring. I hear myself say, with that species of false cheer that sometimes comes in the face of horror, "Good morning."

He neither speaks nor moves. I hear Joseph opening the trunk of the car, and I turn to watch. As I do, the boy takes two steps toward the trunk. Joseph throws him a look, but says nothing as he removes the bags. The man wrapped in the blanket glances at the boy, speaks quietly in Hindi, and points to the bags.

Turning to me, my informant says, "Follow the boy. He will take your bags to your room."

The man in the blanket speaks to the boy once more. The boy responds by walking over to my bags and picking them up. Then, without a word, he heads toward the bungalow across the way. Feeling that something else needs to be said, I hesitate for a moment. But I know it is no use.

Five minutes later, the boy, having placed my bags in the simple room, has gone next door to the room of my informant. I step out onto the porch just in time to see him slip through the screened door and head off across the compound. My informant, standing in the doorway, watches him go.

"What happened to his face?" I ask.

My informant replies, "Six years ago he was attacked by a tiger. No one believed that he would survive." He watches the boy disappear around the corner of one of the bungalows. "But he did survive. His name is Ram. He is an orphan. The man who greeted us just now, the manager, is his uncle."

"He seems shell-shocked. Does he talk?"

My informant regards me in what seems a chastising way and says, "Only when he has something to say."

Thirty-eight

There have been few times in my life when I have felt such sadness, such utter emptiness. For the past two days, K and I have spent almost every waking moment in the forest, walking the trails and the dry streambeds, waiting at the water holes for an animal that now seems to me not real at all but more a product of our imaginations. In this time I have come to see K in a new light, a light that has produced such an alteration in my perception of him as to beggar the imagination. In this place, his persona, the various masks, have fallen away. No, I am wrong about that. A shell remains, a thin veneer, which perhaps no one has ever been allowed to penetrate.

There is in him a sort of anger and desperation. But the anger is not directed toward me. In truth, I am unable to say at whom or at what it is directed. For most of the past two days he has seemed caught up in a kind of frenzy. This morning I had the strangest sensation, a sensation that lasted for several minutes, that he had somehow ceased to be entirely human, and that all that remained was an emptiness.

He spoke again of Anil, his childhood friend. Today, just after noon, as we were sitting in a hide overlooking a nearly dry stream, he told me a story about how, as boys, they had fought. It was he who had started the fight, out of some jealousy he can no longer remember. Though Anil was bigger, it was he who gave Anil a bloody nose. An unexceptional story, just the story of two friends fighting. But it made his eyes brim with tears. One mask at least remains.

We walked nearly all afternoon.

At one point K stopped dead still at an open place in the forest and told me that at that very moment a tiger was staring at us. He looked but saw nothing, and a moment later told me that the tiger was gone. I did not know whether I should believe him, but five minutes later, on the muddy bank of a trickling stream, we found her tracks. "I know this cat," he said. "I know her."

Thirty-nine

ALMOST SUNSET. From where I am sitting, the red-orange blot of the sun looms beyond the black tangle of trees at the top of the ridge. The light has fled, and with it the warmth. To the back of us a nearly full moon shines down on this canyon, these rocks—a world that seems as dead as any I have ever known. Since just past midday we have sat here in the mouth of this rock shelter, next to this stream, maintaining a silent vigil. In the silence of those hours, feeling at times as though I were turning to stone myself, I have begun to understand the mistakes I have made. This canyon, this silence, belong to my companion, belong to his private universe. I am an intruder here.

Because I know this, I am no longer in the least curious about the pugmark we discovered this morning on the muddy border of the small pool twenty yards downstream from where we sit. I have no confidence whatsoever that the tigress who left it there early this morning will return this evening to drink. All I want now is to leave this place and never look back.

From somewhere in the distance comes the chatter of a treepie. Ten feet in front of me, the muscles of my informant's back stiffen at the sound. He looks left, downstream, all his senses directed toward it. Then he turns and looks over his shoulder at me.

Because I am dazed, because my concentration has fled, a long moment passes before it comes to me what he is attempting to communicate: that the chatter of the treepie may mean that the tigress has returned to the pool. An involuntary shiver passes over me. I do not like the feel of any of this. Now it is too late to turn back.

With a nod he beckons me to join him. I do so, and it is only after I have stepped around the boulder that has separated us and am standing next to him that he whispers, "Whatever happens, stay behind me. Say nothing."

I nod, wondering if he has noticed that I am trembling, that the tightness in my chest has left me short of breath. If he has, he gives no indication of it. He turns away, steps down silently onto the flat shelf of rock over which flows a trickle of water, steps across it onto another flat rock, then moves down onto the stream's sandy bank.

Moving slowly, eyes fixed on the ever-broadening prospect of the descending stream, he moves ahead, each step measured with utmost care. My eyes searching every detail of the shadows in the bluing light, I follow. Beyond a large light-gray boulder, the stream turns sharply to the left. The left bank here is a wilderness of rock. The right bank is sandy, the forest vegetation extending almost to the edge of the water. Not more than a few yards ahead, around the bend, is the place where we discovered the pugmark.

He halts, gazes downstream, waits, his eyes scanning the vegetated bank. He takes another step, enlarging his view, and stands waiting. The pool, lost in shadow, is a still, bright mirror in the dying light. A strip of sand not more than a yard wide and ten yards long separates us from it. The forest beyond the pool is a wall of depths and shadows.

Somewhere off in the woods the treepie chatters. My informant turns his head, following the sound. He stands listening, feeling the silence. He takes a step. As he does, a minute movement in the darkness of the trees attracts my attention. I stare. Less than fifty feet away, I see the tigress.

Her face is half concealed behind a small shrubby tree. Before I can move, before I can speak, I know that she is running, the orange of her coat streaking through the shadows, coming straight at us. My body tenses. My lips part to shout.

At the water's edge, twenty feet in front of us, she stops and opens her mouth in a roar so loud I feel the pressure of it in my chest. Then I know that it is the hand of my informant, pushing me back. Twisting her head, the tigress opens her mouth again, releases another roar. Once again the pressure pushes me back. Moving into the water, she takes a step toward us. Roars. Then, as though calculating whether she must kill us or flee, she hesitates, glances across the stream. In a single bound she crosses it, vanishing into the rocks and dead brush.

Then silence.

My informant stands staring after her, trembling, his hand on my chest. He turns to face me. His eyes are wide; his face is covered with beads of sweat. His lips move as though to speak. But he cannot find the words. Saying nothing, he turns and heads back up the gully, stepping quickly from one flat rock to another, moving as fast as he can, running almost, as though his only thought is to escape the rising darkness.

Forty

A GLOW OF LAMPLIGHT, emanating from the window of his room. A pale yellow parallelogram on the dark porch floor. As I step up onto it, I gaze through the screen. My informant is seated on the edge of the bed, elbows planted on his knees, face in his hands. I raise my hand to knock. Then I don't. I open the screen door and step inside.

"Are you all right?"

Lifting his head, he looks up at me and asks, "Are you satisfied now? Have you seen what you needed to see?"

It is then that, the truth, born of suspicions harbored a very long time, comes tumbling from somewhere deep inside me. "You killed him, didn't you?"

He stares. His mouth works, as though to offer a denial. But then the expression softens and he answers quietly, "I did not kill him. But I let him die."

"You don't ha—"

"I loved him, you see. I loved him more than I have ever loved anyone. He knew so much, had read so much—I so wanted to impress him. I wanted him to love me in turn. But hunting was the only thing I knew. He cared nothing for it. He had an abhorrence of violence. But I would not let it go. Week after week, month after month, I begged him to come with me, until at last he consented . . ."

He pauses for a moment, looking into the darkness, then continues. "It was late afternoon. I had shot a chital the day before and left it tied to a stake in the ground, hoping that it would attract the tigress who lived in the area. I had known about the tigress for some time, and hunter that I was, I wanted to kill her. Perhaps because it was still daylight, it never crossed my mind that the tigress would be waiting for us that afternoon. But she was. She had found the chital after all. When she charged, she came up silently behind us.

"I knew nothing of it until Anil screamed. I whirled around and stared. The tigress had grasped him about the waist and was dragging him off. The horror that I felt at that moment—I can still feel it now. I raised my rifle, leveled it at her, and fired. But the shot went wide. And it was just then that Anil shouted my name and cried, "Oh, help me! God, please help me!" I yanked the bolt back, ejecting the spent cartridge, shoved the next cartridge home, but too fast. The cartridge jammed. I yanked at the bolt, pried at the cartridge with my fingernails—but it was no good. There was nothing I could do. Anil screamed, "Oh God, help me! Mommy! Help me!" I froze. I stood there watching as the tigress carried him off. I began to tremble violently. He screamed . . . I couldn't stand it. The rifle dropped to the ground. I clapped my hands over my ears. Then, because I did not want to die, I ran . . . I could hear him calling out my name . . . But I was so afraid. Nothing could have stopped me."

I stare at him, and I have the sickening sense that all his defenses have been stripped away, that now he is nothing more than the child he was then. Aware of a sudden surge of tenderness toward him, I want to walk over to him, put my arm around him, comfort him. But I know that he would not welcome it.

He gazes toward the door. "It was hours before I got back to camp. By that time everyone was frantic. They crowded around me, begging for news of Anil. His parents were there. I looked into their eyes and told them that we had been attacked by a tiger, that I had shot at it and missed, that the tiger had carried him off. I shall never forget the look of horror on their faces. Some of the men spoke of following up the tiger, then and there. But it was agreed that it was too dangerous, that other lives would be placed in jeopardy, that come what may, we must wait until dawn . . .

"That night was the longest of my life. I spent every second of it trying to convince myself that Anil could not be dead, that by some miracle he had escaped, that we would find him alive. Just after first light the next morning, at the place where I had staked out the chital, at the place where he had been attacked, we found the blood—so much blood—a piece of his shirt . . . An hour later, two of the men came upon the tigress and shot at her, chasing her off. There, where she had been standing guard, they found all that remained of Anil."

My informant seems at the end of his strength. I see no reason now that this should continue. But I know that he needs to speak.

"After the cremation," he continues, "I felt dead, as though all the life had drained out of me. But then a kind of anger welled up inside me. I began to convince myself that it was not I who was at fault but the tigress. The tigress was evil. She must be destroyed. Several days passed. My parents begged me to return to Delhi, but I refused. As soon as I was allowed to be by myself, I sneaked away and purchased a bullock from a local farmer. That very afternoon, I led it into the forest to the spot where the tiger had attacked Anil

—all this without my parents' knowledge. I built the simplest of tree machans, and then for six nights I left the house in secret after dark and sat up in the machan, waiting. On the seventh, a night of the full moon, she came, cautiously, quartering the ground in her approach until she was close enough to charge. As I stared down the barrel at her, I cursed her and pulled the trigger. The shot blew away the back of her skull."

My informant looks at me with a questioning gaze. "Perhaps you will not understand what I did next. I climbed down from the machan and in a pool of moonlight I knelt beside her. With my knife, I found a point between her legs and thrust in the blade. I opened her belly. The warm guts and blood came flowing out. If you had asked me at that moment what I was doing, I would not have been able to tell you. But somewhere inside myself, I did know. I was looking for him."

He stares at me with an absolutely blank expression. "Inside her were two fetuses, perfectly formed, each wrapped in a transparent membrane—two sleeping creatures that would never wake. Soaking my hands and arms with black blood, I laid them on the ground next to her. For a long time I just knelt there, rocking back and forth, staring down at them in the moonlight, humming a tune I had learned as a child. Then, from somewhere far away, out of the darkness, I heard a terrible sound. I looked all around me. Then I knew it was coming from inside myself. It welled up—a black scream bursting out of me, flowing over me, over everything, filling the world, drowning me . . . drowning me in darkness.

"It was two days before they found me, wandering in the forest. I was nearly naked. My hands and forearms were rubbed raw from trying to remove the blood. Those who found me I recognized, but vaguely. They seemed no more substantial than dim shadows from another world. You see, by that time I was quite mad."

He stares at me for a very long moment. Then he says, with what seems to me profound bitterness, "If the tiger had killed you today, it would have meant nothing."

I hesitate a moment. "I know."

For several seconds he sits staring. Then, reaching up and touching his forehead in a gesture of utmost weariness, he says, "Now, if you wouldn't mind, I'm very tired. I think I'd like to be alone. We have a long drive back to Delhi tomorrow morning."

Forty-one

IN THE SILVERY PREDAWN LIGHT I pull the door closed behind me. I stand for a moment, breathing in chill air, staring into a world lost in mist. Moving slowly, choosing each step with great care, I cross the veranda, listening to the soft creak of the floorboards under my feet. I step down onto the soft ground and wait and listen, senses trained for any sound or movement. But there is nothing. No one is awake. Without thinking, I turn and cross the open space between the two buildings, then step onto the road that leads into the forest.

The fog is so dense I can see no more than forty or fifty feet. I walk quickly, confidently, my footfall light on the spongy earth, the in-and-out of my breath measured and modulated by the rhythm of my steps. Within a minute the sides of the road have closed in, leaving the world of the lodge behind. There is nothing in the world now except these trees, this road, myself. Everything is just as it should be. Everything is perfect.

The world is silent and still and I am aware of how the moisture of the air has settled over everything, permeating each leaf, each branch, each blade of grass. I feel the cold invading the loose folds of my clothes, as if the dampness, the forest itself, were taking my measure, becoming part of me. I would not resist it. I would sink into this place and remain here forever. I would lose myself in it and never look back.

The road descends, gently at first, then somewhat more steeply through the trees. It crosses a dry streambed littered with smooth round stones. Beside the streambed is a large spreading tree unlike any around it, the tree that marks where the trail begins. I stop beside the tree and look up through its branches, listening to the perfect silence and stillness.

The trail leads off through a patch of undergrowth to a wall of forest. I step onto it and begin to walk. It is little used and narrow, with the branches of ferns and shrubs, heavy with moisture, reaching across it. I push them aside with a hand, feel the chill wetness spattering my trouser leg, soaking instantly through the fabric. But it makes no difference.

The trail begins to climb through the mist and the trees, the dense undergrowth making it impossible to see more than ten feet in any direction. I could come across anything now. I could meet a tiger or a bear. I would not see it until it was directly in front of me. But somehow I know that I won't. I move quickly, silently, pushing the branches aside.

The trail leads down steeply, over rocks and through dense undergrowth, then crosses a glade of ferns before rising slightly at the edge of the trickling stream that feeds into the gorge. I stand for a moment looking down the twisting trail, staring into the stillness, feeling it. I almost step onto it. Then I don't. I turn to the right a little and look downhill, through the undergrowth, where there is no trail. Then I head through the underbrush, skirting the hill, moving as quietly as I can, the only sounds those of my steps on the loose soil, of the wet branches brushing my trousers.

Five minutes later I turn and look back up the hill. The top of it is no longer visible, and I have the odd sensation that I am on an island, floating in a misty void. All my bearings have been left behind. I am lost and it makes no difference at all. I turn and continue down the hill at an angle, toward a sort of clearing where the terrain eases down to a quiet stream, which feeds into the gully where there are several large gray boulders, thickly upholstered with moss. I make my way over to one of them. Looking in every direction, I listen. No sound or movement. I turn and find a flat place next to the boulder and sit.

As I watch, a gash appears in the clouds and the world takes on an almost hallucinatory lightness, brilliant azure beyond the gray. A brief shower of sunlight. Then darkness. Then more sunlight. Light and warmth settle over me and settle into my clothes. Everything in the world is bright and dripping and jewel-like.

Somewhere downstream, a bird sings. It sings once and goes silent. I turn and look. Forty feet away, where the stream turns right at a boulder, a bright bird with an orange breast sits on a branch just above the water. Cocking its head, it says *tick tick tick*.

It flits off its perch and I follow it with my eye. It is then that I see the tigress.

She stands perfectly still, staring directly at me, no more than twenty yards away. Mouth open, eyes fixed, tail slightly elevated, she stares. Breath flooding out of me, I force myself to return her gaze. Looking to the right, as though to determine that I am alone, she seems to ponder for a moment what she must do. She makes her decision. With no warning, she leaps across the stream and vanishes into the undergrowth. A brief rustling. A shivering of leaves. Then silence.

□ □ □

By the time I get back to the lodge, the sky is almost entirely clear and the day has turned warm. I am not sure what I am feeling. Perhaps it is only that curious flatness that always seems to come when a wish has been fulfilled. Although I have seen the tigress on her own terms, that fact seems utterly irrelevant.

When I step off the trail into the clearing, the first thing I notice is that the space where the car was is empty. The whole compound is silent. On the porch just outside my room, the boy with half a face is sitting in the shade, dangling his feet in the dust. He knows I am there, but he does not look up until I am standing just in front of him.

"Where is everyone?"

"Everybody go."

"Where?"

"Away."

"When will they come back?"

"They not come back."

"Did anyone leave a message for me?"

"No message." A smile twists across the side of his face that looks human, the side that has not melted away. He adds, "Everybody go. Only I stay. Only me. Everybody gone. I stay here. All alone now. All alone." Then looking up at me, he laughs, the shape and sound of it the oddest thing I have ever seen. "Mebbe you dead man too. Mebbe you dead now. Mebbe so. Mebbe so . . ."

Epilogue

THE PLACE DES VOSGES is one of the most distinctive and venerable landmarks of Paris. Located in one of the few quarters of the city that have preserved something of their pre-revolutionary character, the handsome steep-gabled, slate-roofed seventeenth-century houses that surround it are a visual delight, there being few examples of architecture anywhere so quietly self-assured and at the same time so eager to please.

A public park occupies the center of the square. Bordered by neat rows of topiary lindens, its center is dominated by a grove of vaulting chestnuts whose leaves in high summer almost, but not quite, obscure an equestrian statue of Louis XIII. On fine days the park is invariably crowded with baby carriages, young children and the nannies who attend them. Almost every afternoon, in all but the most inclement weather, I bring my son, Ben, here in his carriage. In this feminine and infantile world, I am often the only man—a fact that has taken some getting used to. The Place des Vosges, with its sandboxes, slides, and babbling infants, is a long way from the forest.

My life has changed. And I have changed. I can speak now, and with some authority, on such subjects as diaper rash, breastfeeding versus bottle feeding, the emotional life of the one-year-old, and other arcane matters of equal weight. I shop. I feed my child, change his diapers, often rock him to sleep in my arms. And that is simply as it should be.

This particular morning is a little unusual. It is early autumn, the beginning of the season when the skies of Paris can remain gray for weeks at a time. In the last hour the sky has become entirely overcast. Off to the west, rolling black clouds are threatening rain. Because of the weather, the park is nearly empty.

I am sitting on a bench next to the baby carriage where Ben lies sleeping. For the past few minutes, I have been thinking about my journey, and my reasons for doing so are perhaps more compelling than usual. Today, after many long months, the time has come to end my recounting of it.

What I have come to see is that a million years ago, for reasons we will most likely never understand, our time came around. In the history of our planet there was a time for trilobites, a time for dinosaurs. Finally there came a time for us. From the rudest possible beginnings on the plains of Africa, we became the undisputed masters of this planet. With patience and method, we harnessed its latent sources of energy, altered the course of mighty rivers, emptied seas, flattened forests. Most magically of all, in imitation of the birds, we found a way to leave behind the constricting bonds of the earth itself. It would be foolish not to acknowledge the fact that we, as a species, have much to be proud of.

But all this success has come at a price. Without knowing it, we have been living on credit for quite some time. At the end of the millennium, at the beginning of a new era, we find ourselves near the end of a process that will, within the next couple of decades, result in the wholesale destruction of the natural world as it has always existed. The death of the tiger is but a single example of the terrible drama that is about to unfold.

Though it may be hard to accept, the complex series of developments that will lead to the tiger's extinction in the wild within the next ten to fifteen years has already begun. Since 1990, nearly half the surviving tigers in Siberia have been slaughtered, poached for their body parts, and sold to Chinese merchants who turn virtually every square inch of the tiger carcass into "medicines" that can be bought over the counter in Chinatowns in cities the world over. A compelling fund of evidence now suggests that most of the tigers killed in the wilds of Asia eventually end up in Chinese hands. Though it may seem like science fiction, the Chinese lust for tiger parts is so acute that with the extinction of wild tigers now in view, farms designed to raise tigers for slaughter are already operating in Taiwan. The discovery of such farms on the Chinese mainland itself would come as a surprise to no one.

Elsewhere in east Asia the outlook for the tiger is just as bleak. Thailand, Malaysia, and Indonesia, reaping enormous profits while ignoring pleas from concerned conservationists the world over, continue their genocidal war against the world's oldest forests. Openly supported by corporations and financial institutions in Japan, Taiwan, Singapore, Europe, and the United States, Asia's new economic powerhouses have the stated aim of destroying within the next decade all but token fragments of the forests under their control—a goal that now seems easily within their reach.

Nowhere in Asia, however, has the precipitous decline of the tiger been more striking than in India, a country that just a few years ago was considered by many the tiger's last, best refuge. An apathetic government in thrall to the new capitalist orthodoxy, which tolerates corruption at the highest levels, has essentially abandoned the country's parks and refuges to the winds of fate. Because of this, the ultimate destruction of the Indian tiger is now entering its final stages.

In 1992 over half the tigers found in Bandhavgarh National Park and Ranthambor National Park—scores of tigers in all—fell to poachers. In that same year, tiger-poaching bandits overran Manas National Park in Assam state, killing not only an unknown number of tigers but several guards. Most horribly perhaps, in that same crucial year, poachers working in Nagarhole National Park, in the south of India, killed scores of tigers and other animals, burned down the park headquarters, and skinned a warden alive. Since that time there have been other depredations, other deaths.

Having learned all this, one might be tempted to say that this is the end, not only for the tiger but for the natural world of Asia as a whole. Ironically, this does not need to be the case. If the present conservation system is not working, then it ought to be replaced. If the system of *national* parks has not proved efficient in preserving Asia's natural heritage, then a system of *international* parks, paid for entirely by the wealthier nations, must now be instituted. Such a system would create employment on a relatively large scale, and the parks themselves would become objects of pride, not only for the host country but for the world at large, guaranteeing that what remains of earth's natural patrimony is preserved for posterity. Such a system would not be a cure-all, of course. But it would be a brilliant beginning.

In the distance I hear a peal of thunder. Over the rooftops to the west, the sky has grown darker. At the same moment, I am aware that someone is walking toward me across the park. I look up and recognize Christina. She glances to her right at the sky as she approaches, then back at me, and says, "I think you're going to get wet."

"I've been watching it come."

"How long has he been asleep?" she says, looking down at her son.

"Nearly an hour."

"Are you ready for a cup of coffee?"

"Pretty much."

"Did you finish it up?" she asks, looking down at my notebook.

"Almost."

"There are some things we need at the store. Want to wait for me here?"

"Sure."

"And if the rain starts?"

"Then we'll duck under the arcade."

"Okay. I'll see you in a few minutes, then."

Leaning over, she gives me a peck on the cheek, then turns and walks off. I look back at the page I was working on before she came and smile. I see that I have broken the rules. Stories do have rules, after all, rules so severe they might as well be chiseled in stone. It is obviously time for this particular story to come to an end.

That morning when I returned to Delhi, the taxi turned into a street that was wet with rain. Potholes full of water reflected tatters of cloud racing off to the northeast. At the great blue doors, I got out and sent the taxi away. For a long time I just stood there, trying to think what I ought to do. Then at last I reached up, pushed the doorbell.

Within a minute, perhaps, I heard footsteps. The viewing port on the right-hand door slid open and a rectangle framing Joseph's eyes appeared—eyes without emotion, registering no surprise whatever at my presence. Then the viewing port closed and the door opened just a crack. I asked if my informant was at home.

"No," Joseph said firmly. "I am afraid he has gone away."

"Did he leave a message for me?"

"No, no message."

I tried to think of something to say, something that would have some meaning beyond my own desperation. But my mind was a complete blank. I thought he might invite me in, but he didn't. An awkward second or two lumbered by, and then, seeing no alternative, I said, "Well . . . good day, then."

"Good day, sir," Joseph said with a slight nod.

And the door closed.

For several seconds I just stood there, quite unable to move. But at last I turned and headed up the empty street in a kind of daze. Before I walked ten steps, however, I heard music coming over the compound wall, invading the morning silence. It was not at all the sort of music one is accustomed to hearing in a place like Delhi, and it stopped me in my tracks. It was the tremendous merging of voices that is the final "Gloria" of Bach's *Magnificat.* Hesitating for a long moment, I smiled, thinking that I would turn and go back. But then I didn't.

From that moment on, I knew I was on my own.

Author's Note

Of Tigers and Men is a factual account of events that occurred during the years 1986 through 1990. For much of that period I kept a journal in which I recorded many of the events and conversations described in the book. At no time did I use a tape recorder, believing then, as I do now, that people invariably speak and act differently—which is to say, unnaturally—in the presence of the dreaded machine. The conversations reported in *Of Tigers and Men* are therefore not literal transcriptions but reconstructions produced from notes written down generally on the same day on which the conversations occurred. Though I have gone to great pains to capture these verbal exchanges accurately, I had better admit that I do not have an infallible memory. It seems at least possible that certain people may recall conversations somewhat differently from the manner in which I have recorded them. If that proves to be the case, I would like to apologize in advance for any perceived misrepresentation on my part. None was intended.

Because the governments of many of the countries in which the action of this book takes place are democracies in name only and do not as a rule welcome criticism from any quarter, I have taken the precaution of altering the names of a good many people who make a casual appearance in these pages. My reasons for doing this can be simply stated. Given the current political climate in Asia, their association with me, however brief and however innocent, could bring them trouble. Though some readers may regard changing their names as an overreaction, those more familiar with the governments in question and their way of doing business will more likely view it as simple prudence.

In a similar light, I have not given the real name of the person I refer to in the book as "my informant." This was not altogether my decision. Although the gentleman in question has never voiced the slightest objection to my publishing an account of the experiences we shared in the Indian forest, his one abiding concern has always been that his privacy be preserved. Because our friendship is now an old one, extending back almost a decade, and because this book could not have been published in its present form without his blessing, I have obliged him fully on this issue. In view of all that he taught me and all that I owe him personally, I could hardly have done otherwise.

There is a considerable list of people to whom I would like to express my sincere gratitude for kindnesses received both before and during the writing of *Of Tigers and Men*. I would like to thank Mr. and Mrs. Amar Singh for teaching me so much about the Indian natural scene and Indian wildlife in the short time we spent together. I would like to thank Mira and Balram Singh for making two lost travelers feel very much at home in the backcountry of Uttar Pradesh and for revealing, in so doing, a memorably elegant side of Indian life now fast vanishing into history. I would like to thank Raj and Di Singh for their brilliant professional skills and the warm hospitality they showed me in Delhi. I would like to thank Pradeep Sankhala for the excellent job he did in organizing my first professional "recce" into the Indian backcountry.

For editorial assistance and criticism during the actual writing of the book, I would like to extend heartfelt thanks to Julie Harris, Richard Morris, James Luceno, Jill Lloyd, Sherry Bunin, Lynn Bell, Dan Gunn, and Louise Menlo. Whatever success *Of Tigers and Men* may ultimately enjoy will be largely due to their sharp critical faculties and generous moral support. I would also like to express my thanks to Owen Locke, of Random House, who was the first person in the publishing business to give me the hope that I might possibly have something to say as a writer.

No first-time writer could possibly be more fortunate than I in having Jesse Cohen as an editor and Nan Talese as an editor/publisher. *Of Tigers and Men* is a much better book than it would have been in the absence of their extraordinary taste and generous efforts. In a like spirit I would like to extend my thanks to my agent, Murray Pollinger, of London, whose belief in the book and enthusiastic support of it have been unwavering throughout. I should add that a number of details concerning the life and career of Kishan Singh, maharaja of Bharatpur, which would eventually find their way into Chapter 36, were first discovered in Charles Chenevix Trench's excellent *Viceroy's Agent* (Jonathan Cape, London, 1987).

It is an unhappy task to have to report that in mid-1995 the tiger's plunge into extinction continues unabated. The latest news suggests that within the next four to five years, every single Siberian tiger remaining in the wild will have been murdered. Depending on the twists and turns of local and international events, the Sumatran, Indochinese, and Indian races will follow it in only a few years. Though in 1994 the United States imposed limited trade sanctions on Taiwan, these sanctions amounted to little more than a slap on the hand. They will have no effect on the tiger's demise. In view of the present situation, only hopeless romantics can now possibly believe that after another ten to fifteen years have passed, the wild tiger will be anything more than a memory.

In spite of this tragic circumstance—a circumstance that no power in the world seems very interested in averting—I would like to take this opportunity to express my own profound admiration for all the men who have devoted their lives so selflessly to the tiger's continued survival on this planet. In particular I would like to single out "Billy" Arjan Singh and Valmik Thapar. Both of these men deserve infinitely more in the way of encouragement and support for their efforts than they have ever received from any quarter. If there were a Nobel Prize for conservation—and there ought to be—their contribution would have been recognized long ago. Their struggle to preserve the Indian tiger has been valiant, and it continues. Perhaps it is unnecessary to add that they are the true heroes of this book.

In closing, I would like to thank my wife, Christina Lindstrom, for her belief in me and for her constant support over the years it took to write *Of Tigers and Men* and see it into print. She gave me her love. With that came everything.

Paris
July 15, 1995

The Tiger Trust, a registered non-profit organization based in Britain, is at present the *only* organization in the world whose *specific and exclusive aim* is the conservation of tigers in the wild. In 1993 and 1994 it was responsible for devising and implementing the highly successful anti-poaching program, which has brought the Siberian tiger back from the very brink of extinction. The Trust feels confident that it can aid governments in achieving similar results in India and elsewhere. But it needs your help. *Please* send a contribution (whatever you can afford) to *The Tiger Trust*, Chevington, Bury St. Edmunds, Suffolk IP29 5RG, United Kingdom. Tel (+44) 1284-851-001, Fax (+44) 1284-851-002. The tiger *can* be saved.